DATE DUE

			PRINTED IN U.S.A.

TASTE OF
MOROCCO

A TASTE OF MOROCCO

A CULINARY JOURNEY WITH RECIPES

BY
ROBERT CARRIER

PHOTOGRAPHS BY
JOHN STEWART AND MICHELLE GARRETT

Clarkson N. Potter, Inc./Publishers

DISTRIBUTED BY CROWN PUBLISHERS, INC. NEW YORK

Published in the United States of America by Clarkson N. Potter, Inc.,
225 Park Avenue South, New York, New York 10003

Published in Great Britain by Century Hutchinson Ltd., Brookmount House,
62–65 Chandos Place, Covent Garden, London WC2N 4NW

CLARKSON N. POTTER, POTTER, and colophon are trademarks of Clarkson N.
Potter, Inc.

Manufactured in Great Britain

Library of Congress Cataloging in Publication Data
Carrier, Robert, 1923–
A taste of Morocco.
Includes index.
1. Cookery, Moroccan.   I. Title.
TX725.M8C37   1987   641.5964   87-10350
ISBN 0-517056559-5

10 9 8 7 6 5 4 3 2 1

First American Edition

*page 2: Idar presents a tagine called Hergma – calf's feet, chick peas
and cracked wheat – one of the great classics of Moroccan cooking.*

ACKNOWLEDGEMENTS

Many people have helped in the writing of this book. My special thanks to Abouchita Hajouji of the Moroccan National Tourist Office in London, to Abdeslam Ouriaghli and Hamid Benbrahim Elandaloussi of Royal Air Maroc; to his brother, Abdelhak Benbrahim Elandalousii, Director of Transport and Tourism of the O.N.C.F; Mohamed Alami Jemmati, Director of the Hotel Palais Jamai, Fez and A. Kournaf, Director of the Hotel Transatlantique, Meknes; and to Fouzia El Gharbi of Casablanca and her three charming daughters, my friends, who have shared their knowledge of Moroccan cooking with me.

I also owe special thanks to Abdeslam Aarab, Sacha van Dorssen and John Shepherd for letting me use their homes as backgrounds for photography in Marrakech and to Abdeslam, especially, for the many meals we shared with friends both Moroccan and European over the past years.

My thanks, too, to the many Bachas, Fatimas, Mustaphas and other Moroccan friends met on my travels who shared lunches, dinners, snacks and information with me: they have made Moroccan cooking a living adventure.

CONTENTS

*The magic of Moroccan blues in a corner of
the Majorelle Gardens, Marrakech.*

1

THE MAGIC OF MOROCCO

Less than four hours from London is another world. Here, you will find you are deep in another civilization where you will be assailed by new sights, new sounds, new sensations and new flavours. Even the architecture is different: on the walls you will find *zelliges*, glittering mosaic tiles of many colours; *tadillakdt*, a rich hand-rubbed finish made of lime, pigment, black soap and egg yolk that gives a soft, marble-smooth lustre to Moroccan palaces today just as it did in the eleventh century; and *gueps*, carved plasterwork with hand-cut surfaces as fine as lace.

In the bustling streets of the old cities, many of the men and women passing by still wear *djellabahs* (hooded robes of wool or cotton). In the *Souss* or south, men ride donkeys and camels along the country roads just as they did centuries ago, and in

OPPOSITE: *Patterns of Islam. All is rhythm and colour, texture and form in Morocco where lacy-patterned cut plaster and glittering mosaics interact with intricately-worked brass, carved cedar and woven textiles to create a magic world that is close to India and Asia and the Graeco-Persian Empire founded a thousand years earlier by Alexander the Great.*

BELOW: *A phalanx of men on horseback gather in the misty dawn for a fantasia at one of the country* moussems *where it is their custom to gallop straight at the crowds, only to pull up short at the last moment as they fire their muskets into the air. An astounding sight.*

the oases hundreds of date palms tower, rich with golden fruit, against the cobalt sky.

But if you have always thought of Morocco as a 'thousand and one nights' dream of mysterious *casbahs* and castellated cities surrounded by golden sands: forget it. Morocco is a rich, green country with millions of acres of wheat, corn and barley and great forests of cedar, cork, pine and eucalyptus. There are over a hundred million fruit trees in Morocco – oranges, lemons, almonds, apricots, figs, pomegranates, dates and olives. And on a recent trip along the coast from Casablanca to Safi, I saw hundreds of acres of tomatoes growing under plastic constructions to protect them from the hot, bright, African sun. In the north, near Rabat and Casablanca, and at Gherrouane and Boulaouane, I visited extensive modern vineyards where Moroccans are carrying on successfully the production of fresh-tasting Moroccan wines – red, rosé and white – a liquid legacy of the forty years of French rule. And almost everywhere, except of course in urban or highly cultivated areas, you will see fine-looking herds of sheep and goats along the roadsides in the care of smiling young shepherd boys and girls.

Morocco is a land of milk and honey – except that the milk is often buttermilk, and the honey sold on the streets of Marrakech can be just a mix of melted sugar and water. In a land of magic, not everything is what it seems.

The markets of any small Moroccan town are full of booths, shops and tents – even a spot on the open ground – where the market men, raucous and good-natured for the most part, sell every type of product and service imaginable.

I love Morocco for many reasons: because the sun is always hot and the nights are always cool; because in the streets the faces of young and old alike are alive and friendly; because children in my *derb* think I am some sort of strange Father Christmas; because I can swim in the sea, ski in the Atlas mountains and lunch with friends on my patio, all within three hours of each other; and because Morocco has one of the truly great cuisines in the world – not in its restaurants and snack bars, but in its private homes. It is a cuisine which can take its place proudly beside those of France and China, both of which, over the centuries, have influenced it greatly.

In the narrow, winding alleys of the old Arab *medinas* of Marrakech, Fez and Rabat (and even in the old quarter of modern, westernized Casablanca), you will find your first real introduction to the bustle and clamour, the sights, sounds and smells of this magic world. Donkeys bump stolidly into you as you walk through crowded passageways full of colourful open-fronted shops. There are teeming vegetable markets, the stalls of silversmiths and leatherworkers making their wares, and clothes guilds selling beautiful embroidered robes and heavy silks, woollens and damasks by the yard.

Of all the fabled cities of Morocco my favourite is Marrakech, a garden city of tall, curved palms and pointed cypresses, surrounded by orchards of oranges and lemons and acres of silver olive trees, a colourful crossroads between the Sahara and the Mediterranean. Of all the Imperial cities, Marrakech is certainly the most exotic. Showy and exciting, the city was for many centuries an ancient settlement grown from an Arab caravan halt at an oasis. Originally nothing more than a stone-built *casbah* or *ksar* and a collection of tented encampments protected by a stockade, it soon became an important trading settlement on the route across the desert to the north for merchant caravans carrying their silks and spices, ivory, ebony, gems and slaves. This rich Arab trading post was to grow under the Almoravids into an Imperial city of great political significance and dazzling grace, a mediaeval *bazaar* of a town set off from the world by a ring of snow-capped mountains.

What we see today – the miles of fabulous pink walls turning to gold in the sunset, the legendary Koutoubia Tower and the Place Djemmaa el Fna, the meeting place of north and south – has excited more first-time visitors than almost any other city on earth. Here, in one magic bound you will pass the frontier of

The fresh mint seller is a frequent sight on the streets of Morocco: a ready reminder that NÂA-NAA or thé à la menthe (Moroccan mint tea) is the national drink.

A sun-bright sprig of bougainvillaea brings colour and magic to a Moorish arch in a house in the medina.

several centuries. For on this great, sprawling central square you will discover how the common people of Europe used to entertain themselves in the Middle Ages. Walking into the square as evening falls is like a trip into the past. By day, it is animated with crowds of people – merchants and their customers – while later it is alive with the sound of drumbeats and African music, with itinerant jugglers, snake-charmers, acrobats, sooth-sayers, sword-swallowers, monkey-trainers and water-vendors, all gathered to tempt and entertain the passersby. This is no simple show for tourists: this is the true living folklore of another time. If you thrill to the senses of taste, smell, touch and sight, you will savour every moment of your visit here.

Marrakech boasts many beautiful and ancient buildings hidden in the winding streets of the *medina*. One of the most perfect, the Kouba el Baroudiyin (tomb of a thirteenth-century saint), although small, is perhaps the most important building in all Morocco, with its myriad stepped arches set in plain rectangles and crowned by a dome decorated with the zig-zag pattern of a seven-pointed star. The interior decorations of the dome, based on two levels of delicate arches with a luxuriantly carved relief of leaf and shell motifs, lend it an almost baroque voluptuousness quite unlike anything one might have expected from Saharan ascetics of the twelfth century. And the nearby Medrassa ben Yussef, one of the oldest working universities in the world, is one of the most beautiful buildings I have ever seen. Something about its fine filigree of ancient, cedarwood, cell-like rooms for the students, its elegant fountain, and the calm of its shaded courtyards of green and white tiles, makes me return again and again.

Well worth a visit, too, are the eleventh-century Saadian Tombs. Sixty-six Saadi royals are buried in this intensely beautiful necropolis with over a hundred more of the royal family buried just outside the main buildings. This always seems to me a place of pleasure rather than of sadness because of its combination of mood and light, pattern and design. And there are two old palaces, the El Badi and La Bahia palaces. The first, built by Achmed el Mansur at the end of the sixteenth century, was called the 'incomparable' and from the stately ruins and gardens visible today (the scene of a yearly Folkloric Arts Festival), it certainly merits its name. The second, built in the nineteenth century by Abu Achmed who did not like stairways (he had a crippled leg), has a strange 'twisted' charm, for the original palace was extended into the neighbouring houses of the quarter to create a most individual, meandering series of state rooms and courtyards all on one floor.

But, to me, the most interesting place of all Marrakech is the *medina* – a wondrous labyrinth of narrow passages and winding, crooked streets that open suddenly into sunny squares

Brilliant red is a colour constant in Morocco, whether in the crowded streets of the medina, *or in a quiet, tree-shaded courtyard.*

where a lonely fig tree stands guard among the open-fronted shops. Here in the convoluted maze of streets and alleys that form the centre of the Arab quarter, you will be assaulted by a heady succession of smells – the tantalizing aroma of meats charcoal-grilled with cumin, cayenne and cinnamon; the crisp scents of mint and orange; the sensual perfumes of hibiscus and jasmine and the pungent muskiness of cedarwood (there seems to be a woodworker on every corner) contrasted with the faint acrid note of donkey dung – all trapped in the searing heat of the day, bringing home, as no other combination of odours can, that in Morocco the earthy and the sublime are always present.

My house is in the *medina.* All that is visible from the street is a very large door at the end of a narrow *derb.* Behind the door is a secret garden with its jungle of fruit-bearing trees – orange, lemon, thorn lemon, mandarin, fig, banana and a single olive. Bougainvillaea and plumbago hang from the apricot-tinted walls, and the parterres are a jungle of shiny green leaves and bright blossoms. Here it is that I find peace today – cut off from the clamorous rumour of the town – in my little backwater of winding streets. This is my Morocco. A sanctuary where I can work and relax in the sun; where at night when the sky turns from pink to midnight blue, I can hardly distinguish the orange-coloured fruits and the white blossoms against the soft pinks of the walls and the darkening sky. It is then that I feel most at home. Or in the early morning when the *muezzin* sounds, calling the faithful to prayer, and I look out over the garden from my bed to see the silhouettes of three cypress trees in a neighbouring garden, blue-black sentinels against a rose-coloured sky. The morning is crisp and the birds are singing; I can hear Azziz below, watering the garden in the morning's early light. Soon there will be the smell of coffee and the sound of hot yeast doughnuts sizzling for breakfast. My day has begun. It is time to get up and work in the cool of the early morning.

Life here is gentler than in Britain. When the sun becomes hotter, about ten-thirty, I break for a series of household tasks, little duties, like taking the dead heads off flowers, giving instructions for the terraces, setting out for the central market to do the day's shopping. There is time for a drink with friends at the local *café* in the Gueliz (the French quarter). Then it is time for lunch, either at home – just a simple salad followed by a brochette and some fresh fruit, or a more complicated meal with company – or in a restaurant.

Each Friday, it is *couscous*, Morocco's national dish, one of the truly great dishes of the world. *Couscous* here is lovingly prepared, either with seven vegetables, or lamb or chicken – or even with seafood in the manner of Essaouira. Whatever the recipe, it is always a mixture of semolina steamed over a rich bouillon of meat (or fish) and vegetables, the bouillon itself subtly seasoned with Moroccan spices: saffron, ginger, cumin, hot and sweet red peppers. Chick peas and raisins and honeyed onions often find their way into a traditional recipe for *couscous*. Such a meal might begin with an assortment of cooked and raw Moroccan salads and finish off with the fresh, cool note of sliced, peeled, Moroccan oranges garnished with chopped dates and almonds and sprinkled, just before serving, with orange-flower water and a little freshly ground cinnamon . . .

Nowhere is the magic of Morocco more apparent than in the sleepy sun-washed streets of the old towns where a man finds time to sit and dream.

2

AN INTRODUCTION TO MOROCCAN FOOD

Moroccan cuisine, more than that of almost any other country, has been shaped by the history of the country itself. Throughout the centuries the Maghreb, the coastal strip along the southern shores of the Mediterranean (which now comprises the modern states of Morocco, Algeria and Tunisia), was subjected to many invasions, rulers and influences. The indigenous Berbers, the nomadic Arabs, the Phoenicians and Carthaginians all played an early part, and then much of Morocco was absorbed for a while into the Roman Empire.

But it was after Mohammed's death in AD 632 that the military, cultural and religious influence of the Arabs, of Islam, grew like a single gust of wind from the desert to envelop the then-known world. First Persia, Syria and Egypt, then Turkey and North Africa fell to the Moslem armies. In the eighth and ninth centuries, Spain, Sicily and parts of France were conquered, a foothold the Moslems maintained for hundreds of years. And by the thirteenth and fourteenth centuries, Islam ruled as far as India, Indonesia and China. Even today one can see evidence of this heterogeneous mix in the people of Morocco: the Berber fair skin, light hair and fine features; Mongol and Asiatic types; the darker skin of the Arab; and the admixture of slave-market negro blood. A rich blend in which the instincts of savannah and forest have mingled with the most austere traditions of the desert.

And it is apparent, too, in the food of modern-day Morocco. The diet of the nomadic Bedouin Arabs included dates, milk, *smen* (a cooked and aged butter), and grain, still basics of

OPPOSITE: Tagines *for an outdoor luncheon at the Hotel Transatlantique in Meknes.*

ABOVE: Le petit déjeuner de l'Emir – *a wonderful Moroccan breakfast in the classical manner – served at the Palais Jamai in Fez.*

eating and cooking in Morocco. They had early discovered the infinite possibilities of grain as a versatile and nourishing food. First they left the grain to soften in water and made the happy discovery of fermentation. Then, when cooking pots had been developed, they began grinding grain between two stones to make a finer dish, a sort of floury soup or gruel made from soaked grains; in those days it was usually millet or spelt (a primitive kind of wheat), or chick peas. At some stage this floury soup may have been overcooked into a more solid mass or may have fallen on to the hearth and been baked into a bread. This was made more palatable when the fermented flour, salt and water mixture of the day before (what we know today as sourdough or natural 'starter') was worked into the newly ground flour to make a 'riser'; and Arab bread, which still plays a central role in all Arab cuisines, as well as Morocco, was born.

It is said, too, that dried pasta may have been invented by the Arabs as a way of preserving flour during the long caravan routes across the desert. They certainly introduced it into Sicily and the southern regions of Italy from whence it spread to other Mediterranean regions. Interestingly, in southern Italy, there is still a dish of Arabic origin called *circeri e trii*, which combines cooked chick peas and strips of soft pasta dough simmered in a vegetable broth. With the addition of chicken and saffron, the dish is served to this day in Morocco, where it is known as *trid*. It is reputed to have been the Prophet's favourite dish – as indeed it is one of mine.

The Berber influence was as great. The most famous dishes of the present-day Moroccan cuisine include *couscous*, *tagines* (long-simmered stews of meat, poultry or vegetables), and *harira*, the thick pulse soup which has become the commonest 'break fast' meal of the Islamic Lent, Ramadan.

After the centuries spent in southern Europe, particularly in Spain, the Moors brought back to North Africa the style of Andalusia – the use of olives and olive oil, the incorporation of nuts, fruits and herbs into dishes. Almond and olive trees, and many fruit trees – oranges, plums and peaches among them – crossed the Mediterranean at this time, and their fruits were soon enhancing Moroccan dishes, echoing the sweet-sour mixtures characteristic of China, and the sweet-savoury dishes of Persia and other countries of the Middle East.

Spices are a major feature of Moroccan cooking. The Arabs had long been the leading spice merchants of the world, as a result of their intrepid expeditions carrying the laws of the Koran to the world. They had brought back from the Moluccas or Spice Islands of New Guinea nutmeg, cloves, cinnamon, ginger, saffron (which they planted commercially in Spain along with sugar) and curcuma or turmeric. Until the thirteenth century, they had kept the secret of their source of

OPPOSITE: *Spices play an important part in Moroccan cooking. No visit to Morocco is complete without a visit to the spice souks where you will find every spice you have ever heard of and many that you never imagined.*

supply so closely guarded that the West did not discover where these riches could be obtained until Marco Polo visited the Orient. His written account of his three voyages astonished the western world. As a result, Columbus set out from Spain on the voyage of exploration that was to end in the discovery of the islands of the Caribbean and of America; Vasco da Gama rounded the continent of Africa to reach India for the first time by sea; and Magellan, after two years of hardship and adventure, discovered the Spice Islands for himself.

Other ingredients, now so characteristic of aspects of Moroccan food, were only incorporated after the discovery of the New World, when the Old World was introduced to the colours and flavours of tomatoes, peppers both sweet and hot, edible gourds and potatoes. Powdered sweet peppers and hot chilli (chili) peppers – paprika and cayenne respectively – play an enormous part in almost every single aspect of Moroccan savoury cooking.

The major recent cultural and culinary influence on Morocco has been that of the French, who, along with the Spanish, ruled Morocco as a Protectorate from 1913 to 1956 until independence under King Mohammed V, now succeeded by his son, King Hassan II. The French language is spoken by a large number of Moroccans, a French sophistication pervades many aspects of Moroccan city life, but culinary influences have been more subtle. The use of tomato concentrate (purée) is thought to be attributable to French and Spanish cuisine, and the introduction of an entrée course and a distinct dessert course are reflections of a more western approach to eating. In restaurants, this is particularly apparent, while it is in the homes in the country and in the towns that the true traditions of Moroccan eating and cooking are kept very much alive.

LEFT: *Forty years of French rule have left a lasting legacy of French cheeses and French wines in Morocco. Shops in the larger cities present a variety of cheeses produced in Morocco and ripened to perfection. You'll find them served in the major restaurants and hotels with light Moroccan wines of great distinction.*

ABOVE: *Moroccan food is rich in flavour, rich in history. This dinner in Marrakech features sea bass cooked in the Moroccan manner with onions, almonds and black raisins,* tagine *of lamb with saffron-tinted potatoes and red olives and a mixed salad of lettuce and tomatoes with Moroccan dressing.*

3
EATING IN MOROCCO

The food of Morocco is among the most exciting in the world. Not yet, I am afraid, in the hotels and restaurants of the major cities, but in the country's palaces and private homes, where cooking is still considered an art, something to talk about, well worth the rapt attention of every member of the family. I have been lucky enough over the past ten years to share with my Moroccan friends their love of their culinary heritage. Moroccan food is among the most visually striking in the world – rich in flavour, rich in history and rich in the myriad influences of black Africa and the Orient and the later influences of Andalusia and the forty-year French Protectorate.

Bringing the *Taste of Morocco* to life has been a most exciting exercise. For months, with photographers John Stewart and Michelle Garrett, I have been travelling through the different regions of the country to taste and record the flavours of its rich and varied cuisine.

The visitor to Morocco is blessed, for none of the Moroccan traditions of food preparation or dining habits have disappeared. All the colour, charm and beauty of Morocco's living cuisine is still very much in evidence.

Moroccans are notably generous, open-hearted and hospitable. They hold open table today – much in the way our ancestors did – and enjoy sharing their meals with friends and family. The traditional family celebrations – betrothals, weddings, births, circumcisions and religious feast days – give them the chance to indulge their desire to share their generosity and the magnificence of their table. Even in the simplest home a *tagine* or two – or a great heaped platter of *couscous* – is provided as the centre-piece of the meal, probably accompanied by Moroccan salads and almost certainly ending with fresh fruit and freshly brewed mint tea.

ABOVE: *Flat-leafed parsley, coriander, fresh lemons, red-skinned onions, garlic and spices add accent and flavour to long-simmered Moroccan dishes.*

OPPOSITE: *Luncheon in an indoor garden with its orange and lemon trees and luxuriant vegetation is a special pleasure in Morocco. An ancient fountain splashes musically, caged birds sing and the house cat stretches lazily in the African sun.*

Although Moroccans produce some superb wines, devout Moslems do not drink alcohol. Sidi Harazam (still) and Oulmes (sparkling) are the two excellent bottled waters that replace wine at table. As do home-made soft drinks of almond milk, pomegranate juice and grape juice, often flavoured with a hint of rosewater or orange-flower water.

Parties have a way of growing in Morocco. It is not unusual for a simple luncheon or dinner planned for six to become – in a matter of a few telephone calls – a banquet with fifteen to twenty guests. Sounds impossible? Not in Morocco where meals are usually served at low, round tables so that it is easy to fit in unexpected guests – and if there are too many for one round table, another is quickly brought in. No panic; no fuss. Just open-hearted hospitality. And it's all quite easy, thanks to the way that Moroccan meals are planned around one or two generous *tagines* (delicious long-simmered stews of meat, poultry or game combined with fruits or vegetables).

On the brightest day, or on the coolest of summer nights, a profusion of raw and cooked vegetable salads and meat salads rounds out the meal, each platter or bowl coolly shining thanks to the contrast of colourful ingredients: diced green peppers and tomato; sliced oranges and black olives; cubed cucumber and potato; grated beetroot (beets) with watercress; diced lemon, parsley and onion; cooked brains or liver and spiced cooked carrot chunks with plumped-up raisins.

Dessert is usually a series of home-made little pastries and honey-dipped sweets or a great platter of carefully arranged chilled fresh fruits – black and white grapes, pointed wedges of melon and watermelon, peaches, plums, apples, pears and prickly pears (Barbary figs).

Whatever the menu, the spread is quickly assembled so that each guest can enjoy a taste or two of each ingredient, using the three fingers of his right hand in the traditional Arab fashion; a spoon or fork; or more probably, a piece of crisp flat Arab bread to carry succulent bits of meat or poultry to his mouth, or to dunk happily in the generous sauce.

I well remember a festive dinner where the number of guests magically increased from twelve to twenty-two. They all found their places in the approved manner around three large low tables set out in the cool patio surrounded by comfortable banquettes with cushions brought out for the occasion. The first course – little hot pastries of pounded pigeon and lemon-flavoured eggs; minced lamb seasoned with onion, garlic and spices; and cooked rice flavoured with cinnamon and studded with chopped almonds – was followed by steaming bowls of soup (chick peas, lentils and bits of diced chicken in a rich broth prickled with spice in which I could discern ginger, cumin and cinnamon). Then came a regal series of Moroccan *tagines* –

lamb with onion, tomatoes and sweet spices; chicken with saffron, preserved lemons and green olives; and cinnamon-flavoured beef with almonds and prunes – all easily eaten by the guests with fingers, a spoon, or with 'dipping' pieces of crusty Arab bread. There were no problems of extra plates, extra silverware: everyone ate from the central dishes. Even the dessert – a towering edifice of choux pastry and flavoured butter cream hastily ordered for the occasion from a neighbouring restaurant – was handed around and guests delicately broke off delicious bits to nibble with chilled glasses of fragrant mint tea (the chilling is an innovation) or small cups of hot black coffee while watching the musicians and dancers brought in for the evening's entertainment.

There are many dishes in Morocco's rich and varied cuisine that can be compared favourably on the highest scale of world culinary inventions. To name but a few:

Harira

This is certainly one of the great soups of the world – a combination of diced lamb, lentils and chick peas in a delightfully flavoured and thickened broth enriched with the accents of tomato, onion, parsley and coriander. *Harira*, traditionally served as the 'break fast' soup during the month of Ramadan, is also finding its place today on modern Moroccan menus.

Moroccan appetiser salads

These are made from raw or cooked vegetables, often supplemented by brains and cubed liver. Fresh-tasting, colourful and exotic, and interestingly spiced, they are served as appetizers in the European manner, but are often left throughout the meal as tasty exclamation marks to freshen the palate between richly flavoured *tagines* of fish, poultry or meat.

B'stilla

This legendary *milles-feuilles tourte* or pie of *warkha* pastry encloses a mediaeval mix of pounded pigeon, lemon- and honey-flavoured eggs, chopped almonds and raisins. Possibly Persian inspired, and brought to Morocco via Andalusia in Spain, it is the great party piece of every Moroccan banquet.

M'choui

A whole lamb is roasted in the open air until crisp and golden on the outside, moist and butter tender within. It is not carved on to plates but served in the centre of the table so that each guest can pull hot bits from the bone with the help of pieces of crisp-textured Arab bread. *M'choui*, often seasoned with saffron and hot red pepper, is served with ground cumin and coarse salt.

Moroccan tagines

I like, too, the many *touajen* of Moroccan cooking – long-simmered, highly flavoured *ragoûts* of chicken, pigeon, turkey or lamb, flavoured with saffron, garlic, coriander, cumin and the three red peppers (*felfla hlouwa*, sweet red pepper; *felfla soudania*, hot red pepper; and *felfla harra*, spicy red pepper). There is a huge variety from which to choose. *Kedra* is a favourite way of preparing chicken in Morocco: the bird is rubbed with saffron and paprika, and sometimes crushed hot peppers, sautéed in butter until golden and then simmered in chicken stock with chick peas, thinly sliced onions and rice. The saffron colours and flavours the stock of this simple dish. *Djed Mefenned* is golden braised chicken, covered immediately before serving with paper-thin *crêpes* flavoured with finely chopped herbs and freshly ground cumin.

There are many *tagine* specialities to try when you visit Morocco: *Tagine de foie de mouton* is lamb's liver cut into thin slices and marinated in olive oil and lemon juice with crushed red peppers and garlic pounded to a paste with powdered cumin, chopped coriander and flat-leafed (Italian) parsley. The strips of marinated liver are then lightly sautéed in butter, cut into dice and simmered in the marinade juhces until meltingly tender.

For similar dishes with lamb, poultry or fish, the main ingredients of the dish are cut into segments and marinated in olive oil with finely chopped onion and garlic, saffron, cumin, crushed red peppers, finely chopped coriander and flat-leafed (Italian) parsley. The meat, fish or poultry is then simmered in the marinade juices until tender.

Vegetable dishes

Moroccans use vegetables – tomatoes, onions, peppers sweet and hot, dried beans (pulses) and chick peas, courgettes (zucchini), aubergines (eggplant), artichokes and okra – alone or in combination with meats or other vegetables in many ways. But one thing they always have in common: they are flavoured with olive oil or butter, garlic, onion, sweet and hot red peppers, cumin and chopped fresh green coriander and flat-leafed (Italian) parsley.

I am intrigued by Moroccan cooks' imaginative use of fruits – apples, quinces, pears, prunes, dates and grapes – in combination with chicken, lamb, pigeon and turkey; and by their sweets which are delicate mixtures of milk, honey, flour and pounded almonds, flavoured with orange-flower water, rose-water, or aniseed or sesame seeds. But best of all I love their exciting use of spices and herbs: a mix of red peppers to heighten the flavour of a casserole; the unusual combination of cinnamon and saffron in savoury dishes; the fabulous mixture of twenty-four spices known as *ras el hanout*, a highly flavoured, finely ground mixture of dried roots, berries, pods and grains, mixed by the 'head of the shop' from which this potent (supposedly aphrodisiac) mix gets its name. You'll find a generous pinch of this mixture does much to add hot, spicy flavour to Arab casseroles and stews of meat and fish and vegetables. And who knows?

Couscous

Any meal of substance always ends with a gigantic *couscous*. My favourite is *couscous aux sept légumes*, with seven vegetables, in which carrots, turnips, tomatoes, onions, courgettes (zucchini), red *courge* (first cousin of our pumpkin, but more richly coloured and intensely flavoured), and that long, twisted, pale green squash the Moroccans call *slaoui*, all play their part. I also enjoy the *couscous k'dra* with a garnish of chick peas, raisins and honeyed sliced onions that Moroccan cooks add for favoured guests and the very special *couscous aux poissons* that is a speciality of Essaouira and Safi.

Add to this the galaxy of fruit desserts, honeyed sweets and pastries that have swept the eastern Mediterranean and you will have an idea of the pleasures in store. To mention just a few:

Orange salad with dates and almonds

One of the freshest-tasting fruit salads I know, combining slices of fresh orange with lemon juice, orange juice and orange-flower water; garnished with chopped dates and slivered almonds and sprinkled, just before serving, with powdered cinnamon.

Cornes de gazelle

The ubiquitous (and quite delicious) horn-shaped crescents called gazelle's horns. Filled with a richly flavoured almond paste, the thinnest-ever crisp pastry is dipped (at its best) in orange-flower water and coated with a thick, white dusting of icing (confectioners') sugar.

M'hanncha

A perfect coil of orange-flower and rose-petal flavoured almond paste, wrapped in the thinnest of pastry leaves, coiled like a snake into a perfect round and baked until crisp and golden. It is served dusted with powdered sugar and cinnamon.

A great dish of SFFA (sweet couscous) as served in the Moroccan restaurant of the Palais Jamai in Fez, one of Morocco's most beautiful hotels.

Sweet b'stilla

Crisp fried leaves of *warkha* pastry, piled mountain high, each two layers sprinkled with a mix of ground almonds, crushed sugar and pounded cinnamon; the whole bathed just before serving with a slightly thickened almond milk.

Sweet couscous

Yes, *couscous* comes 'sweet' too . . . and delicious it is, when dusted with trails of icing (confectioners') sugar and powdered cinnamon, and decorated with patterns of raisins, prunes or dates. Sweet couscous is served hot with accompanying bowls of cool buttermilk, milk or almond milk to moisten it with.

4

THE MOROCCAN KITCHEN

Modern Moroccan kitchens are heavily influenced by the French and have no need to envy their international counterparts. In the kitchen of my Casablanca friend, Zoubida el Gharbi, there are all the modern conveniences – a refrigerator, a freezer, a four-burner gas stove with twin ovens, a sink, set in colourful tiled counter tops, and shelves of glowing bottled preserves, but I noticed that the *khlii* – the sun-dried meat (see page 68) that was used to flavour the lentil salad included in our selection of appetizer salads (see page 117) – was kept in the larder without benefit of refrigeration, and the two *tagines* that we were to enjoy for luncheon – chicken with lemons and olives, and lamb with glazed quinces and artichokes – were being cooked in aluminium saucepans on charcoal braziers on the floor!

My kitchen in Marrakech is long and narrow, with walls of the old house at least a metre/39 inches thick to protect it from the extreme heats of summer and the cold of winter. Tiled both on floors and work surfaces, it is an uneasy cross between a European and a Moroccan kitchen. High ceilinged, it has rows of saffron tinted cedarwood shelves against the rough, pale-blue washed plaster of the walls. There are two refrigerators – one for fruits, vegetables, butter, milk and cheeses, and the other, fan-cooled to hang meats for ten to fourteen days.

At the far end of the room is a Provençal *hotte* (a raised open fire with hood and open chimney), inspired by the one I had in my St Tropez kitchen so many years ago. Used by me to cook brochettes and grill spatch-cocked chickens and pigeons or butterflied legs of lamb, it is virtually ignored by my maid Bacha who prefers to cook squatting happily over a series of small round braziers in the tiled courtyard outside the kitchen door.

She is happy to use the oven for roast poultry and fish and the top burners of the stove for her subtly flavoured *tagines* of

ABOVE: *Cooking is a moveable feast for Marrakshi cook Bacha.*

OPPOSITE: *Robert Carrier's kitchen in Marrakech is a cross between a European and a Moroccan kitchen.*

1   2   3

meat, poultry or fish. But when it comes to grilling, the charcoal brazier is the only thing. I am always amused to see her rather large bulk posed on a tiny raffia-covered stool aerating her semolina for *couscous* in a hugh *gsaa*, placed on the floor, or mixing the dough for the countless little Arab pastries my guests and I are offered at any time of the day with a glass of refreshing *nâa-naa* (hot mint tea).

And Bacha is not alone for when I lunched one day with Najua Alaui in her modern house in Rabat, I noticed that the *tagines* which were later served in attractive glazed earthenware *tagines* were being prepared in metal saucepans over the ubiquitous charcoal brazier on the kitchen floor (see picture on page 31).

Tradition lasts long in Morocco and in the usual country kitchen the cooking pots are earthenware or tin-lined copper; the mixing bowl is a large flat wooden or earthenware platter with a 10cm/4 inch sloping lip. The heating unit is a small round charcoal brazier which is specially designed to hold the rounded bottom of a *tagine* safely in place with its three high-rising points. And it is charcoal which serves as the heating element to cook the brochettes and allow the richly flavoured sauces of Moroccan cooking to simmer gently over the heat.

There are no chairs in the traditional Moroccan kitchen and often no table; a stool or two perhaps, or even an old carpet folded to act as a seat for the cook, the only attempts at comfort.

8

32

5

6

1 Chtato A flat sieve or *tamis*, with silk or nylon base.

2 Gdra The bottom part of a *couscoussier*. Used to cook meats, fish, poultry and vegetables. Exists in tin, aluminium, stainless steel and, in country districts, earthenware. **Kskas** or **Keskes**, the top part of a *couscoussier*, has a perforated bottom that allows flavoured steam from meats or fish, vegetables and aromatics cooking in the *gdra* base to permeate and flavour the grains of *couscous*.

3 Gsaa A large round dish of unglazed pottery (or wood). It is used to mix dough for breads, cakes and pastries, and to mix and aerate semolina grains for *couscous*. (In England I use a large, wide, flat-bottomed wooden salad bowl.)

4 Kanoun or **Mjmar (Mishmihr)** The ubiquitous charcoal brazier, usually round and made of unglazed pottery.

5 Midouna or **T'beck** A large flat basket. Used to roll or to separate semolina grains for *couscous*.

6 Tagine slaoui A round flameproof dish made of glazed earthenware with a pointed glazed earthenware cover, which is used to cook Moroccan stews of meat, fish, poultry or vegetables, also generically known as *tagines*. They are used as well as the serving container for stews which have been cooked in another pot or casserole. I use mine to keep bread fresh (the conical lid seems to help in some magic way) or to keep ice cubes from melting in the hot months of summer. Excellent, too, without its cover, to present fruits or vegetables.

Moroccan cooks usually use *tagines* over charcoal – a low, even heat. When using a *tagine* on top of a direct heat in a western kitchen – over gas or electricity – always make sure to use a heat diffusing mat to protect it.

7

7 Mehraz A brass mortar and pestle. Used to pound spices, grains or herbs.

8 T'bicka A large basket with decorated conical lid, used to serve bread.

T'bsil dial warkha A round flat metal dish with a shallow rim (see p. 85). It is used (bottom side up) to bake *warkha* pastry leaves and (bottom side down) to bake *b'stilla*.

5

THE TEA CEREMONY

It has been said that Morocco is a land that yields its meaning only to those who are able to take the time to draw water and make a pot of tea. There is always time to sit with a friend and sip a glass of tea: time to watch the sprigs of fresh green mint being pushed into the round-bellied pot, the cane sugar carefully broken off and added before the boiling water; time to let the mint and tea leaves infuse; time for the pale amber-green liquid to be poured from on high into the little coloured glasses in which it is served; and time for the glass to cool slightly so that it can be picked up in the fingers and enjoyed.

Mint tea has become inseparably associated with Morocco, and yet tea was introduced there only in 1854 when, during the Crimean War, British merchants were obliged to seek new markets for their wares. They disposed of large quantities of tea in Tangier and Mogador, and the Moroccans took to the new drink with alacrity and enthusiasm. They adapted it, however, and made it their own – as they have done so successfully with many other foreign imports – by adding sprigs of the fresh mint that grows so bountifully throughout the country. This they had been infusing with water for centuries, making a herbal tea or *tisane* with absinthe or wormwood, *verveine* and marjoram. (Interestingly, absinthe, now banned in many countries because it affects the nervous system, is also occasionally used in small quantities, dried, in *tagines* and soups.)

Now tea making is almost as much a ritual in Morocco as it is in China or Japan, as is tea drinking, a ceremony in itself, whether served at the end of a meal or shared with a friend in a simple street *café*. Time seems to stand still in the Arab market towns of the south, and its infinitely slow passage is marked in the tiny *cafés* lining the *souks* only by the arrival of successive glasses of hot mint tea without which no Moroccan business deal is ever discussed or brought to fruition. Even road workers

ABOVE: *A circular beaten brass tray contains the pot-bellied teapot, sugar and fresh mint leaves which are used for the ritual of tea-making.*

OPPOSITE: *The tea ceremony at the elegant Dar Marjana restaurant in Marrakech. Abdel Azzis, dressed in his Berber robes, complete with turban and Berber knife, kneels before the guests in the old courtyard of the Arab palace on a rug set with trays of Moroccan silver.*

Street scene in the medina *of Marrakech. Itinerant pedlars of freshly picked mint are an everyday sight in Morocco.*

stop for their mid-morning break of hot mint tea, bread and a few olives. From a tattered piece of newspaper or cloth in their pocket they bring out a precious pinch of tea, break off a lump of cane sugar, and stuff a few sprigs of fresh mint into a carefully washed metal teapot. Then, at their feet, over a small open fire made of a few twigs or over a one-burner kerosene stove, they brew the tea, pouring the fragrant liquid into small glasses.

I've sometimes shared with the various masons working on my house in the *medina* a sample of their lunch-time cooking: sliced onions and tomatoes, a little chopped parsley and fresh coriander, a pinch of salt, cumin and hot red pepper, the whole simmered for a moment in oil before a few bits of lamb are added – for flavour, really – and some roughly cut potatoes for bulk. We all sit around the communal pot, break off some bits of flat Arab bread and dip in. *Bismillah.* This simple fare is delicious. And so is the tea that accompanies it: pale green, fragrant and refreshing. 'A gift of Allah', they say. And one to be truly thankful for.

Tea can be all things to all Moroccans. It is used to soothe the excited and help the restless to sleep. On the other hand, it is held to waken the senses and rouse the drowsy. It has been used as a medicine and as a placebo to quiet the restless young, to relax the tensions of the mature, and to ease the discomfort of the aged.

Mint tea, *thé à la menthe* or *nâa-naa* is the ritual drink of Moroccan hospitality, and is served rather like coffee in the

West, in offices, in the humblest homes, at the barber or hair-dresser and, often, in shops. It has pride of place, though, at the end of a meal. It must be very sweet and, according to tradition, it is the master of the house who breaks sugar from a large sugar loaf and plunges it into the teapot into which he has just put the tea. He then adds a handful of garden mint and fills the pot with boiling water. The tea is left for moments to infuse, the mint is crushed, then a glass is drawn out, then poured back in. It is also traditional for guests to drink three cups of tea.

ABOVE LEFT: *The neighbourhood café in Morocco functions like a men's club in London. The men who frequent it consider it as an extension of their homes.*

ABOVE: *A glass of* thé à la menthe, *steaming hot, so hot one's fingers cannot at first touch the glass, the vivid green of the mint leaves clearly visible: a drink that makes the eyes shine, the breath sweet, the digestion easy. NÂA-NAA – a gift from Allah.*

MINT TEA

The tea ceremony at its simplest as demonstrated at the olive-pressing station of the Domaine Ouled-Aissa near Taroudant.

1 Measure 2–3 teaspoons green tea into pot.

2 Pour in boiling water; then quickly strain out water to clean tea of dust.

3 Pour in more boiling water and place teapot in the embers to steep for 1 minute.

4 Wash mint leaves and stuff tightly into pot.

5 Place teapot in embers to steep for a few seconds more.

6 Add lumps of sugar to the pot.

7 Pour out one glass of tea, then pour it back into the pot.

8 Repeat this operation and then serve tea in little glasses, pouring with the pot held high to aerate the hot tea. Deliciously fragrant and – surprisingly enough – not too sweet.

6

STREET FOOD

A wandering subculture of itinerant street sellers provides needed services and local colour in the streets of major Moroccan cities. A host of shoe-shine boys and sellers of rugs, *djellabahs* and Berber knives roam the streets in search of sales, as does the lemon-wood man with his bicycle strung with dozens of wooden spoons and whisks and stirrers of all kinds, fashioned from the wood of lemon trees, and a selection of outlandish straw hats. Another street specialist sells tall jars of mountain honey. But it is the ambulant hard-boiled egg vendors and the hot chick pea or broad (fava) bean merchants that interest me the most. From the former, a shelled hard-boiled egg with a small paper square with salt and cumin powder to dip your shelled egg in; from the latter, a heaped mound of steaming hot chick peas or broad (fava) beans served with a liberal dusting of coarse salt and powdered cumin. Each for only a *dirham* or less than 7 pence (about 4 cents): wonderful provender – with a drink or a glass of mint tea – for literally pennies.

My first Moroccan street food of any consequence was four twisted metal skewers of tiny bits of lamb's liver and fat, grilled over an open fire, the cook turning the skewers and fanning the charcoal with an old piece of tattered cardboard. The brochettes were seasoned with a mix of powdered cumin, hot red pepper and coarse salt. Then, with a flourish, the meats were stripped into a quarter round of flat, crunchy, chewy Arab bread. A pinch or two more of the magical seasoning and I was lost; my senses ablaze with new savours, new mysteries, new sights and new aromas. For around me as I delightedly munched my simple feast were a whole series of wooden tables and benches set up every night in the square where people, tightly gathered, were eating brochettes like mine or choosing from an array of colourful vegetable salads, gleaming piles of savoury chick peas or lentils flavoured with finely chopped onion and garlic, and seasoned with sweet red pepper, hot red pepper, and the (new to me at that time) completely different taste of *kasbour* (fresh

ABOVE: *The harira stall in an open street market offers sustenance at low cost.*

OPPOSITE: *Open-air street restaurant in Place Djemaa el Fna in Marrakech where visitors to the desert oasis can feast on* tagines *of lamb and chicken with lemon, saffron-flavoured potatoes and a host of grated vegetable salads.*

39

At the fish stalls they serve chunky fish steaks of white-fleshed moustele *(dredged in a saffron- and salt-flavoured flour before being fried in bubbling oil) with a side order of chips (the French influence), two rounds of fried aubergine and a fried hot green pepper for accent.*

green coriander). Saffron-scented whole chickens were there with preserved lemons or violet coloured olives, and flat earthenware dishes of beef and lamb cooked with raisins and prunes and almonds. As were deep-fried chunks of fresh fish brought that morning from the nearby ports of Safi, Agadir and Oulidia. Dipped first in a salt- and saffron-flavoured flour and then deep-fried in cauldrons of bubbling oil until crisp and golden, the fish is served – one large piece per customer – with a side helping of crisp-fried potatoes (the French influence), two rounds of fried aubergine (eggplant) and a hot green pepper. Ambrosia. If you are more adventurous – I certainly am – you'll try, too, the rich-flavoured *tagines* of sheep's or calf's feet simmered with chick peas and cracked wheat, or the savoury stews of lamb or beef with saffron, cumin, prunes, raisins and almonds.

There is one special stall on the square that my friends and I often visit just for a glass or two of chilled fresh yoghurt thickened in the traditional way (with chokes of baby wild artichokes) which gives it a fresh and delicious flavour. Here, too, on the tiny terrace above the square, you can sit at long tables and order brochettes of *kefta* (seasoned minced lamb), or lamb or beef liver, and bits of lamb or beef. Precede this, as we did one night during *Aid el Kebir* (the Great Feast), with a nourishing bowl of *harira* (the traditional 'break fast' of Ramadan) and follow with a glass or two of fresh yoghurt and you'll have a meal to remember. All for less than a pound.

Aladdin had opened his cave of mystical delights for me right in the heart of the Place Djemmaa el Fna – an array of wonderfully colourful street food ready to be enjoyed in the midst of a Middle Ages scene of story-tellers, fortune-tellers, monkey-trainers, water-sellers, acrobats, musicians and dancers. This was the entertainment of our ancestors and this was the food they ate. If the essence of food is its flavour, its texture and its aroma, its spirit is in the people who create it, enjoy it and rely on it for their own sense of identity. Moroccan street food fulfils all of these ideals.

Eating out in the port at Essaouira is one of the many pleasures of this little seaside town. The freshly grilled fish – sardines, pageot *and the occasional lobster served with a fresh-tasting salad – are superb. Bring your own wine, and a bottle opener, and you'll have a meal to remember.*

Street markets

No visit to an Arab city is complete without a visit to the out-door street markets to see at first hand the beautiful arrays of fresh vegetables and fruits available to everyday shoppers: the best tomatoes I have ever seen, sweet, firm, thin skinned and slightly irregular in shape, richly flavoured and literally running with juice; purple, pink and white onions, and wild onions set out in Matisse-like swatches of primitive colour with glossy green and yellow and red peppers, pale white-green bulbs of fresh fennel, long perfectly shaped new carrots twinned with new turnips and baby courgettes (zucchini) all exactly the same size. There are fresh green lettuces, a choice of *sucré*, limestone, oak leaf, *frisé* and batavia; and wild herbs and baskets of Moroccan truffles, morels and ceps from the mountains. At one tiny stall of the market, you will find thin, crisply elegant stalks of wild asparagus; pungent piles of fresh coriander and flat-leafed (Italian) parsley nestle with stacks of dandelion leaves and the ragged, dark, almost black-green wild watercress that our ancestors must have known. Here, too, are baskets of live snails, and a farmer in for the day from the country, holding a brace of live rabbits by the ears or with a live turkey in his arms.

Freshness is the keynote here: from the round woven baskets of fragrant green and purple figs to what seems like acres of melons and oranges, blood oranges, tangerines and mandarins. Oranges sent to market right from the trees are delicious in Morocco. And I particularly like the small green Moroccan lemons called *limouns* (not quite lemons and not really limes) that have a sharp, sweetly pungent flavour all their own. Then there are loquats, those intriguing, slightly bruised-looking fruits that seem to be a cross between an apricot and a small quince with a funky, spicy mango flavour that is hard to describe.

The stand-keepers vie with each other to present their fruits and vegetables in the most pleasing way possible. Around the broad areas of fresh produce are little shops selling cheeses, spices, nuts, coffee and wine, as well as butchers', florists' and grocers' shops. Most exciting of these, perhaps, are the Moroccan spice and conserve stalls which display attractive bowls of green, black, red and violet coloured olives with their different dressings (dried herbs and brine; diced orange, carrot and hot red pepper; or a mouth-searing *harissa* spice mixture made of chopped tomatoes, garlic and hot red peppers). I like, too, the tall, glistening jars of salt-preserved, smooth-skinned Moroccan lemons and tiny oranges, perfect in their serried ranks, so necessary for traditional Moroccan *tagines* of chicken, lamb and fish, and an absolute 'must' for the fresh-tasting diced raw onion, tomato and salted lemon salad that I first tasted with freshly grilled fish in the old port of Essaouira (see page 102).

OPPOSITE: *Visiting the markets and* souks *is one of the great pleasures of Morocco.*
FROM LEFT TO RIGHT AND TOP TO BOTTOM: *Mountain of turnips for sale in a country market near Taroudant; sun-ripened melons – wonderfully juicy and full of flavour – are sold in the open village markets for a few pennies a pound; a country booth at a* moussem *selling flavoursome* tagines *of meats and poultry; a shopkeeper in the old city of Fez shows his wares; a butcher's shop in one of the new towns on the road to the Sahara; tomato sellers in the market at Marrakech; and spices on aromatic display in the spice* souk.

Herbs and spices

Moroccan cooks have used the finely ground barks, seeds, roots and berries in their cooking for hundreds of years. These riches are at our fingertips today, fresh or dried, ground or whole, ready to impart a magic touch to even the simplest dishes. For it is a mistake to think that simple cookery requires nothing more than a pinch of pepper and salt to make it palatable. There are so many more aromatics that we can call on to bring out the utmost in flavour in our everyday fare. And Moroccan cooking will bring you flavouring accents – *savant* combinations of aromatics, spices and herbs – that will affect your whole culinary palette. *Chermoula*, for instance, the brilliantly flavoured Moroccan seasoning mixture, is now an everyday flavour intensifier in my kitchen, especially for fish and poultry. This simple seasoning – a combination of finely chopped onion, garlic, flat-leafed (Italian) parsley and fresh green coriander, sparked with saffron, sweet and hot red pepper (and in the case of pigeons, turkey, duck or game), a hint of cinnamon instead of saffron – will add immeasurably to your cooking.

The three roots – garlic, onion and ginger – were the essentials for a healthy and potent life according to the ancient philosophies of India and China. To these potent aromatics,

CHERMOULA – *a classical seasoning agent made of chopped onion, garlic, flat-leafed parsley and coriander, enhanced with salt, black, sweet and hot red peppers and saffron – is a 'must' for all Moroccan recipes for cooking fish and poultry. This seasoning blend is also used to lend excitement and flavour to brochettes of lamb, beef or fish. When combined with certain other additives, such as cinnamon and honey and raisins, it can be used for game.*

Moroccan cooks add fresh green coriander, flat-leafed (Italian) parsley and the five basics of Moroccan cooking: saffron, cumin, sweet and hot red peppers and cinnamon.

Moroccan cooks use bountiful amounts of chopped fresh herbs and powdered spices to enhance, blend or accent the flavours in a dish, to stimulate appetite, aid digestion and add aroma, colour and texture to the foods they cook.

These magic powders, leaves, berries and seeds are the secret of fine cooking in Morocco. But western cooks are advised to use them sparingly until accustomed to their effects in cooking. It is always easier to add extra seasoning, but it is very difficult to subtract. When trying out a new recipe in which you use herbs and spices, use half quantities only, and then – if you like the flavour – add the rest (or even more) towards the end of cooking time.

ABSINTHE

Absinthe, used fresh in conjunction with several varieties of fresh mint, *verveine* and marjoram, provides the basis for a rich blend of herbal tea in Morocco. Used dried in *tagines* and soups, it is said (because of its bitterness) to provoke increased production of saliva. Good for digestion and stimulates the appetite. Excellent, too, for liver ailments.

ANISEED

A light, pleasantly liquorice flavour when used with a gentle touch in cooking. Aniseed, well known to ancient Chinese medicine, is used widely in Moroccan confectionary and cake making today. Moroccan cooks sprinkle aniseed on cakes, breads, sweet breads and sometimes pound it with sugar and cinnamon to flavour cakes, milk drinks and creams. Use it in the Moroccan manner – combined with cinnamon and ginger – to add flavour and excitement to fish and game. Moroccan cooks say it aids digestion and, believe it or not, increases the intellect!

CARDAMOM

Similar in flavour to ginger and allspice, but with a fresher, more pungent, almost citrus, flavour. It is used in Morocco as one of the prime ingredients of *ras el hanout*, the legendary Moroccan spice mixture used in 'warming' winter *tagines* of meat, poultry and game. Cardamom goes particularly well with orange. Try a little, too, sprinkled on melon, or just a hint of this fragrant spice to give a touch of the *bazaar* to after-dinner coffee in the Arab manner. Good for digestion.

CINNAMON

When used in moderation, its fragrant odour and sweet spicy flavour are the perfect foils to fish and fish sauces. Combine

The spice shops in the medina *are especially interesting to the food lover. Row after row of tiny shops sell every possible spice and herb.*

45

cinnamon with pepper, ginger, cloves and mace. Use this spicy mix as a 'dry marinade' to rub on game before cooking. Combine ground or powdered cinnamon with pounded sugar and ground almonds for a tantalizingly spicy-sweet flavouring and crunch for the *milles-feuilles* Arab pastries of the famous *b'stilla*.

Its highly fragrant odour and sweet aromatic flavour are a must for cinnamon toast in the Arab manner (see page 75).

CORIANDER

Sweet yet tart in flavour, coriander seed is a favourite ingredient in Morocco for dry marinades of sun-dried meats. Rubbed on the salted meats after salting, it is a must for *khlii* and for certain *tagines* of dried pulse vegetables and soups.

Fresh green coriander, once difficult to come by, is now found in most oriental food stores, supermarkets, Indian and Greek shops, and many supermarkets. The stems and leaves should be washed to remove any grit or dirt and then shaken dry. They can be kept successfully for a week in the refrigerator, standing in a jar or glass of water and with their tops covered with a plastic bag; or, more simply, in a plastic bag into which some drops of water have been sprinkled to provide moisture.

It makes a very determined contribution to every dish it touches which, to some, is an acquired taste. Fresh green coriander is used in practically all cooking in Morocco where it is called *kasbour*. Its exotic, funky flavour is the highlight in *kefta*, brochettes of lamb, beef or fish, and in all salads and salad dressings.

CUMIN SEED

Cumin seed – along with hot and sweet red peppers – is perhaps the most commonly used spice in Moroccan cooking. Its strong aromatic scent and pungent flavour (similar to caraway seed but much stronger) are made use of extensively in Moroccan cookery. It is a delicious flavourer for barbecued or steamed lamb and is a must for charcoal-grilled brochettes or *kefta*. In Morocco, I like to use the seeds whole, or ground, as an attractive and flavourful 'wrapping' for cubes or balls of creamy white goat's cheese.

GINGER

One of the earliest oriental spices to be known to Morocco, ginger originally came from southern China, where the ripe roots were carefully selected, oiled in several waters to remove some of their fire, and then dried and ground.

This extremely pungent spice should be creamy white in colour when ground. Try blending ground ginger, black pepper and crushed salt, and rubbing this over cubed beef before grilling. Also good with lamb. Use it fresh too, peeled and grated or finely chopped.

OPPOSITE: *A selection of spices used in Moroccan cooking photographed in front of colour drawings taken from an old travel book on Morocco.*

PEPPER

Pepper is the most widely used spice in Morocco. Black pepper – one of the first spices to be introduced to Europe – lends flavour and excitement to most foods. It quickly loses its flavour and aroma when ground. I prefer to grind it (or crack it) as I need it. Sweet red pepper (paprika to us), warmly aromatic and a rich red in colour, is used a great deal in Moroccan cookery. Use this mild sweet cousin of hot red pepper to add colour and flavour to all Moroccan *tagines*, grilled (barbecued or broiled) fish, meat or chicken dishes, and to flavour salad dressings for cooked and raw Moroccan salads. I like to use it, too, as a colourful 'wrap' for cubes or balls of creamy white goat's cheese. Hot red pepper (or cayenne pepper) – the most pungent of all spices – is very hot and biting. Use it to lend excitement to fish and shellfish, to pick up salad dressings and for all the hot stews and *ragoûts* of North Africa.

SAFFRON

Saffron – one of the world's most costly flavouring agents – comes from the stamens of a certain kind of crocus. Greatly esteemed in Morocco as a flavourer of bread, cakes, soups and stews, saffron lends its special flavour and colour to *chermoula* mixtures for fish and poultry, fish soups and stews and the famous 'break fast' soup, *harira*.

Although this expensive spice is often used in Moroccan recipes, only a small amount of saffron is used, sometimes in conjunction with a little powdered turmeric, salt and sweet red pepper to make it go further.

SALT

Salt is important in Moroccan cooking, used as an integral part of the flavoursome spice and herb mix known as *chermoula* which gives savour to Moroccan dishes. It is also provided in small bowls with twin bowls of powdered cumin to accompany grilled brochettes and *kefta* and roasts and grills of lamb and poultry.

RAS EL HANOUT

This, roughly translated as 'shop-keeper's choice' or 'head of the shop' – is a warming blend of many spices and herbs. *Ras el hanout* is available packaged commercially in France and loose in Morocco. In Britain you will have to make do with fewer – as in the following simple recipe – or with the 'magic' thirteen: pepper, grains of Paradise, lavender, thyme, rosemary, cumin, ginger, nutmeg, mace, cardamom, cloves, fenugreek and cinnamon. In some Moroccan mixes you will also find arcane ingredients unknown elsewhere, such as *harmel*, *jusquiane*, and even rosebuds, belladonna and cantharides (Spanish fly).

RAS EL HANOUT

A simple version!

$1\frac{1}{2}$ teaspoons black peppercorns
1 teaspoon each of powdered ginger, cumin, cinnamon and coriander
$\frac{1}{4}$ teaspoon each of powdered nutmeg and hot red pepper
4 cardamom seeds
4 cloves

Pound all these in a mortar to a powder and use in recipes as directed.

MOROCCAN GRILLED KEFTA

450g/1lb minced (ground) lamb
100g/$\frac{1}{4}$lb lamb fat
1 egg
1 tablespoon sweet red pepper
1 teaspoon powdered cumin
$\frac{1}{4}$ teaspoon each hot red pepper and powdered cinnamon
fresh mint leaves, chopped
1 small bunch fresh green coriander, chopped
1 Spanish onion, peeled and grated
2 tablespoons each olive oil and water
salt and freshly ground black pepper

1 Mix all the ingredients, adding salt and freshly ground black pepper to taste. Knead for 15 minutes. Chill in the refrigerator for 1 hour.

2 Prepare charcoal fire, or preheat grill (broiler).

3 When ready to cook, form *kefta* mixture into little round patties 5–6cm/2–2$\frac{1}{2}$ inches in diameter and 1.5cm/$\frac{3}{4}$ inch thick. Cook over or under high heat for a few minutes on each side. Serve grilled *kefta* with additional salt and powdered cumin.

Serves 4

MOROCCAN BROCHETTES I

350g/$\frac{3}{4}$lb lamb, cut into 1cm/$\frac{1}{2}$ inch cubes
350g/$\frac{3}{4}$lb lamb fat, cut into 1cm/$\frac{1}{2}$ inch cubes
1 teaspoon each salt, powdered cumin and crushed black pepper
$\frac{1}{4}$ teaspoon each hot red and sweet red peppers
2 tablespoons olive oil

1 Place lamb and fat cubes in a large bowl. Combine salt and spices and sprinkle over lamb and fat cubes, turning them as you do so. Add olive oil and mix well. Leave lamb to marinate for at least 2 hours.

2 Prepare charcoal fire, or preheat grill (broiler).

3 When ready to cook, place meat on metal skewers alternately with lamb fat. Sprinkle any remaining marinade sauce over skewered lamb and grill over charcoal, or under preheated grill (broiler), until done, turning skewers frequently during cooking. Serve brochettes with additional salt and powdered cumin.

Serves 4

Brochette stalls where for the price of a cigarette you can enjoy three brochettes of cubed liver and lamb fat seared over the open fire, generously seasoned with a magical mix of powdered cumin, hot red pepper and coarse salt and then deftly inserted into a quarter round of crisp crusted Arab bread: a revelation of fabulous texture and flavour that literally explodes in the mouth.

There are three main sorts of brochettes served on street stalls: BOULFAF (pieces of sheep's liver skewered and grilled over charcoal and strewn with cumin, invariably served with a hot sauce for dipping); KEBAB (a grander version of boulfaf) is made of fillet of lamb or beef, marinated, spiced and grilled with interlarding strips of fat (both illustrated); and KEFTA (grilled minced lamb with spices) which can be really delicious.

MOROCCAN BROCHETTES II

350g/$\frac{3}{4}$lb lamb, cut into 1cm/$\frac{1}{2}$ inch cubes
350g/$\frac{3}{4}$lb lamb fat, cut into 1cm/$\frac{1}{2}$ inch cubes
$\frac{1}{2}$ Spanish onion, peeled and finely chopped
1–2 cloves garlic, peeled and finely chopped
2 tablespoons chopped fresh green coriander
4 tablespoons chopped flat-leaved (Italian) parsley
1 teaspoon salt
$\frac{1}{2}$ teaspoon sweet red pepper
$\frac{1}{4}$ teaspoon each powdered cumin and hot red pepper
2 tablespoons olive oil

1 Place lamb and fat cubes in a large bowl. Combine remaining ingredients and spoon over lamb and fat. Mix well. Leave to marinate for at least 2 hours.

2 Prepare charcoal fire, or preheat grill (broiler).

3 Place meat on metal skewers alternately with lamb fat and grill and serve as above.

Serves 4

MOROCCAN LIVER BROCHETTES
BOULFAF

This recipe requires a special ingredient called caul, lace fat or *crépinette* that is rarely, if ever, found in supermarkets. It is available, however, in fine butchers' shops. Ask for lamb caul if you can get it, otherwise (not very Moroccan as they don't use pork products) use pork.

700g/1½lb lamb's liver, cut into slices 1cm/½ inch thick
lamb caul, well washed and drained and cut into strips 2.5cm/1 inch wide by
5cm/2 inches long

SPICE MIX
1 teaspoon each sweet red pepper and salt
½ teaspoon powdered cumin
¼ teaspoon hot red pepper

1 To prepare brochettes, cut the liver slices into 1cm/½ inch cubes. Place in a large colander and pour boiling water over them, tossing from time to time. Allow to drain, then pat dry.

2 Combine spice mix ingredients in a small bowl. Mix well and then dredge liver pieces with it.

3 Prepare charcoal fire, or preheat grill (broiler).

4 When ready to cook, wrap each piece of liver in a piece of caul and place six parcels on each metal skewer. Grill over charcoal, or under preheated grill (broiler), until done, turning skewers frequently during cooking. Serve with additional salt, powdered cumin and hot red pepper.

Serves 4

STREET MARKET FRIED FISH

4 large thick slices flat fish, 5cm/2 inches thick (see below)
flour
salt
powdered saffron
1–2 pinches hot red pepper
freshly ground black pepper
oil for deep-frying
Pommes Frites (see page 119)
8 aubergine (eggplant) slices, deep-fried
4 hot green peppers, deep-fried

1 Rub thick flat slices of fish (*mostelle*, bonito, *palomete* or monkfish in the Moroccan street restaurants; try turbot or monkfish) with a mixture of three parts flour to one part salt, flavoured with powdered saffron, hot red and black peppers to taste.

2 Deep-fry saffron-floured fish in bubbling oil until crisp and golden on the outside but still moist and tender within (about 10–15 minutes).

3 Serve each fish slice with a portion of Pommes Frites, and garnish with a couple of slices deep-fried aubergine (eggplant) and a deep-fried hot green pepper, for flavour accents.

Serves 4

7

OLIVE OIL
AND OTHER FATS
USED IN
MOROCCAN COOKING

Many small villages in the pre-Sahara are surrounded by their own olive groves from which the ripe olives are harvested in December and January for making the olive oil for which Morocco is so famous. Not one of the biggest producers in the Mediterranean, Italy or Spain dispute this honour, Moroccan olive oil – at its best golden in colour with a fresh fruity flavour – is one of the finest oils I know.

Setting off early on a visit to southern Morocco, in the still dark central square of Taroudant's walled *medina*, we saw a group of thirty or so men dressed in dark cloaks and armed with long wooden staves. In the gloom they seemed somehow threatening, like a group of mediaeval *samurai* or brotherhood of armed monks about some secret business. On closer inspection we could see that their hooded dark cloaks were woollen *djellabahs*, a necessary protective covering against the still crisp air, and their threatening staves, long wooden sticks to knock olives from the branches of the olive trees.

Excited by the prospect of seeing an olive harvest, we gave up our plans for an early start to the Souss, and followed the trucks carrying the pickers, huddled together in silence. The men seemed uncomfortable at the idea of harvesting the olives in the rising mist, and could not be sent up into the trees until the sun was high enough to dry the dew. The women in their bright dresses came to join them, walking out from the *medina* with sacks and baskets for the ripe fruit.

Then, suddenly, magically, it was time and the men were high in the trees with their tall ladders rattling against the

ABOVE: *The olive harvest. Black olives must be harvested in a dry season and are beaten down with sticks by men who climb up into the trees. They are then carefully sorted on the ground.*

OPPOSITE: *Olives, like dates, were almost sacred to the early Arabs. The green-tinted oil was used not only for cooking but as the chief fuel to light the lamps of their homes and mosques and as a healing balm in cases of illness or old age.*

boughs, and the sound of the long staves beating on the branches to make the olives fall was like castanets. The women on the ground below gathered the olives one by one, picking only the best fruits to place on the cloths laid out near the trees.

The harvest seemed a happy event with the women singing and giving out the extraordinary piercing musical cry, a drawn-out ululation, with which they express great joy and great sadness, or use in time of war to drive their men on. The men scampering among the tall branches of the old trees kept time with their sticks to the singing below.

We stayed with the harvesters all morning, until it was time for them to break for early lunch – quarters of lamb cooked over an open fire with ripe tomatoes and green peppers grilled in the ashes. Crisp round loaves of bread from the local bakery, a beaker of olive oil for the vegetables, tiny packets of salt and powdered cumin for the lamb, and the meal was complete.

As they sat down for their feast, the *mallem* who was directing operations led us off to the nearby olive press where we found they were still using the age-old method of crushing the ripe olives for oil – a great round stone trough, measuring at least 2.25 metres/8 feet across, around which a small blindfolded donkey was turning a heavy stone wheel to crush the olives.

In Morocco, the fruit is crushed into a pulp in the sort of mill which was used in Apicius' time and probably even before. And from the pulp is pressed the best quality 'virgin' olive oil – light green to golden amber in colour, fruity and warm with a unique bouquet – making it perfect for salads and marinades and for the spice and herb mixture called *chermoula* which is one of the great secrets of Moroccan cooking.

Cold water is added to the residue of this first pressing for the second and third pressings to replace some of the moisture that has been squeezed out. The oil from these pressings, though not of the ultra top grade of the first 'virgin' pressing, is still of excellent quality. These stronger, more acid oils are used in the cooking of the countless *tagines* of meat, poultry, fish and vegetables that make up the basis of Moroccan menus.

That absolutely everything is used from the olive is proved

ABOVE: *Olive trees vary enormously in size. The trees in and around Taroudant are as big as oak trees but the olive plantations of Marrakech, and further south near Agadir, raise trees small enough so the tender fruits can be gathered by hand.*

RIGHT: *All twigs, moss and leaves are removed by the women on the ground below before the olives are transported to the olive press.*

FAR RIGHT: *Olives are pressed in these rustic mills where, by the light of a lantern, a blinkered donkey may be observed turning the heavy stone wheel.*

by the fourth pressing; this time the oil is used in the manufacture of beauty products, soaps and shampoos, and the dry residue of the pulp is used for fertilizer. Even the pits are used to provide a lubricating oil and the tight-grained wood of the olive tree, golden in colour and beautifully marked with darker whorls, is used to make beautiful olive wood salad bowls and servers.

The olive trees that one sees on the rocky southern slopes of Morocco – with their dusty green leaves, silvery white on the underside – have been growing there since paleolithic times, imported in all probability from the Middle East. The olive's origins have been lost in legend: the Egyptians knew it and attributed it to Isis, sister-wife of Osiris, the Greeks to Pallas Athene from the island of Crete and the early Romans to Minerva. But it was probably the Etruscans who first brought the olive from Asia Minor.

In Islam, the olive tree is associated with light, the symbol of the Prophet, and of virility. In certain tribes men drink olive oil to increase their powers and it has been an integral part of Moroccan life and cooking since early times.

Olive classifications

Olive verte: a fresh bright green in colour.

Olive cassée: tender green or yellow green in colour.

Olive tournante: slightly rose or wine red in colour turning to brown or a deep reddish brown.

Olive mure: a brilliant black colour, or matt violet tinted black, or a deep brown red, not only its skin, but in all the thickness of the flesh.

Of all the oils used for cooking – and for salad dressings – groundnut, sunflower, sesame, mustard, corn, hazelnut, walnut – my favourite is olive oil.

Olive oil must be perfectly clear, brilliant in colour and without impurities. At its best, a clear golden yellow, leaning a little towards green, its soft savour giving a fruity taste, light or accentuated. The new oil is a little 'troubled' at first, it clears as its fermentation makes it transparent.

Unrefined oils that are cold pressed (so called because no artificial heat is applied in the extracting process) are the richest in colour and flavour, and unrefined oils are best from the nutritional point of view as well.

A flavoured oil that is much used in Morocco is red pepper oil. Steep 20 hot red peppers in a bottle of olive oil for two weeks and use the oil to add piquant flavour to Moroccan *tagines*, soups, sauces for *couscous* and for salad dressings.

Argan oil

One of the most picturesque sights of the pre-Sahara areas of the Souss are the herds of little black and white goats that are pastured among the argan trees on the roads from Agadir and Taroudant to the desert. Here the Berbers often cook with a highly flavoured oil extracted from the nuts from these trees. Argan oil is, as far as I'm concerned, an acquired taste, but the goats love the acid, pungent flavour of the nuts and literally climb high into the trees to harvest them.

Argan oil is often mixed with thick almond paste and local honey to make an intriguing almond spread called *amalou*. Served with hot breads or as a filling for *rghaif* and *beghrir* (see pages 79 and 78), it is a famous southern dish.

ARGAN OIL: *Among the more picturesque sights of the south are the herds of goats which literally climb the argan trees to harvest the pungently flavoured nuts.*

8

CONSERVES AND OTHER BASICS OF MOROCCAN COOKING

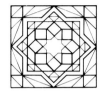

There are certain basic preparations – conserves of fruits and vegetables for the most part – preserved olives with aromatics, cut vegetables in brine, preserved sweet and hot red peppers, preserved lemons, and the special salted butter called *smen* without which no *couscous* is complete – which are absolute 'musts' if you want your cooking to have an authentic Moroccan flavour.

Add to these simple basics, Moroccan yoghurt made with the thistles of wild artichokes, the delicious preserved meat called *khlii*, a special sourdough 'starter' for flat round loaves of Moroccan bread, yeast-raised pancakes, *rghaif* and *beghrir*, both savoury and sweet, and the paper-thin leaves of pastry called *warkha* that are used for such diverse recipes as *brik* and *trid* (see pages 95 and 90) and to enclose the legendary spiced *milles-feuilles* pastry of pigeon mixed with eggs, sugared spices and lemon called *b'stilla* which is served as the traditional first course of every Moroccan banquet.

Olives

Jars of identical olives neatly packed on supermarket shelves in Britain give no clue to the enormous variety to be found loose, piled in colourful mounds in the market stalls of every Moroccan city. Here you can make your choice daily from tiny crinkled black olives with a pungent salty taste for snacks, salads and hors d'oeuvres, glossy green olives in brine, stone-cracked green or wine red olives soaked in brine for cooking, cracked green olives flavoured with diced preserved lemon peel and dried herbs, cracked rosy-hued olives flavoured with diced bitter

OPPOSITE: *No visit to the* souks *is complete without a stop at the conserves stall. Here you will find certain basic preparations – mainly conserves of fruits and vegetables – which are most useful if you want your cooking to have an authentic Moroccan flavour.*

TOP ROW, LEFT TO RIGHT: *Tiny preserved* Marrakshi *lemons, preserved lemons and pickles in brine.*

MIDDLE ROW, LEFT TO RIGHT: *Black olives, olives with aromatics, cut vegetables in brine.*

BOTTOM ROW, LEFT TO RIGHT: *Cornichons, spicy harissa mixture and capers.*

orange, raw carrot, fennel and hot red pepper, or cured black olives set like ebony beads in a hot red pepper sauce called *harissa*.

The olive probably was first cultivated in Syria six thousand years ago, and the practice slowly spread around the shores of North Africa, reaching Spain and Portugal at the time of the Arab conquest. The ancient Greeks and Romans grew the olive and used its precious oil for food, medicine and for anointing their bodies.

The olive – green when immature, turning tan, rose-hued, violet, wine red and finally black as it ripens – gives us a multiple harvest. For green olives in brine or oil, the fruit is picked early. For black olives, it is allowed to mature on the tree but not to become soft. For oil, the fruit is allowed to ripen fully.

Olives fresh from the tree, green or black, are intensely bitter. In the home preserving process the fruit is soaked for six to ten days in as many changes of water to remove the bitter taste. Commercially, it is soaked first in a lye solution to remove the bitterness and then washed thoroughly to remove the lye. In either case the olives are next soaked in a strong salt brine where they are left for quite a while before being soaked in fresh water to remove excess salt.

PRESERVED OLIVES WITH BITTER ORANGES

To make this conserve, choose olives that are violet coloured, just turning from green to black.

1 Crack olives with a flat stone just hard enough to break the flesh but not so hard that you crack the stone (pit).

2 If using fresh olives from the tree, put them in a large earthenware, enamelled tin or stainless steel bowl, add cold water to cover and leave overnight. Repeat this process, changing water each time, for 7–10 days, or until olives have lost their bitterness. Drain. (If using bottled or packaged olives, crack olives as above and then put in cold water overnight only. Drain.)

3 To make a bitter orange brine, peel Seville oranges, making sure that you remove all traces of pith, then chop flesh coarsely and place in a mortar. Add coarse salt and pound vigorously to extract all the juice. Add more salt to taste and $\frac{1}{2}$ teaspoon hot red pepper. Mix well and strain this highly flavoured orange brine into a clean bowl.

4 Divide olives between sterilized Kilner (Mason) jars; and do the same with the orange brine. Add enough cold boiled water to cover olives. Cover jars and let olives marinate in this mixture for 2–3 weeks.

Use in *tagines* of lamb and veal with vegetables or in Moroccan appetizer salads – delicious, for example, with sliced oranges, artichoke hearts or endive (chicory), or a combination of two or more of these.

GREEN OLIVES WITH MOROCCAN MARINADE

1 Cure the green olives as opposite.

2 Soak cured, cracked green olives overnight in cold water to remove excess salt. Drain.

3 To prepare the Moroccan marinade, combine 6 tablespoons each chopped flat-leafed (Italian) parsley and fresh green coriander with 2 cloves peeled and finely chopped garlic, $\frac{1}{2}$ teaspoon hot red pepper flakes and $\frac{1}{4}$ teaspoon powdered cumin. Add 4–6 tablespoons olive oil, and lemon juice to taste.

4 Cover olives with the flavoursome marinade, and keep in the refrigerator for at least a week. Moisten with olive oil and toss well before serving.

GREEN OLIVES WITH GREEN HERB MARINADE

You'll find this delicious recipe – first tasted in the street market in the old city of Fez – a refreshing variation on the preserved olive theme.

1 Cure the olives as opposite.

2 Soak cracked cured green olives overnight in cold water to remove excess salt. Drain.

3 To prepare the green herb marinade, combine 8 tablespoons each chopped flat-leafed (Italian) parsley and fresh green coriander with 2 cloves peeled and finely chopped garlic. Add the peel of $\frac{1}{2}$ preserved lemon (see page 64), cut into thin strips 2.5cm/1 inch long, and thin strips of hot red and green peppers. Add juice of preserved lemon to taste.

4 Cover olives in sterilized jars with this marinade.

One of the most popular Moroccan hors d'oeuvres *or snacks is the olive: wrinkled, fresh, black olives that you see heaped high in giant metal bowls in Moroccan grocery or conserve shops; or cracked green olives flavoured with wild thyme and conserved lemons; or even better, black olives spiked with fiery hot* harissa; *or, my favourite for serving with drinks, violet-hued olives flavoured with hot red pepper, pieces of bitter orange and raw carrot flavoured with a hint of lemon or vinegar.*

BLACK OLIVES WITH PRESERVED LEMONS

1 Cure the olives as on page 60.

2 Soak cured black olives overnight in cold water to remove excess salt. Drain.

3 To make the marinade, combine diced peel of 1 preserved lemon (see page 64) with 1 teaspoon dried oregano and the juice squeezed from preserved lemon flesh. Add ¼ teaspoon hot red pepper and fresh lemon juice to taste.

4 Cover olives with this marinade and keep in sterilized jars indefinitely, if well covered.

BLACK OLIVES WITH HARISSA

1 Cure the olives as on page 60.

2 Soak cured black olives overnight in cold water to remove excess salt. Drain.

3 Combine in bowl with *Harissa II* (see page 66), and keep in sterilized jars in the refrigerator.

A typical display of olives and conserves in a favourite shop in the Marrakech medina.

Home-made Moroccan butters

Butter – especially the clarified 'aged' butter called *smen* – and olive oil are favoured for cooking in Morocco, although ground-nut (peanut) oil can be used for general frying, particularly pastries.

ZEBDA

This is a fresh-tasting butter made in the spring. It is much appreciated in Morocco where it is made from fresh milk which has been allowed to curdle slightly by leaving it for 2–3 days in an open jug. The 'turned' milk is then poured into a churn called a *khabia* where it is churned until the golden butter begins to separate from the *lben* (buttermilk). The butter particles are patted into cheese-like rounds and left to cure in the cool buttermilk. *Lben*, the fresh buttermilk left over from making *zebda* is also much appreciated by southern Moroccans who serve it as an accompaniment to breakfast cakes or pancakes, or as a thirst-quenching drink flavoured with orange-flower water. It is also served at Moroccan banquets as an accompaniment to sweet *couscous* (see page 201).

SMEN

This is a cooked butter made from *zebda* to which a little salt and sometimes a little thyme, oregano and *za'atar* (a wild herb from the scrubby wastes of the pre-Sahara) have been added. *Smen*, although a trifle strong-tasting to be consumed as butter for European palates (including my own), is absolutely delicious when used to lend its fragrant, cheese-like flavour to *couscous* or *k'dras* (stews of chicken or lamb simmered in *smen* with vegetables, chick peas and almonds). I can always tell when we are cooking *couscous* or *k'dra* in my house for the tantalizing aroma of *smen* –delicate, buttery, with perhaps a hint of Dolcelatte or Gorgonzola to it – permeates the house.

In Fez and Berber households, it is the custom to keep *smen* packed away in sealed jars like old wines for years, with the aged *smen* becoming more amber-tinted and more potent with each year that passes. It is possible to make a reasonable sort of *smen* at home.

HOME-MADE SMEN

450g/1lb unsalted butter, diced
1 tablespoon coarse salt
¼ teaspoon herbes de Provence

1 Melt the diced butter over a moderate heat, stirring frequently to avoid colouring it. Bring the butter to the boil, then lower heat and simmer, without stirring, for 30–40 minutes, or until the butter is clear and separated from the solids at the bottom of the pan.

2 Sprinkle the salt and dried herbs into a muslin (cheesecloth)-lined strainer. This will give a little added flavour to the *smen*.

3 Spoon the clear liquid little by little into the muslin (cheesecloth)-lined strainer and then strain again into a sterilized jar. Cover jar and store in the refrigerator until ready to use to add flavour to a *couscous*, a hot soup or for making any of the *k'dra* recipes. You will find your *smen* will keep for at least 6 months.

4 You could, as a way of approximating the flavour of an aged Moroccan *smen*, cool the clarified butter, and then mash in a little Dolcelatte cheese to taste (one part cheese to five or six parts *smen*). Another way is to use a mixture of butter and olive oil with a little added salt and black pepper, sweet and hot red peppers and cinnamon to taste. Both these are good with *couscous*.

Jars of Moroccan conserves in their serried ranks make an attractive kitchen display.

MOROCCAN PRESERVED LEMONS
CITRONS CONFITS

One of the prime ingredients of Moroccan cooking, preserved lemons can be bought ready-made in Morocco, packed in jars or loose, for use at home. But many Moroccan cooks prefer to make their own from a mixture of small, thin-skinned lemons (*doqq*) and tart bergamot lemons (*boussera*). In Britain, look for ripe, smooth, thin-skinned lemons, without flaws for the best results. Thick-skinned lemons are not suitable.

Only the peel is used in cooking, plus the juice from the pulp (which is discarded), and the flavour is quite unique. The peel has lost its bitter taste, and brings a different, pungent, even 'sexy' taste to countless Moroccan dishes.

16 small ripe lemons, thin-skinned if possible
coarse salt
lemon juice

1 Scrub lemons with a stiff brush, then place them in a large glass, plastic, stainless steel or glazed earthenware container. Cover with cold water and allow lemons to soak for 3–5 days, changing water each day.

2 Drain lemons. Then, using the point of a sharp knife, insert knife 6mm/$\frac{1}{4}$ inch from the bud end of each lemon and make four incisions lengthwise to within 6mm/$\frac{1}{4}$ inch of the other end. Then cut through incisions in each lemon so that lemons are cut completely through both sides, but still held together at both ends.

3 Insert $\frac{1}{4}$ teaspoon coarse salt into centre of each lemon, squeezing them open, then arrange lemons in sterilized Kilner (Mason) jars. Sprinkle lemons in each jar with 1 tablespoon coarse salt. Add strained juice of 1 lemon to each jar and pour in enough boiling water to cover lemons.

4 Leave lemons to steep in this mixture for at least 3 weeks before using them. You'll find that the salty, oily pickling juice is honey thick and highly flavoured. Use it in salads instead of vinegar; use it, too, to add savour to *tagines*. The lemons will keep in this mixture indefinitely if stored in a dry place.

5 To use preserved lemons, remove lemon from jar, and rinse well under cold running water. Cut away pulp from each quarter (squeezing juice from pulp to use in recipe) and discard. Use quartered preserved peel for delicious *tagines* of lamb, chicken or fish, or cut peel into thin slices, julienne or tiny dice to use in vegetable *tagines*, with fish or in salads. Never touch preserved lemons in the jar with an oily or greasy spoon, as fat will spoil the pickling mixture. Don't worry if a white film forms on preserved lemons in the jar; just rinse it off before using lemons.

Harissa

Harissa (or *arhissa* as it is sometimes called) is a fiery condiment based on hot red peppers, olive oil and garlic, common to the Maghreb countries of Morocco, Tunisia and Algeria. An excellent sauce for saffron-flavoured fish soups and stews, I like to use it, too, to spice sun-dried meats, *tagines* of meat and poultry, or meat and vegetable soups. Use it to add savour to a sauce for *couscous* as well. I like to add a touch of *harissa* to a stew of tomatoes and red peppers used as a savoury base for poached eggs or the little fresh sausages called *merguez* (originally Tunisian but which one finds in the street-market restaurants in Morocco today). Sliced sausages or Spanish *chorizo* would be a good substitute, but do try the following recipe.

A good *harissa* should be thick, with the consistency of a light mayonnaise. Serve it in a little side dish with a very small spoon.

The food stalls and the brochette vendors in the *souk* make a wet 'dipping' sauce of skinned, seeded and finely grated tomatoes and water, flavoured with salt and a little *harissa*, to serve with grilled *kefta* or brochettes of heart or liver. Try it.

Preserved lemons and olives play their part in many Moroccan tagines. *This is* CHICKEN MQUALLI, *chicken simmered with aromatics and spices, preserved lemons and olives.*

HARISSA I

100g/¼lb (2 cups) hot dried red chilli (chili) peppers
6 cloves garlic, peeled
4 tablespoons coarse salt
6 tablespoons coriander seeds
4 tablespoons cumin seeds
8–10 tablespoons olive oil

1 Remove the stems from the dried red chilli (chili) peppers and remove seeds. Put red peppers in hot water until they are soft.

2 In the meantime, pound garlic cloves in mortar with half the salt until smooth. Remove from mortar and reserve. Add drained red peppers to mortar and pound to a smooth paste with remaining coarse salt. Remove and add to pounded garlic.

3 Combine coriander and cumin seeds in mortar and pound until powdered. Return pounded garlic and hot red peppers to mortar, add a little olive oil, and pound until smooth. Continue this process, adding more olive oil, until sauce is smooth and well blended. It will keep indefinitely in a sealed jar in the refrigerator.

HARISSA II

2 fresh red peppers, grilled (broiled or barbecued) and skinned (see page 105)
25g/1oz (⅓ cup) hot red chilli (chili) pepper, or 15g/½oz (1 tablespoon) dried hot
red peppers
2 cloves garlic, peeled
2 teaspoons cumin seeds
½ teaspoon coriander seeds
coarse salt
olive oil

1 Drain the skinned, rinsed fresh peppers, and cut in quarters, discarding stems, but reserving seeds. Chop pepper segments coarsely and add to seeds.

2 Slice hot red pepper thinly; if using dried red peppers, soak them in hot water for 1 hour. Slice thinly.

3 In a mortar, combine chopped skinned fresh pepper, pepper seeds, garlic, cumin and coriander seeds, and salt to taste. Pound to a smooth paste, adding a little olive oil if desired.

4 Add chopped hot red pepper and continue to pound until well amalgamated into the mixture. Add a little olive oil to give smoothness to the sauce if desired. Spoon into sterilized Kilner (Mason) jars and cover with a layer of olive oil, then seal jars and refrigerate.

MERGUEZ

These are delicious when served with a *harissa*-spiked sauce of tomatoes and red peppers.

350g/¾lb beef, cut into cubes
100g/¼lb beef fat, cut into cubes
1–2 cloves garlic, peeled and chopped
2–4 tablespoons water
salt and freshly ground black pepper
1 teaspoon sweet red pepper
¼ teaspoon each hot red pepper, powdered cinnamon (or nutmeg), powdered cloves
and crumbled thyme
casing for sausages

1 In a food processor, process beef, beef fat and garlic until well mixed.

2 Moisten the meat with a few tablespoons of water, then add the remaining ingredients, and process again. Correct seasoning, adding a little more salt, pepper and spices if desired. The mixture should be highly flavoured.

3 Force the seasoned meat into a casing, tying at 5cm/2 inch intervals, and hang the sausages in an airy place to dry for 24 hours.

4 The sausage is cooked in boiling water, pan-fried or grilled over charcoal, and is eaten hot or cold.

OPPOSITE: *Preserved lemons (in the foreground) in their amber-tinted syrup made from the natural oils of the lemon peel infused in brine, black olives (just behind) in spicy* harissa, *and preserved olives.*

KHLII
SUN-DRIED PRESERVED MEAT

This age-old method of preserving meat in Morocco pre-dates the age of canning and freezing by many centuries, and it is still in use today. Moroccan cooks rub strips of lamb or beef with salt, spices, garlic, oil and vinegar and then hang them in the open air to dry in the hot summer sun for up to 7 days. The meat is thoroughly dry when it is no longer soft when cut. Absolutely no moisture must come out when meat is pressed with your finger.

The sun-dried meat is then cooked for 2–2½ hours in lamb fat and water until all the water has evaporated and the strips of meat are glazed with the flavoursome fat and cooking juices.

Khlii is used, much as we use bacon or *petit salé* (lightly salted pork fat), to flavour *tagines* of fresh or dried vegetables, or a winter *couscous* or soup.

1

2.25kg/5lb beef
50g/2oz (¼ cup) coarse salt
450g/1lb lamb (or beef) fat
1.2 litres/2 pints (5 cups) water
250ml/8fl. oz (1 cup) groundnut (peanut) oil
150ml/¼ pint (⅔ cup) olive oil

SPICE AND GARLIC PASTE
75g/3oz (6 tablespoons) coriander seeds, ground
50g/2oz garlic, peeled and crushed
2 tablespoons vinegar
50ml/2fl. oz (¼ cup) olive oil
50g/2oz (¼ cup) coarse salt

1 To prepare spice and garlic paste, combine all the ingredients together in a bowl. Mix well and leave to rest for 24 hours.

2 In the meantime, cut the meat into long thin strips. Rub the strips well with the coarse salt. Cover with a piece of muslin (cheesecloth) to protect from insects, and leave to absorb the flavours for 24 hours.

3 Then, take each strip of salted meat and cover it with a layer of spice and garlic paste, rubbing it in well with your fingers. Cover with muslin (cheesecloth) and leave to absorb flavours for a further 24 hours.

4 On the following day, take each piece of meat and hang it over a washing line (see picture) or, with needle and thread, take thread through the end of each strip and tie thread into a loop. Insert a broomstick through each loop, and hang the pole horizontally in the sun, covering the meat with a strip of muslin (cheesecloth) as above. Make sure that each strip is well covered with spice and garlic paste, and pat on a little where needed. Repeat this process over 3 or 4 more days, or until meat is thoroughly dried. Make sure you bring meat indoors at sunset, to keep it away from any possible mist or moisture in the night air.

4

5 When the meat is dried, remove it from the line or pole. Cut it into even-sized pieces and simmer it with its aromatics in melted fat, water and the oils, until all the water has been absorbed. The richly flavoured fat will be left in the pan. Stir often to ensure that meat does not stick to the bottom of pan or scorch.

6 When the meat is tender, remove it from casserole or stock pot and allow to cool completely in a large shallow container. Strain fats through a muslin (cheesecloth)-lined sieve into a container. Allow to cool completely. It must still be liquid.

2

3

KHLII: *The age-old method of preserving meat in Morocco, predating the age of canning or freezing and still used today, is to rub the strips of meat with salt, spices, ground coriander and cumin, finely chopped garlic, oil and vinegar and then to hang them in the open air to dry in the sun for seven days. The meat is taken indoors every night after the first two days to protect it from moisture. The sun-dried meat is then cooked for 2½ hours in lamb fat and water until the water has evaporated and the strips of meat are covered with fat. Khlii is used to flavour tagines of fresh vegetables, dried lentils and haricots blancs, or couscous much as we would use bacon or petit salé which it resembles a little in taste.*

7 Fill sterilized Kilner (Mason) jars loosely with meat, then pour over strained fat. Leave jars open for 2 hours, then seal.

8 Reserve the remaining bits or crumbs of meat and spice and garlic paste in a jar to use in savoury *beghrir* or *rghaif* (see pages 78 and 79).

KHLII WITH EGGS

I like *khlii* in one of the ancient recipes for royal breakfasts as served at the Palais Jamai in Fez.

175g/6oz khlii
1 tablespoon fat from the khlii
1 tablespoon olive oil
2 ripe tomatoes, skinned, seeded and chopped
¼ teaspoon sweet red pepper
⅛ teaspoon hot red pepper
freshly ground black pepper
4 eggs

1 Cut the *khlii* into small dice. Put dice in a *tagine* or small frying pan with the fat and olive oil, and simmer over a low heat for a few minutes.

2 Remove meat and keep warm. Add chopped tomatoes to *tagine* (or pan) and sauté until moisture has evaporated. Season tomatoes with sweet and hot red peppers, and freshly ground black pepper to taste. Return meat to pan and warm through.

3 Just before serving, carefully break eggs (1 per person) over meat and tomatoes, cover, and cook until whites of eggs are set. Serve immediately.

Serves 4

9

KHOBZ AND OTHER MOROCCAN BREADS

ABOVE: *Window in a little backstreet bread shop in the* medina *of Essaouira on the Atlantic coast of Morocco.*

OPPOSITE: *Old man selling bread in the* medina *of Marrakech.*

Bread is the mainstay of all meals in Morocco, with an almost religious significance. 'Give me bread in the name of Allah' is a cry heard from door to door in the *medina*. And if a Moroccan sees a crust of bread in his path, he will stop and carefully set it aside where it will not be trodden upon.

In my house, each flat round crisp-crusted loaf is blessed in the name of the Almighty before it is cut into the traditional wedges for each meal. And my cook Bacha brings it to the table herself and serves it personally to each guest so that, as she says, there will only be happiness in the house.

Bacha makes bread every morning, carefully setting out her large, round, wooden *gsaa* in which she kneads her dough. First, she measures out the unbleached wheat flour, adds a little salt and a little cornmeal (for crunch) and mixes it well across the breadth of the bowl.

Then she adds a tablespoon of peanut oil and a little warm water, works it in lightly with her fingers and then adds her secret ingredient – a sourdough 'starter' – which adds a wonderful flavour to the bread. She then kneads the dough energetically with both hands, adding a little warm water from time to time until the dough is smooth and pliable and pulls away from the bowl easily. Then she separates the dough into four parts (three to make loaves for the day and one to serve as the next day's 'starter').

It is all part of the bread *mystique* that forms such an important part of Moroccan home and street life. Of course, we have to buy extra loaves from time to time to supplement Bacha's three or four home-made creations, but here too, ritual plays its part. They are bought, on Bacha's orders, from one special woman

who sits in a high *kiosk* just inside the gate of Bab Doukkala.

On special occasions, Bacha scents the dough with sesame seeds or green anise seeds; at other times she brushes the loaves with egg yolk and water, or lightly dusts them with a little ground cornmeal for an extra crunchy crust. I confess I like these extra touches and the country blends of strong flour, cornmeal and barley that I first found in the *bled* or country – an altogether more lusty, simpler version than the sophisticated breads of the cities.

Bread – like Bacha's – is made each morning in most of the houses in my neighbourhood, and baked by the local neighbourhood baker. Each family marks the uncooked loaves with a fork or a special mark to enable them to pick out their own loaves. The uncooked loaves are carried to the baker by little boys or girls, usually the youngest child in the family, on special wooden boards covered with scraps of coloured cotton to protect them from the dust on the trip through the crowded streets. The loaves are baked in a wood-fired oven, each cotton covering also serving as a sign of ownership at the bakery, to distinguish it from that of the neighbours.

Bread is the 'staff of life' in Morocco, providing – with a few olives or dates, or a bit of cheese, and a glass of the ever-present mint tea – a complete meal for country labourer or shepherd tending his flocks in the *bled*.

BELOW LEFT: *My young neighbour Mohamed is a special friend who delights in running errands, not least of which is the morning trek to the local baker.*

BELOW RIGHT: *Moroccan bread is prepared in the home every morning and baked in the local baker's oven. Usually made of plain flour, sometimes with a little added barley flour or cornmeal, it stays fresh for 24 hours. Always round and flat in shape, the loaves are crisp crusted and golden in colour. Before sending bread to the neighbourhood baker, each family marks the loaves with a special mark to enable them to pick out their own loaves.*

YEAST DOUGH 'STARTER'

100g/¼lb plain flour (scant 1 cup all-purpose flour), sifted
2 tablespoons yellow cornmeal
8–10 tablespoons warm water
groundnut (peanut) oil

YEAST
7g/¼oz dried (active dry) yeast
1 teaspoon sugar
1 tablespoon plain (all-purpose) flour
4 tablespoons lukewarm water

1 In a small bowl, combine yeast, sugar, 1 tablespoon flour and lukewarm water. Stir and leave until frothy.

2 In the meantime, sift the 100g/¼lb (scant 1 cup) flour and the cornmeal into a larger bowl. Add the dissolved yeast and 8 tablespoons warm water and mix well with a wooden spoon until all the flour is incorporated and a small ball of dough is formed.

3 Remove dough from bowl and knead until well mixed. Add 1 tablespoon water and knead again until dough has absorbed it. Then add 1 more tablespoon water and knead again until it is absorbed, and the dough is smooth again, shiny and elastic (10–20 minutes).

4 At this point, dough will adhere to board and fingers, so remove and add to bulk of dough. Then sprinkle dough with a little extra sifted flour and gather into a ball, adding more sifted flour as required, until it is possible to hold ball of dough in hands.

5 Lightly oil a small bowl, place ball of dough in it, and brush with more oil. Put bowl, covered with a cloth, in a warm place to rise for 1–1½ hours, or until dough has doubled in bulk. Use in recipe for Moroccan bread (below).

NATURAL SOUR DOUGH 'STARTER'

100g/¼lb plain flour (scant 1 cup all-purpose flour), sifted
2 tablespoons yellow cornmeal
8–12 tablespoons lukewarm water
groundnut (peanut) oil
1 clove garlic, peeled

1 Sift flour and yellow cornmeal into a mixing bowl. Add 8 tablespoons lukewarm water and 1 tablespoon groundnut (peanut) oil and mix well with a wooden spoon to form a dough.

2 Remove dough from bowl, and knead until dough is well mixed. Add 1 tablespoon water and knead again until dough has absorbed it and is elastic. Add 1 more tablespoon water and knead again until it has been absorbed, and the dough is smooth again, shiny and elastic (10–20 minutes). (1 or 2 more tablespoons water may be added in this way, if desired, kneading dough each time until dough has absorbed extra water.)

3 Sprinkle dough with a little extra sifted flour and gather into a ball, adding more sifted flour as required, until it is possible to hold ball of dough in hands. Insert the garlic clove into the centre of the ball.

4 Lightly oil a small bowl, place ball of dough in it, and brush with more oil. Put bowl, covered with a cloth, in a warm place to rise for at least 12 hours, or overnight, or until dough has doubled in bulk. Remove garlic clove and use dough in recipe for Moroccan bread (overleaf).

MOROCCAN BREAD

Usually made of unbleached flour or strong (hard) flour – with sometimes a little barley flour or cornmeal added – Moroccan bread stays fresh for 24 hours. In the country, cooks often make bread completely of barley flour or cornmeal, or a mixture of two or three flours. Always round and flat in shape, the loaves are crisp crusted and golden in colour.

This recipe makes 2 flat round loaves with enough dough 'starter' left over for the next baking.

450g/1lb plain flour (3 cups plus 2 tablespoons all-purpose flour)
4 tablespoons yellow cornmeal
1 recipe yeast dough or natural sour dough 'starter' (see page 73)
1 tablespoon salt, diluted in a little water
350–450ml/12–15fl. oz (1½–2 scant cups) warm water
1 tablespoon sesame or anise seeds (optional)

1 Sift flour and cornmeal into a *gsaa* or large shallow bowl. Add 'starter' of your choice (see recipes on page 73) and salty water. Add a little warm water (about half the total quantity) and mix well with both hands, sprinkling with water from time to time as you beat, until dough is smooth and pliable.

2 Knead dough energetically several times, then work dough for 10–20 minutes, or until it is consistent in texture and elastic enough to pull away from bowl easily.

3 Divide the dough into three equal pieces and form each piece into a round ball with lightly oiled hands. Two balls to make two loaves for baking, and one leftover for the next baking's 'starter'.

4 To finish loaves, flour a flat surface, and place on it two balls of dough. Sift a little flour over each ball, then flatten each gently with your hand into two rounds about 13cm/5 inches in diameter.

5 Cover rounds with a clean cloth and then a piece of blanket reserved for making bread and leave dough to rise for 1–1½ hours in a warm place.

6 Meanwhile, preheat oven to 400°F/200°C/Gas 6.

7 To test whether loaves are ready to be baked, press your thumb gently into one of the rounds. The loaves are risen enough if the dough returns to its original shape when you remove your thumb.

8 When dough is well risen, prick each loaf in three or four places with the prongs of a fork, sprinkle with sesame or anise seeds if you like, and bake in a preheated oven for 50 minutes or until crisp and golden.

Makes 2 loaves

TAGINE BREAD

Moroccan cooks have a wonderful recipe for making *tagine* bread. It is made in the same way as the plain Moroccan bread above but is baked in a glazed earthenware *tagine* with live coals on top and underneath for heat.

Make a round of bread dough about 5cm/2 inches smaller in diameter than the *tagine*, and place in the bottom of the *tagine*. Put on the heavy *tagine* cover and set it to rise for 1–1½ hours either within faint warming distance of the fire, or out in the sun. The heat for baking, when the bread has risen, must be handled carefully. Too little heat means pale doughy bread, and too much means over-crisped bread of an unpleasant brown colour. When properly baked, the bread is feather light, a lovely golden brown and of a flavour achieved under no other circumstances.

KHOBZ M'CHEFARA
FRIED MOROCCAN BREAD WITH CINNAMON

This is the delicious fried cinnamon bread I had every morning at breakfast when I stayed with Mohamed and Ruth Bari in their home in Casablanca.

½ loaf French bread
1–2 eggs
250ml/8fl. oz (1 cup) milk
½ teaspoon salt
½ teaspoon vanilla essence (extract)
butter
sugar
powdered cinnamon

1 Cut French bread in half lengthways, then cut each half into 10cm/4 inch segments.

2 In a shallow bowl, beat eggs until well mixed, then add milk, salt and vanilla essence (extract) and beat again.

3 Melt butter in frying pan (skillet or griddle) and heat.

4 In a shallow bowl, combine equal quantities of sugar and powdered cinnamon.

5 Dip several pieces of bread into egg and milk mixture and then fry in melted butter until crisp and golden on both sides. Dip fried bread segments in sugar and cinnamon mixture until well coated on both sides. Repeat with remaining pieces of bread, adding a little more butter, as necessary.

Serves 4

KHOBZ BISHEMAR
MOROCCAN BREAD 'PACKAGES' WITH SAVOURY
FILLINGS

The dough is pricked before it is cooked on a griddle so the envelopes of raised dough can cook in the fat which escapes from the filling. Eaten as a snack *khobz bishemar* is a delicious bread almost like a pastry or even, if it contains tomato and a little *brebis* cheese, an enclosed Moroccan pizza.

1 recipe Moroccan bread (see page 74)
groundnut (peanut) oil
butter

SAVOURY FILLING
75g/3oz lamb or beef suet, finely chopped (¾ cup finely chopped lamb or beef suet)
3 tablespoon finely chopped onion
3 tablespoons chopped flat-leafed (Italian) parsley
1 dried hot red pepper, finely chopped
1 teaspoon sweet red pepper
½ teaspoon each powdered cumin and salt

1 Make dough as in steps 1 and 2 of recipe for Moroccan bread.

2 Form dough into four equal pieces and with lightly oiled hands, form each piece into a round ball.

3 Flatten each piece into a rectangle approximately 20 × 30cm/8 × 12 inches.

4 In a small bowl, combine ingredients for the savoury filling. Spread a quarter of the filling down the centre of each rectangle. Then fold over right, then left side, to make rectangular 'package' of 7.5 ×20cm/3 ×8 inches high.

5 Flatten 'package' out until it is 20 × 30cm/8 × 12 inches again. Then fold over dough as above to make rectangle 7.5 × 20cm/3 × 8 inches. Repeat this procedure with remaining balls of dough and filling.

6 Place the four bread 'packages' on a buttered baking sheet and cover with a clean cloth, and then a piece of blanket reserved for making bread. Leave dough to rise for 1 hour in a warm place.

7 Heat griddle (or iron frying pan/skillet) and brush with butter. Prick package with a fork four to six times on each side. Fry each dough 'package' for 8–10 minutes on each side until crisp and golden. Brush with a little extra butter just before serving.

Makes 4

LITTLE SPICED BREADS

These delicious spice-scented home-made snacks, of about 10cm/4 inches in diameter, are eaten for breakfast or throughout the day.

1 recipe yeast dough 'starter' (see page 73)

DOUGH
100g/¼lb (cup) butter
450ml/¾ pint (2 cups) hot water
4 tablespoons orange-flower water
450g/1lb plain flour (3 cups plus 2 tablespoons all-purpose flour)
100g/¼lb icing (1 cup confectioners') sugar
¼ teaspoon salt
4 tablespoons sesame seeds
1 tablespoon anise seeds

EGG-WASH GLAZE
1 egg yolk
water

1 Make the yeast dough 'starter' as described on page 73.

2 To make the dough, combine butter, hot water and orange-flower water in a small bowl, and leave butter to melt. Sift flour, icing (confectioners') sugar and salt into a large flat mixing bowl. Add sesame seeds, anise seeds and yeast dough 'starter'. Add half the warm butter/water mixture and beat energetically with hands, sprinkling with additional butter/water mixture from time to time as you beat, until dough is smooth and sticky.

3 Cover dough with a clean cloth and then a piece of blanket reserved for making bread and allow to rise in a warm place for 1–1½ hours, or until doubled in bulk.

4 Punch dough down and knead for 5–7 minutes or until mixture leaves sides of the bowl, adding just enough extra flour to prevent sticking. Divide dough into twelve small balls and flatten them with oiled fingers into small rounds about 5cm/2 inches in diameter. Place rounds 5–7.5cm/2–3 inches apart on a buttered baking sheet, cover with a clean cloth and then blanket (as above) for making bread, and leave to rise for 1 hour in a warm place.

5 When dough is well risen, prick each loaf in three or four places with the prongs of a fork and brush them with egg-wash glaze.

6 Bake loaves in a preheated oven (375°F/190°C/Gas 5) for 15–20 minutes or until they are crisp and golden brown.

Makes 12 little breads

Beghrir, Rghaif and Sfenj

The Moroccans have the same love for their sweet pancakes – *beghrir* and *rghaif* – as the Americans do for their pancakes and waffles, and the English for griddle cakes and scones. Until fairly recently, these pancakes were served only at breakfast time, or occasionally as a snack at mid morning. Today in many Moroccan restaurants and modern Moroccan homes they have been up-graded to dessert status, and are served warm with honey and melted butter, or honey, chopped walnuts and lemon juice at the end of a meal. And delicious they are, too.

The *sfenj* or doughnut maker – a magical figure in Moroccan street life and much loved by children – is usually located in a little booth near an open market or bus station, or at the centre of a *souk*. To watch him is a delight as he takes a piece of smooth, pliable, moist dough in his right hand, squeezes it out between his thumb and forefinger, catches it deftly on his left forefinger, twirls it instantly into a ring and drops it into the hot fat. Then he takes a hooked piece of iron – especially conceived, it seems, for this purpose – and moves it in a quick circle to keep the hole in the dough open as it puffs up in the hot fat. Four or six *sfenj* are quickly cooked to crisp, puffed-up golden circles, slipped on a thin circlet of bamboo, weighed, and handed to you. You then walk through the busy streets, with the little loop of bamboo carefully clasped in your fingers, to the terrace of a nearby street *café* to eat the crisp-fried hot doughnuts with a little pounded sugar and a glass of *thé à la menthe* or *café cassé* (a glass of dark Moroccan coffee 'broken' with an equal amount of hot milk), or home for breakfast.

A circlet of crisp-fried SFENJ *(Moroccan doughnuts) with crunchy coarse sugar for dipping makes a heart-warming mid-morning treat by the pool.*

BEGHRIR
HONEYCOMB PANCAKES

These pale gold pancakes are cooked on one side only so that the little holes that prick the topmost 'uncooked' side give an attractive honeycomb effect. Cooked on a griddle or flat earthenware pan, these Moroccan pancakes are very light and can be served with honey and melted butter or with the savoury crusts and melted fat from sun-dried *khlii* (see page 68).

Fatima cooks her *beghrir* on a tile instead of a griddle pan and that is the way we have photographed them for this book. Try a *crêpe* pan, a griddle pan, a thick iron frying pan (skillet), an electric *crêpe* pan – or, like Fatima, a 15cm/6 inch tile.

450g/1lb plain four (3 cups plus 2 tablespoons all-purpose flour)
¼ teaspoon salt
1 egg
300ml/pint (1¼ cups) water (or a mixture of milk and water)
salad oil

YEAST STARTER
1 tablespoon dried (active dry) yeast
1 teaspoon sugar
6 tablespoons warm water

TO SERVE
melted butter
hot honey
orange-flower water (optional)

1 To make the yeast 'starter', mix yeast with sugar and sprinkle over warm water. Stir until well mixed. Set aside in a warm place for 10–15 minutes, or until bubbly.

2 To make the pancakes, sift flour and salt into a large shallow bowl and make a well in the centre with your hands.

3 Beat egg with half the water (or milk and water), and slowly pour the mixture into the flour well, stirring constantly with your hand until well mixed. Then, add the yeast mixture and beat with your hand, adding a little more water from time to time, until mixture is runny smooth (like thick cream). Set aside to rest for 1 hour.

4 When ready to cook, rub your chosen pan with a piece of kitchen paper soaked in salad oil and heat over a medium heat.

5 Pour 1 small ladle (3–4 tablespoons) batter on to pan, smooth into a perfect circle with the bottom of the ladle, and cook until little bubbles appear over the surface of pancake. Place pancakes in a large heatproof shallow bowl in overlapping circles (do *not* stack them, or they are liable to stick), and keep warm until ready to serve.

Serve with melted butter and hot honey flavoured with a little orange-flower water if desired.

Serves 4–6

BEGHRIR, *cooked* (TOP) *on a tile over a gas flame, are pale-gold Moroccan pancakes cooked on one side only so that the little holes that prick the topmost side give an attractive 'honeycomb' effect not unlike English muffins.* MIDDLE: *The gently cooked beghrir is lifted off the hot tile (you can use a frying pan, omelette pan, griddle or electric* crêpe *pan) and transferred to a serving plate.* LEFT: *Pile pancakes in overlapping circles to prevent them sticking together and keep them warm until ready to serve.*

RGHAIF

LAYERED MOROCCAN PANCAKES

These are often called *crêpes feuilletées* (flaky pancakes) by Moroccan housewives who like to serve them with honey or caster (superfine) sugar as a rich breakfast dish or dessert. It is a folded yeast-raised dough, made much like puff pastry, which is then deep-fried in oil. They can also be stuffed, with a tiny amount of filling spread on before the folding, so that the flavour of the filling permeates the whole 'pancake'. Stuff with grated onions and *khlii* sautéed in the rich aromatic *khlii* fat. I also occasionally substitute a little *kefta* mixture and grated onions.

450g/1lb plain flour (3 cups plus 2 tablespoons all-purpose flour)
¼ teaspoon salt
300ml/½ pint (1¼ cups) warm water
groundnut (peanut) oil

YEAST 'STARTER'
1 tablespoon dried (active dry) yeast
1 teaspoon sugar
6 tablespoons warm water

TO SERVE
butter
hot honey

1 Make the yeast 'starter' as for *beghrir* (opposite).

2 To make the pancakes, sift flour and salt into a *gsaa* or shallow wooden or earthenware bowl. Add yeast 'starter' and enough warm water to make a soft ball of dough. Knead dough energetically with your hands, adding a little more water from time to time to keep dough sticky and soft as you knead it to a smooth, elastic dough.

3 To form *rghaif* 'packets', oil the *gsaa* or working surface, and your hands as well. Divide dough into 16–20 little balls. Coat each ball with oil and pat it out on oiled surface to a 20–25cm/8–10 inch circle. Fold two outside edges of circle in towards centre; and then fold in the two other edges of the circle to make a pastry rectangle about 15 × 20cm/6 × 8 inches.

4 Fold narrow ends of this rectangle into centre so that they meet; repeat with other sides and then flatten out again to a rectangle 10 × 15cm/4 × 6 inches.

5 To cook, pour groundnut (peanut) oil into a large frying pan (skillet) to the depth of 1cm/½ inch. Fry the *rghaif* in hot oil, one by one, until crisp and golden on both sides. Serve with butter and hot honey.

Makes 16–20

SFENJ

DEEP-FRIED MOROCCAN DOUGHNUTS

The doughnut maker may be a favourite stopping-off place for a street snack or breakfast, but *sfenj* are fun to make at home too. While I cannot promise you will be as deft and sure in your movements as the *sfenj* maker himself, the results will be delicious.

This traditional recipe for *sfenj* uses no lightening agent other than yeast, and as a result is not as light as an Austrian *cruller* or American doughnut. To my mind it needs none. It is wholesome and satisfying enough as it is.

450g/1lb plain flour (3 cups plus 2 tablespoons all-purpose flour)
200–250ml/7–8fl. oz (1 cup) warm water
oil

YEAST 'STARTER'
4 tablespoons warm water
1 tablespoon dried (active dry) yeast
2 tablespoons sugar
½ teaspoon salt

TO SERVE
crunchy coarse sugar

1 To make the yeast 'starter', measure the warm water into a small bowl, add yeast, sugar and salt, and stir until well mixed. Set aside in a warm place for 15 minutes.

2 Sift the flour into a large shallow bowl and make a well in the middle with your hands. Pour in the yeast 'starter' and begin to mix in the flour with your hand, adding a little warm water from time to time as you mix, until it is the consistency of a stiff dough.

3 Knead dough for 10–15 minutes, pulling dough away from bowl, slapping it down and kneading it into bowl again with the heel of your hand, until dough is smooth and elastic. Then, little by little, add remainder of water, sprinkling 2 tablespoons at a time into bowl. Knead the dough in bowl until water is dissolved, continuing until dough is spongy, very elastic and very sticky.

4 Oil a mixing bowl lightly. Oil your hands and push dough down into centre of original bowl with oiled hands until you can easily pick it up and transfer to the oiled bowl. Wipe any dough that might stick to your hands, dip fingers in oil again, and turn dough over in bowl. Then cover with a clean kitchen towel and a folded blanket or bath towel, and allow dough to rise in a warm place for 1–1½ hours.

5 When dough is risen, punch it down in bowl with your fist. Heat frying oil in a deep fryer.

6 To fry doughnuts, oil fingers of both hands. Take dough in your right hand and, squeezing your hand slightly, force a piece of dough the size of an egg out through the hole made between thumb and forefinger. Then, with the forefinger of your left hand, make a hole in the dough and twirl circle of dough made in this way around forefinger to enlarge the hole to the size of a golf ball. Plunge ring of dough into hot fat and fry until dough puffs up, turning it once or twice so that it becomes golden on both sides. Keep the hole open and circular while frying with the aid of a metal hook (see picture) or handle of a slotted spoon.

7 As *sfenj* begins to firm in hot fat, make other dough rings as above, plunging them into the hot fat, turning them rapidly so that they swell and brown uniformly on both sides. As each *sfenj* cooks to a smooth golden brown, remove with metal hook or slotted spoon, and allow to drain dry on kitchen paper.
  Serve hot sprinkled with crunchy coarse sugar.

Makes 12–16

OPPOSITE: *Children in the streets of the* medina *have an unusual beauty – a touch of mystery – that is ageless. This little girl is bringing home* sfenj *(crusty Moroccan doughnuts) from the local* sfenj *maker.*

10

B'STILLA
AND OTHER
WARKHA PASTRY
DISHES

Was it of Persian origin, I wonder, or Byzantine, or even from Spanish Andaluz as is sometimes claimed, this highly spiced, highly flavoured mixture of the meat of pigeons mixed with creamy lemon-flavoured eggs and almonds, sparked with cinnamon and saffron, sweetened with pounded sugar and encased in a hundred onionskin-thin layers of pastry, so thin, in fact, that you can actually see through one before it is cooked as if it were made of the finest worked lace. Or did this legendary mediaeval *tourte* come from some magic Samarkand, brought on a warm soft wind from the desert, an intricately wrought dish from black Africa? Suffice to say that *warkha* pastry is made today in the major cities of Morocco by black travelling ladies from the Sudan whose skill at making the impossibly fragile pastry leaves up to 60cm/2 feet in diameter is one of the modern facts of Moroccan culinary history.

B'stilla – sometimes known as *pasteeya, bisteeya,* or even *pastela* – is one of the truly great dishes of Morocco. Its crisp golden pastry leaves, finer than Austrian *strudel* pastry, Chinese *shao mai* pastry or Greek *phyllo* pastry, are made by tapping a loose wet mixture of flour and water against a special overturned cooking pan called a *t'bsil dial warkha* in Marrakech.

When I first heard about it, I imagined a copper bowl overturned over a charcoal brazier, its rounded bottom used as a base to pat out the paper-thin concentric circles of dough that make up the paper-thin pastry leaves called *warkha*. In reality, it is a large flat-bottomed metal dish with a raised rim – not unlike in shape our own pyrex pie dishes or French metal *tourte* pans. The pan has a double use. First, turned 'bottom side' up

OPPOSITE: *Flaky, unbelievably rich* B'STILLA – *pounded pigeon, almonds, spices and creamy, lemon-flavoured eggs (or chopped hard-boiled eggs) in a* mille-feuilles *casing of Moroccan pastry – is virtually the national dish.*

over a charcoal brazier, it is used as the base for making the thin *warkha* pastry leaves. Then, it is turned right side up again to form a lipped baking pan for the *b'stilla* itself to cook in.

Who was the first cook to realize that by touching a ball of dough eighteen or twenty times in quick succession on a hot metal surface over a charcoal brazier, one could create a wide sheet of the thinnest and most delicate pastry imaginable? And did the pastry and leaves evolve many centuries ago, I wonder, from the thin sheets of dough – like that for lasagne or ravioli – that the Moroccan cook uses to make *trid*, the favourite dish of the Prophet? At any rate, *trid* is often called the poor man's *b'stilla*, a country man's version of this famous dish.

B'stilla is one of the great dishes of the Maghreb – forty cartwheel-sized sheets of the thinnest pastry I have ever seen. The onionskin-thin pastry rounds are made by tapping a small ball of yeast-raised dough in a series of concentric circles on to the upturned metal pan, making sure the dough circles overlap each other slightly to form a lacy sheet of pastry. You'll need patience to make one sheet of *warkha* pastry: it takes about eighteen taps of the ball of dough to make just one circle. And a good-sized *b'stilla* requires twenty-four sheets of *warkha* pastry!

In England and America, cooks use Greek *phyllo* pastry or Viennese *strudel* pastry – but neither of these comes anywhere near the delicacy of the Moroccan *warkha*. So, I have given the step by step directions for making *warkha* as demonstrated by a *Marrakshi* neighbour of mine called Fatima, who is famous among the locals for the *finesse* of her *warkha* leaves and for the many delicious dishes – *b'stilla*, *trid*, *briouats* and *boureks* and *briks* that she makes from them.

Fatima begins making warkha *pastry leaves in the classical manner – on the floor.*

WARKHA PASTRY

Traditionally the pastry is made over charcoal as I describe below, on a *t'bsil*, but I have used a griddle pan and the bottom of a shallow steel frying pan (skillet). Best of all, however, is a thermostatically controlled electric *crêpe* pan. It makes a perfect cooking surface, and the temperature is easily controllable.

The first thing to do if you're attempting to make *warkha* pastry leaves traditionally, is to prepare the charcoal brazier. Fatima uses a traditional small round charcoal brazier called a *mishmihr* to hold the charcoal fire, half filling the brazier with ashes to serve as a base for the charcoal to burn on. A second trick is to pile the charcoal up on a flat piece of metal before lighting it so that the charcoal catches fire immediately; then she transfers it to the brazier, packing the flaming charcoal in tightly with a small shovel. A third trick is to cover the charcoal with a little more ash to 'soften' the heat of the fire, before using it to make the *warkha* leaves. (A newer – and almost revolutionary – way of cooking the delicate pastry was suggested to me recently by Mohamed Alami Mejjati, assistant director of the world-famous Palais Jamai Hotel at Fez. He uses steam to heat the pan on which the pastry is made, to achieve a more even heat.)

> 225g/½lb strong flour (1½ cups plus 1 tablespoon hard or bread flour)
> 450g/1lb plain flour (3 cups plus 2 tablespoons all-purpose flour)
> 1 tablespoon salt
> warm water
> 5–6 tablespoons salad oil

1 Sieve the flours and salt into a container, then shake it gently into a large, shallow bowl. (Fatima uses the same traditional shallow *gsaa* for making dough for *warkha* as she does when making bread or preparing *couscous*.)

2 Make a well in the centre of the flour with your hands, and add 150ml/ ¼ pint (⅔ cup) warm water and 2 tablespoons salad oil. Knead dough with your hands, adding more warm water from time to time, until a wet, soft dough is formed.

3 To aerate dough, scoop it up into the air with both hands and then let it fall into the bowl. Knead the dough down into the bowl.

4 Add 2 more tablespoons oil and knead again.

5 Lift dough up in air again to aerate it, then knead it down into bowl once more.

6 Moisten hands with a little water and clean off excess dough from fingers by rubbing dough on to sides of bowl. Add remaining oil and pat moisture and bits of dough into surface of dough. Allow dough to rest in bowl for 1 hour.

7 When you are ready to make the pastry leaves, heat up the chosen surface – the *t'bsil* over charcoal, or switch on the *crêpe* pan.

8 When your cooking surface has reached the right temperature (about the same as for making thin French *crêpes*), knead dough once more. Then wet your right hand, take up a handful of dough and gradually shape it into a ball. Then have a little practice at tossing the ball of dough in the air a few times, catching it quickly again with your hand, and rotating it gently as you toss and catch. This is the trick of making *warkha*, for it is necessary to keep giving a new surface to the dough each time it touches the hot pan. Tap the ball of dough down to touch the surface of the hot pan quickly and lightly; then, quickly pull your hand back into the air again; rotate the ball of dough and bring it gently down to touch the hot surface again; pull back quickly, rotate ball of dough again and continue this quick tapping/pulling back/rotating process until you have covered the surface of your pan with small thin circles of overlapping

MAKING WARKHA PASTRY LEAVES. TOP: *The soft mix, held loosely in the right hand, is deftly tapped on to the overturned* t'bsil *pan kept at a hot, even heat over charcoal.* MIDDLE: *Fatima covers the hot surface with concentric dabs of paper-thin pastry.* BOTTOM: *The lacy* warkha *sheet is peeled away from the hot pan.*

dough to make a large transparent *crêpe* as thin as an onion skin. (So thin, in fact, that you can actually see through one before it is cooked as if it were made of the finest worked lace.) Tap against any 'holes' or 'tears' or places where your little circles of dough have not quite joined up.

9 Allow your thin film of *warkha* leaf to dry slightly around the edges, for a second or two only, and then carefully lift it up, picking up the edges to loosen it from the pan. When you have picked up one-quarter of the leaf you will be able to peel off the remainder quite easily.

Now, don't get impatient if you don't succeed the very first time. I once saw Fatima try seven times before the pan had become properly 'seasoned', just right to make a perfect thin *crêpe* without tears or holes. So be patient. Even when making French *crêpes*, it sometimes takes three or four tries before the pan is just right and you perfect your *tour de main*. Making *warkha* leaves is just the same, but even more so! Always wipe off any mistakes from pan with a clean cotton or paper towel.

10 The *warkha* leaf is cooked on one side only, and once you have managed to remove it from the pan, place on a folded tea towel, shiny side uppermost.

11 If you want to use the leaves as perfect circles in dishes, stack the pastry leaves, four at a time, and fold in half then in half again. Cut round the wider edges to make a perfect circle, then unfold and use.

The finished sheet of warkha *pastry, for use in making* b'stilla, brik briouats *or even* trid, *is onion-skin thin.*

NEW WAYS OF MAKING WARKHA PASTRY

A revolutionary new way of making *warkha* pastry leaves is the modern manner given to me by my friend Said Alaoui of Kenitra whose mother prepares a very liquid mixture to make her *warkha* leaves and then 'paints' the heated *tbsil* pan with a thin layer of the mixture using a large, flat brush to spread the mixture evenly over the pan. She then proceeds to bake the *warkha* pastry leaves in the traditional manner.

SAID'S MOTHER'S RECIPE FOR 'BRUSHED ON' WARKHA LEAVES

300g/10 oz plain flour (2 cups all-purpose flour)
150g/5 oz strong flour (1 cup hard or bread flour)
600–750ml/1–1¼ pints (2½–3 cups) water
4 tablespoons salad oil
1 teaspoon salt

MAKING WARKHA PASTRY IN ELECTRIC CRÊPE PAN

After testing this revolutionary new way of making *warkha* leaves, I had an inspiration: I added 50ml/2fl. oz (¼ cup) water to the above mix, sieved it into a large, flat dish, dipped the surface of an electrically heated crêpe pan for an instant into the very liquid mix (just enough to coat the surface of the pan lightly) and then allowed the thin *warkha* layer to dry out on the pan for a minute before turning it out on to a plate. The thin *warkha* sheet literally slid off the hot pan. I then brushed each *warkha* pastry leaf lightly with salad oil to keep the pastry leaves from sticking together and continued as above until all the mixture was used.

Warkha leaves made in this manner will keep in the refrigerator for a day or two if wrapped in foil or kitchen paper. They may be used to make smaller *b'stillas* for 2 or 3 people (the leaves are only as big as the circumference of your pan) and for making *briks, trid, briouats* or *cornes de gazelle*. (See recipes on pages 90–95, 202–4.)

B'STILLA AUX PIGEONS

24 warkha pastry leaves (see page 85)
melted butter
2 egg yolks, beaten with a little water
groundnut (peanut) oil

PIGEON FILLING
6 young pigeons, boned and quartered
pigeon giblets
salt
100g/¼lb (½ cup) butter
900ml/1½ pints (3¾ cups) water
icing (confectioners') sugar
1 packet (heaped ½ teaspoon) powdered saffron
powdered cinnamon
6 hard-boiled eggs, shelled and chopped

CHERMOULA
1 Spanish onion, peeled and coarsely grated
4 cloves garlic, peeled and finely chopped
1 packet (heaped teaspoon) powdered saffron
1 teaspoon powdered ginger
6 sprigs flat-leafed (Italian) parsley, chopped
6 sprigs fresh green coriander, chopped
1 teaspoon freshly ground black pepper
1½ teaspoons coarse salt
6 tablespoons olive oil

SUGARED ALMOND MIXTURE
450g/1lb (4 cups) ground almonds
6 tablespoons icing (confectioners') sugar
4 tablespoons orange-flower water
1–2 teaspoons powdered cinnamon

BUTTER AND ORANGE-FLOWER SAUCE
6 tablespoons melted butter
3 tablespoons orange-flower water

GARNISH
icing sugar
powdered cinnamon

1 The day before you want to serve the *b'stilla*, rub the pigeon quarters and giblets with salt, leave for 1 hour, then wash off salt, drain and dry. Place pigeon quarters and giblets in a large bowl.

2 To make the *chermoula*, combine all the ingredients in a bowl, then pour over pigeons and giblets. Rub in well, then leave to marinate for at least 2 hours or overnight.

3 To make the sugared almond mixture, combine all the ingredients in a bowl.

4 On the following day, transfer the pigeon pieces and giblets to a large flameproof casserole with *chermoula*. Add butter and water, and sprinkle with 2 tablespoons icing (confectioners') sugar. Cover and simmer for 20 minutes. Add saffron and cook for 30 minutes more. Transfer pieces to a plate, remove any loose bones and reduce pan juices over a high heat until a third of original volume. Reserve.

5 To assemble the *b'stilla*, brush the bottom and sides of a 30–35cm/12–14 inch round pizza pan (or large tart tin with removable bottom) with melted butter. Place a *warkha* pastry leaf in the centre, shiny side down, then place five more pastry leaves in overlapping circles over the edges of this central sheet (like the petals of a flower) so that they cover the bottom of the pan, but half of each leaf in the outer circle overhangs the edges of the pan (to tuck round the filling later).

6 Repeat this process to add one more layer of five pastry leaves (one in the centre and four overlapping 'petals').

7 Sprinkle centre of this shell of pastry with half the sugared almond mixture, spreading it to cover base of leaves in pan evenly, leaving a 1cm/½ inch space all around edge of pan.

8 Place two more pastry leaves in centre over sugared almond mixture.

9 To make the butter and orange-flower sauce, combine the melted butter with the orange-flower water and sprinkle two-thirds of this over pastry leaves in pan.

10 Cover with two more pastry leaves, sprinkle with 2 tablespoons icing (confectioners') sugar and then arrange the cooked pigeon meats and reduced juices in centre, again leaving a 1cm/½ inch edge of pastry in pan free. Sprinkle with ½–1 teaspoon powdered cinnamon.

11 Sprinkle pigeon with chopped hard-boiled egg and top with two more pastry leaves. Sprinkle with remaining sugared almond mixture, with remaining butter and orange-flower sauce, then with 2 tablespoons icing (confectioners') sugar.

12 Turn up the overlapping sides of the pastry leaves, sealing them together in the centre with a little beaten egg yolk.

13 Add two more layers of pastry leaves (as in Steps 5 and 6) with five circles to each layer (shiny side *up* this time), allowing pastry leaves to overhang edges of pan as before.

14 Fold overhanging leaves neatly *under* towards the centre of the pie. Brush top and sides of pastry with groundnut (peanut) oil and then with beaten egg yolk and water, to form a glazed *tourte* about 7.5–10cm/3–4 inches thick.

15 To bake the *b'stilla*, place in a hot oven (425°F/220°C/Gas 7) for about 20 minutes, or until pastry is golden brown. Run a metal spatula under pie to loosen it from pan, pour off excess butter if necessary (reserve it), and place a large flat serving dish over top of pan. Carefully invert the pie on to the plate and then replace, bottom side up, in the pan. Brush with reserved melted butter and return to oven to continue baking for another 10–15 minutes, or until golden brown.

16 Remove the *b'stilla* from the oven and pour off any excess melted butter. Invert the pie as before out of the pan on to a large serving dish. Remove excess butter from pie with a paper towel and dust the top with icing (confectioners') sugar. Decorate with a lattice of strips of powdered cinnamon as a last touch.

B'STILLA AU POULET ET AUX OEUFS CITRONNÉS

24 warkha pastry leaves (see page 85)
melted butter
1 egg yolk, beaten with a little water
groundnut (peanut) oil

CHICKEN FILLING
2 frying (broiler/fryer) chickens, boned and quartered
chicken giblets
salt
900ml/1½ pints (3¾ cups) water
100g/¼lb (½ cup) smen (or butter)
icing (confectioners') sugar
1 packet (heaped ½ teaspoon) powdered saffron
4 tablespoons lemon juice
8 eggs, well beaten

CHERMOULA
1 Spanish onion, peeled and coarsely grated
2–4 cloves garlic, peeled and finely chopped
1 packet (heaped ½ teaspoon) powdered saffron
1 teaspoon powdered ginger
6 sprigs flat-leafed (Italian) parsley, chopped
3 sprigs fresh green coriander, chopped
1 teaspoon cracked black pepper
1½ teaspoons coarse salt
6 tablespoons olive oil

SUGARED ALMOND MIXTURE
350g/¾lb (3 cups) ground almonds
6 tablespoons icing (confectioners') sugar
4 tablespoons orange-flower water
1–2 teaspoons powdered cinnamon

BUTTER AND ORANGE-FLOWER SAUCE
4 tablespoons melted butter
3 tablespoons orange-flower water

GARNISH
icing (confectioners') sugar
powdered cinnamon

1 On the day before you are to make *b'stilla*, rub chicken pieces and giblets with salt. Leave for 1 hour, then wash off and drain dry. Place chicken pieces and giblets in a large bowl.

2 To make the chermoula, combine all the ingredients in a bowl, then pour over chicken pieces and giblets. Rub in well, then leave to marinate for at least 2 hours or overnight.

3 To make the sugared almond mixture, combine all the ingredients in a bowl.

4 On the following day, transfer chicken pieces, giblets and *chermoula* to a flameproof casserole. Add water and *smen* (or butter) and sprinkle with icing (confectioners') sugar. Cover casserole and simmer for 20 minutes. Add saffron and cook for 30 minutes more. Transfer chicken pieces and giblets to a large plate, remove any loose bones, and reduce sauce over a high heat, to a third of its original volume. Add lemon juice and beaten eggs and cook, stirring continuously for 5 minutes more. Remove from heat and reserve.

5 To assemble the *b'stilla*, follow the instructions in steps 5 to 10 of the previous recipe. After arranging the cooked chicken pieces and giblets in the centre of the *b'stilla*, top them with the cooked egg mixture.

6 Cover the chicken and eggs with two more *warkha* pastry leaves, sprinkle with remaining sugared almond mixture, remaining butter and orange-flower water sauce, and 2 tablespoons icing (confectioners') sugar.

7 Continue as in previous recipe from step 12 up to and including step 14.

8 Bake and serve as in previous recipe, steps 15 to 16.

TRID MARRAKSHIA

This *trid* is more traditional than the former, with stew and *warkha* leaves layered and baked together as in *b'stilla*.

1 roasting (broiler/fryer) chicken, about 1.5–1.75kg/3½–4lb, cut into 8 serving pieces
chicken giblets
coarse salt
300ml/½ pint (1¼ cups) water
2 teaspoons each sugar and powdered cinnamon, mixed together
8 warkha pastry leaves (see page 85)

CHERMOULA MARINADE
1 Spanish onion, peeled and finely chopped
1 tablespoon cracked black pepper
1 packet (heaped ½ teaspoon) powdered saffron
4 tablespoons finely chopped flat-leafed (Italian) parsley
2 tablespoons finely chopped fresh green coriander
4 tablespoons each olive oil and water

1 Wash chicken pieces, marinate in above *chermoula*, and cook with marinade and water (this time 300ml/½ pint/1¼ cups) as in previous recipe.

2 To assemble *trid*, place 1 small ladle of the pan juices in the bottom of a *tagine* or shallow flameproof casserole. Set *tagine* (or casserole) over a medium heat and cook, stirring constantly, until sauce begins to sizzle. Cover bottom of *tagine* with two rounds of *warkha* pastry and sprinkle with 1 teaspoon sugar-cinnamon mixture. Cover with two more rounds of *warkha* pastry, spoon over a small ladle of pan juices and sprinkle with 1 teaspoon sugar-cinnamon mixture.

7 Arrange chicken pieces on top of *warkha* rounds, and cover with another two rounds of *warkha* pastry. Moisten with pan juices and pat pastry down with a wooden spoon around chicken pieces.

8 Sprinkle pastry with sugar-cinnamon mixture, and cover with remaining two *warkha* pastry rounds. Pat down as above, pour over remaining pan juices, and sprinkle with remaining sugar-cinnamon mixture.

9 Heat through in the preheated oven (375°F/190°C/Gas 5) for about 20 minutes, and serve immediately.

Serves 4

HADDA'S TRID. *There are almost as many ways of making* trid *as there are cooks in Morocco. Trid Marrakshia is my favourite.*

90

ABOVE: HADDA'S TRID. *Hadda's recipe for* trid *cooks the chicken as in the first three steps of the recipe on this page but she then rips up the* warkha *leaves to cover the bottom of a large heated* tagine *or serving dish. She then arranges chicken pieces and giblets on top of pastry leaves; spoons over the hot stock (broth); sprinkles the dish with 1–2 teaspoons each of powdered ginger and sugar and serves immediately.*

OPPOSITE: MAKING BRIOUATS. TOP: *Put 2 teaspoons of the filling of your choice at the top of each strip of pastry.* MIDDLE: *Fold over into a triangle.* BOTTOM: *Fold over again and continue to do so until you have reached the end of the pastry strip. If the pastry strip is too long, snip off the end with pastry shears; brush inside of last fold with egg yolk and fold end into pastry fold to seal.*

TRID MOULAY HASSAN

This is a sort of 'do-it-yourself' *trid*, with the stew and *warkha* leaves served separately.

1 roasting (broiler/fryer) chicken, about 1.5–1.75kg/3½–4lb, cut into 8 serving pieces
chicken giblets
coarse salt
600ml/1 pint (2½ cups) water
12–16 warkha pastry leaves (see page 85)

CHERMOULA MARINADE
2–4 small cloves garlic, peeled and finely chopped
1 large Spanish onion, peeled and finely chopped
1 teaspoon each cracked black pepper and powdered cinnamon
½ teaspoon powdered ginger
1 packet (heaped ½ teaspoon) powdered saffron
100g/¼lb (½ cup) smen, or clarified butter
4 tablespoons chopped flat-leafed (Italian) parsley
2 tablespoons chopped fresh green coriander

1 Wash chicken pieces and giblets with coarse salt and water. Rinse and dry well.

2 Combine *chermoula* marinade ingredients in a *tagine* or flameproof shallow casserole, then add chicken pieces and giblets. Rub well with *chermoula* and leave to marinate for at least 2 hours, or overnight.

3 When ready to cook, simmer over a medium heat for 30 minutes. Add 600ml/1 pint (2½ cups) water and continue to cook for 15 minutes more.

4 To prepare *trid*, stack *warkha* pastry circles on a round serving dish and warm in a low oven. Remove chicken from stock (broth), and keep warm in oven (325°F/160°C/Gas 3). Strain stock (broth) into a clean saucepan and cook over a high heat until reduced to half its original volume.

5 To serve *trid*, pour hot stock (broth) into a heated bowl, arrange chicken pieces on a heated serving dish, and arrange stack of *warkha* leaves on a heated serving dish. Guests help themselves to a few pieces of *warkha*, place some pieces of chicken on it, and then pour over some hot stock (broth).

Serves 4

BRIOUATS

These triangles of *warkha* pastry leaves are filled with sweet or savoury fillings and baked or deep-fried.

8 warkha pastry leaves, cut into 20cm/8 inch circles (see page 85)
1 recipe filling of choice (see overleaf)
1 egg yolk, beaten with a little water
groundnut (peanut) oil (optional)
hot dark liquid honey (optional)

1 Cut each *warkha* pastry circle in half. Fold over a third of each half round at both sides to the centre to make a narrow strip about 5cm/2 inches wide. Trim top and bottom ends flat.

2 Put 2 teaspoons of the filling of your choice at the top of each strip of pastry. Fold over into a triangle (see picture), fold over again similarly and continue to do so until you have reached the end of the pastry strip, and you have a fat triangle shape.

3 Brush inside of last fold with egg yolk (with your finger), and fold end into pastry fold to seal *briouat*. Continue with other pastry strips.

4 Preheat oven to moderate (350°F/180°C/Gas 4) and bake for 20–30 minutes or until puffed and golden brown on both sides. Or, more traditionally, fry in peanut oil until golden, turning once.

5 Just before serving rice or peanut *briouats*, dip in simmering dark honey for a minute or two to glaze them.

Makes 16

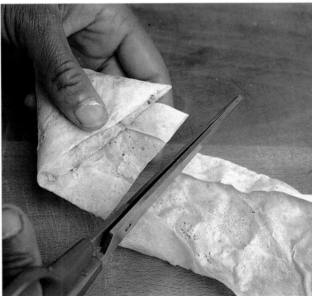

FISH BRIOUAT FILLING

100g/$\frac{1}{4}$lb minced (ground) fish
$\frac{1}{2}$ teaspoon chopped fresh green coriander
$\frac{1}{2}$ teaspoon chopped, flat-leafed (Italian) parsley
$\frac{1}{4}$ teaspoon finely chopped garlic
$\frac{1}{8}$ teaspoon each powdered cumin, sweet red pepper and salt
1–2 tablespoons olive oil

Combine the fish, herbs, garlic, spices and salt. Mix well and sauté for 1 minute in olive oil.

KEFTA BRIOUAT FILLING

100g/$\frac{1}{4}$lb minced (ground) lamb
$\frac{1}{2}$ teaspoon chopped fresh green coriander
$\frac{1}{2}$ teaspoon chopped flat-leafed (Italian) parsley
$\frac{1}{8}$ teaspoon each freshly ground black pepper, powdered ginger and salt
1–2 tablespoons butter

Combine the lamb, herbs, pepper, ginger and salt. Mix well and sauté for 1 minute in butter.

RICE BRIOUAT FILLING

100g/$\frac{1}{4}$lb (scant 1 cup) cooked rice, drained, rinsed in cold water, and drained again
2 tablespoons orange-flower water
$\frac{1}{2}$–1 teaspoon icing (confectioners') sugar
$\frac{1}{4}$–$\frac{1}{2}$ teaspoon powdered cinnamon

Combine all the ingredients.

PEANUT BRIOUAT FILLING

100g/$\frac{1}{4}$lb peanuts, chopped ($\frac{2}{3}$ cup chopped peanuts)
2 tablespoons orange-flower water
2 tablespoons icing (confectioners') sugar
$\frac{1}{4}$ teaspoon powdered cinnamon
1 tablespoon butter

Combine first four ingredients. Mix well and sauté for 1 minute in butter.

BOUREKS AU PÂTE DE WARKHA

12 warkha pastry leaves (see page 85)
450g/1lb minced (ground) lamb
$\frac{1}{4}$ Spanish onion, peeled and coarsely grated
2 tablespoons olive oil
$\frac{1}{4}$ teaspoon each of crushed black pepper, hot red pepper and powdered cinnamon
salt
4 eggs

4 tablespoons chopped flat-leafed (Italian) parsley
4 tablespoons chopped fresh green coriander
2 tablespoons butter, or smen
oil, for frying

GARNISH
lemon segments

1 To prepare the lamb filling, sauté the onion in olive oil until transparent. Add lamb, pepper, spices and salt to taste, and continue to cook, stirring constantly, until meat changes colour.

2 To prepare the runny omelette, beat eggs in a small bowl until frothy. Add chopped parsley and coriander and beat again until well mixed. Melt a little butter (or *smen*) in a large frying pan (skillet), pour in egg and herb mixture, and cook until omelette just begins to set. Remove from heat and turn omelette out on to a plate. Cut into strips.

3 To assemble *boureks*, place a tablespoon of lamb filling at the end of each round of *warkha* pastry. Cover with a small strip of omelette and fold over two outside edges of pastry sheet to form a rough rectangle. Then, starting at filling end, roll up pastry rectangle into the form of a cigar. Reserve. When ready to cook, plunge *boureks* into hot oil – three or four at a time – and deep-fry until crisp and golden. Drain on paper towels and serve immediately with lemon segments.

Serves 6

BRIKS

These are deep-fried pastry triangles, stuffed with eggs, fish or *kefta*. If the *warkha* pastry is too thin use two sheets instead of one for each *brik*.

6–12 warkha pastry leaves (see page 85) or 6–12 sheets of phyllo pastry, cut into
rounds 20–23cm/8–9 inches in diameter
oil, for deep-frying
6 eggs
4 tablespoons chopped, flat-leafed (Italian) parsley
2 tablespoons chopped fresh green coriander
6 tablespoons minced (ground) raw fish, or kefta (see page 49)
salt
powdered cumin
hot red pepper

GARNISH
lemon segments
fried parsley sprigs

1 Heat deep-frying oil in a shallow casserole or large frying pan (skillet).

2 Place one round of *warkha* pastry (or *phyllo* pastry) over a flat soup plate, indenting the pastry slightly into the plate. Break an egg gently into the indented centre of pastry round, sprinkle with a little chopped parsley and coriander, and add 1 tablespoon minced (ground) raw fish, or *kefta*. Season with a pinch each of salt, cumin and hot red pepper.

3 Fold the pastry circle in half, and then in half again to form a triangle. Press edges lightly together to contain stuffing, and deep-fry in hot oil until crisp and golden on both sides, about 2–3 minutes. Drain on paper towels. The runny egg yolk becomes a sauce for minced fish or *kefta*. Serve immediately with lemon segments and fried parsley.

Serves 6

11

SALADS
AND OTHER
MOROCCAN
VEGETABLE DISHES

Salads are a way of life in Morocco, where the city and the country markets are filled with wonderfully inexpensive vegetables and fruits brought in daily from the neighbouring countryside. A selection of vegetable salads is often served as a first course and then left on the table throughout the meal to serve as refreshing accompaniments to the richly flavoured *tagines* of meat, poultry and fish that make up the Moroccan menu.

Moroccan salads are not salads as we know them, but seem instead to be direct imports from the Middle Ages or some fabled twelfth-century Andaluz. Colourful combinations of simple vegetables – tomatoes, cucumber, sweet onion and green pepper – are often combined with black olives, cooked artichoke hearts or preserved lemons, always moistened with an olive oil dressing rich with the spiky flavours of chopped Moroccan garlic and the pungent leaves of fresh green coriander and flat-leafed (Italian) parsley. The dressing is sharpened by the addition of a little vinegar, or, better still, lemon juice from the tart little green and yellow lemons native to Marrakech that the

MOROCCAN SALAD LUNCHEON. FROM LEFT TO RIGHT: SPICY AUBERGINE SALAD: *the aubergines are scored, sliced in half and sautéed in olive oil until almost charred. They are then seasoned with chopped garlic, powdered cumin, sweet red pepper, chopped green coriander and lemon juice.* MOROCCAN CARROT APPETIZER: *the carrots are boiled with garlic, drained and seasoned with lemon juice, sweet and hot red pepper, cumin and chopped green coriander.* LEMON, ONION AND PARSLEY SALAD: *the flesh of the fresh lemons is diced and combined with equal quantities of chopped sweet onion and flat-leafed parsley and seasoned with salt only.* ORANGE AND BLACK OLIVE SALAD (*in large bowl in centre*) *is flavoured with lemon juice, sugar, salt and orange-blossom water.* SAUTÉED GREEN PEPPER AND TOMATO SALAD (*in wooden bowl in centre*) *is flavoured with lemon juice, powdered cumin, hot red pepper and chopped garlic, green coriander and flat-leafed parsley. And in the green bowl, bands of diced, peeled and seeded tomatoes blend with diced, charred green peppers. The middle row is a* SALAD OF SLICED CUCUMBERS.

Marrakshi call *limouns*. Add to this a sprinkling of coarse salt and both fiery hot and sweet red peppers and you have a passionate mix which leaves my European and American friends literally gasping with pleasure.

There is enormous variety in the cold appetizer salads that are available in each Moroccan household. Shades of Russian and Turkish cold tables and Greek *meze* feasts fade into insignificance before the richness of the dishes available in Morocco. Vegetables, of course, are cheap . . . and it does not take great skill or a fattened purse to make the most of fresh garden produce.

Often, my lunch is nothing but a delicious Moroccan salad, inspired no doubt from its Mediterranean cousin, *Salade Niçoise*, or its Tunisian brother, *Salade Tunisienne*. In this case, the salad is composed of fat slices of ripe tomato, thick slices of peeled cucumber, thin rings of green pepper (a trifle hotter than our own sweet green pepper) and thin slices of sweet-tasting red onion, with liberal quantities of chopped fresh Moroccan garlic, red skinned and gently pungent, chopped flat-leafed (Italian) parsley and fresh green coriander in an olive oil and vinegar dressing, spiked with salt, pepper and sweet red and hot red peppers. Segments of Moroccan canned anchovies and black olives (soaked overnight in olive oil to fatten them up) give texture and flavour contrast to the salad. The dressing is always mopped up to the last drop with crisp, crunchy Arab bread.

Remember that just as a salad ought to be crisp, so cooked vegetables must never be taken beyond the stage where textures break down to a uniform, lifeless mush except in the case of some of the mashed cooked vegetable salads: carrot and aubergine (eggplant). They should be neither raw, nor overcooked, but kept at the stage at which texture and, as a result, flavour are at their peak.

Most of the recipes are composed of easily obtainable and economical ingredients. Such salads are a boon to the hostess for much of the preliminary preparation can be done the day before.

Make your salads with the best and freshest ingredients only and with a watchful eye for colour, taste and texture contrast. They make a wonderful cold beginning to summer meals.

In Morocco, dishes of fried aubergines (eggplant), chopped or served whole or in halves, provide a spicy, dark contrast to the shredded carrots or cucumbers sweetened with orange-flower water, lemon juice and sugar that often make up a Moroccan salad course. Orange sections served with thin slices of artichoke heart or black olives; *Schlada*, a delicious first cousin of *Andaluz gazpacho*, is a combination of diced, skinned and seeded tomato and diced charred flesh of green pepper, a sort of 'soup salad' that is a standby with Moroccan grills or brochettes. The

Three refreshing Moroccan salads are kept cool by the tiled fountain on the terrace of the Hotel Transatlantique, Meknes. LEFT TO RIGHT: MOROCCAN GLAZED CARROT SALAD, DICED TOMATO, CUCUMBER AND ONION SALAD, BEETROOT APPETIZER SALAD.

same salad is often served, too, with the addition of the diced skin of a preserved lemon (see page 64).

A more rustic version than the diced tomato and green pepper mentioned above, sautés green peppers whole with halved tomatoes in olive oil; pours off excess oil and dresses the dish when cool with lemon juice which is flavoured with chopped garlic, fresh green coriander and flat-leafed (Italian) parsley, salt, freshly ground black pepper and the merest hint of powdered cumin.

Other salads – simpler to make but more exotic to our western palates – are the grated carrots, grated long radishes and grated cucumber (peel and flesh, but no seeds) which rely on a hint of sugar and salt, a squeeze of tart lemon juice and a spoonful or two of fragrant orange-flower water for their cooling effect.

One of the most unusual of the Moroccan salads is the salad made of diced fresh lemon, coarsely chopped sweet onion and flat-leafed (Italian) parsley. Piquant, wonderfully green and refreshing, this is an appetite whet of the first order. I like to serve it, too, in the western manner, on a salad of sliced ripe tomatoes: moisten sliced tomatoes with a little virgin olive oil; sprinkle with salt and spoon a colourful trail of Moroccan lemon salad down the centre of each serving. Or, with fillets of raw fresh sardines 'cooked' in lemon juice and olive oil, with a few green peppercorns, and a spoonful or two of Moroccan lemon salad as a garnish for each plate.

More exotic salads are often added to the simpler vegetable salads noted above. Fresh lamb's brain salad, for instance, is simmered in a broth enhanced by chopped garlic, chopped green coriander and flat-leafed (Italian) parsley, powdered cumin, sweet red pepper, olive oil and lemon juice, the cooked brains mashed or cut into small pieces before being served. A diced liver salad, the liver either marinated, and served raw or cooked in the marinade, is dressed in a flavoursome dressing; and spiced aubergine (eggplant) salad consists of halved and scored aubergines (eggplant) sautéed in oil if they are small enough, or sliced, sautéed and mashed or cut into small pieces if large. In either case the richly flavoured aubergines (eggplant) are further enhanced with a mix of powdered cumin, sweet red pepper, finely chopped garlic, coriander and lemon juice. In Moroccan spiced carrot salad, the carrots – cut into eighths lengthwise, or into chunky slices, simmered in garlic-flavoured water until just tender – are drained and then dressed with a spicy-sweet coating of sugar, cinnamon, cumin, sweet and hot red peppers, olive oil and lemon juice. You'll find recipes for these salads on the following pages.

All the salad recipes in this section will serve four to six people if they are offered along with one or two other appetizer salads. The greater the selection of salads, the more revered your guests!

Moroccan Salad Dressings

In a land where the olive is plentiful, olive oil is relatively inexpensive as a result, and Moroccans use great quantities of delicious fruity olive oil in their cooking and in their salads. Guests of mine have exclaimed over the flavour and consistency of the local virgin olive oil, declaring it 'good enough to drink'. A slight exaggeration, perhaps, but indicates its flavour.

Salad dressings use an inordinately greater quantity of chopped garlic, flat-leafed (Italian) parsley and fresh green coriander – as well as a heady seasoning of Moroccan spices – hot red and sweet red peppers and, sometimes, a hint of cinnamon and ground cumin – to spark up the combinations of vegetables. There is a large selection of varied dressings attached to individual recipes, but the following is a favourite.

BACHA'S MOROCCAN SALAD DRESSING

2 tablespoons lemon juice or wine vinegar
8 tablespoons olive oil
4 tiny garlic cloves, peeled and finely chopped
$\frac{1}{2}$ teaspoon sweet red pepper
$\frac{1}{8}$ teaspoon hot red pepper
salt and freshly ground black pepper
4 tablespoons each chopped flat-leafed (Italian) parsley and fresh green coriander

Simply mix all these together, leave for a while to allow the flavours to blend, then use.

DICED PEPPER, TOMATO AND ONION SALAD

The grilled peppers give a smoky taste to this salad. Diced cucumbers, salted and rinsed, could also be added instead of, or with, the peppers.

2 large green bell peppers (or 4 long thin green peppers), grilled (broiled or barbecued) and skinned (see page 105)
3 ripe tomatoes, skinned and seeded (see page 105)
1 large Spanish onion, peeled
6 tablespoons olive oil
2 tablespoons vinegar
1 clove garlic, peeled and finely chopped
salt

1 Prepare the vegetables. Stem and seed grilled green peppers, then wash and cut flesh into 6mm/$\frac{1}{4}$ inch dice. Cut tomatoes into 6mm/$\frac{1}{4}$ inch dice. Add to diced green peppers. Cut onion into 6mm/$\frac{1}{4}$ inch slices, then cut slices into dice. Add to diced green peppers and tomatoes. Mix well.

2 Combine olive oil, vinegar and finely chopped garlic. Add salt to taste, and mix well. Pour over salad ingredients and chill.

3 Just before serving, strain off excess juices and arrange in a salad bowl.

Serves 4–6

ESSAOUIRA SALAD

This, a great salad to accompany grilled (broiled or barbecued) sardines or other fish, is served at the quay-side restaurants of the old port of Essaouira. Delicious.

1 recipe Diced Pepper, Tomato and Onion Salad, (see page 101)
1–2 preserved lemons (see page 64), peel only, cut into 6mm/¼ inch dice
1–2 tablespoons preserved lemon juice

Make salad as above, and add diced preserved lemon peel and a tablespoon or two of the juices in which the lemons were preserved. Mix well and chill.

Serves 4–6

DICED PEPPER AND TOMATO SALAD

The smoky taste of the green peppers permeates the entire dish, giving a most unusual flavour to this typically Moroccan salad, whether served as an appetizer, or as a cooling, pungent accompaniment to grilled (broiled or barbecued) brochettes of lamb or fish.

3 large green bell peppers (or 6 long thin green peppers), grilled (broiled or barbecued and skinned (see page 105)
6 ripe tomatoes, skinned and seeded (see page 105)
2 cloves garlic, peeled and finely chopped
salt

1 Rinse and drain the skinned green peppers, remove core and seeds, and cut flesh into small dice. Cut skinned and seeded tomato flesh into dice the same size as peppers.

2 Combine diced peppers and tomatoes in a bowl, add finely chopped garlic and salt to taste, and chill.

3 Drain off excess liquids before serving.

Serves 4

Vegetables

It is hard to believe that before Cortes discovered Mexico, there were no tomatoes, green and red peppers, potatoes and sweet potatoes in Moroccan cooking. But these colourful vegetables, so evident in Moroccan cooking today, did not appear until the sixteenth century.

Moroccan vegetables are cooked in the same manner as meats, fish and poultry: with diced or grated onion, peeled, seeded and diced tomato, finely chopped garlic, chopped flat-leafed (Italian) parsley and fresh coriander. Salt, pepper, sweet red and hot red peppers are added to these tasty dishes, with sometimes a hint of saffron or cumin added for extra savour. These are superb vegetable dishes in the Mediterranean manner, well worthy to be a course on their own, and, of course, wonderful too as accompanying vegetable dishes to complement roasts or grills of lamb, beef or poultry.

OPPOSITE: *Washing vegetables on the road to Tiznit.*

AUBERGINES (EGGPLANT)

The Arabs brought aubergines (eggplant) from India to Spain, Portugal, southern France and southern Italy in the fifteenth century. These purple, shiny, long vegetables are excellent when salted and rinsed to remove bitterness, fried in olive oil and mashed; or braised or stuffed or baked in the oven. The Moroccans make deliciously rich appetizer salads out of them, dressed with a chopped garlic, onion, parsley and fresh green coriander dressing. And they use a combination of sliced sautéed aubergines (eggplant) and hot green pepper to dress up fried fish in the street food stalls.

OKRA

Okra seems to be the Cinderella among vegetables. To bring this vegetable to its glamorous fulfilment, only the very small tender young pods are used. These are left with the stem end uncut and are cooked for 5–6 minutes in rapidly boiling salted water. Serve them arranged like flowers on individual small plates, with small bowls of spicy Moroccan tomato sauce set in the centre of each plate. The okra is lifted by the stem end, dipped in the hot spicy sauce and eaten with gusto. The flavour is unique. Try this, too, with tiny aubergines (eggplant), cut like flowers and served as above.

My favourite salad stall in the Gueliz market of Marrakech. Wild mushrooms, fresh eggs, fresh snails, fresh herbs and every sort of wild salad you can imagine are available here.

SWEET RED ONIONS

Flat wine-red Moroccan onions are a year-round delight in Moroccan markets. Sweet-tasting and juicy, they lend their attractive colour and gentle onion flavour to a Moroccan luncheon salad along with anchovies and black olives.

TINY RED-SKINNED GARLIC

The diminutive cloves no thicker than 3mm/$\frac{1}{8}$ inch are pungently alive in flavour, yet gentler and less bitter than garlic in Britain. All recipes in this book have been adapted to use the larger European and American garlic cloves.

FIERY-TASTING LONG GREEN MOROCCAN PEPPERS

These are quite unlike our sweet green peppers. Glossy skinned and dark bright green in colour, they are elongated and slightly irregular in shape, with a hotter, more intense flavour.

Peppers are usually roasted over an open fire in Morocco, turning them over three or four times until skins are charred on all sides, and then steamed in a double steamer or *couscoussier* or, more easily, in a plastic bag. This combination of roasting and steaming leaves the peppers tender and digestible.

To prepare peppers for skinning, to be used in salads and other dishes, grill them, turning so that they char evenly on all sides. Either rub off the charred skin under running water, seed the pepper and drain; or put the grilled peppers in a plastic bag and rub between your hands to remove the charred skin, then seed, rinse and drain.

HOT RED PEPPERS

When preparing fresh or dried hot red or chilli (chili) peppers, always wash your hands directly after handling and make sure you do not put your hands near your eyes before you do so.

To seed a fresh hot red pepper, hold the stem end in one hand and, using a sharp pointed knife, cut through both sides of pepper. Then, scrape out the seeds with the point of the knife.

To seed a dried hot red pepper, cut off the base of each pepper at the stem end and roll the pod between thumb and forefinger to loosen the seeds. Shake seeds out the open end of pepper.

SLAOUI

Moroccan farmers raise an ethereal relation of the squash family, called the *slaoui*. The pale green *slaoui* is the shape of an elongated, slightly curved cucumber, pale jade green in colour. Peeled, sliced and parboiled, it can be served as one of the deliciously subtle vegetables of a lamb *tagine*, or as one of the prime requisites of a *couscous* of seven vegetables.

TOMATOES

The tomatoes in Morocco are sweet and full of flavour. To prepare them for skinning, plunge into boiling water for a moment, then skin with a sharp knife and gently press out seeds.

Highly flavoured Moroccan garlic cloves are red-skinned under their white outer casing.

DRIED VEGETABLES (PULSES)

Lentils and chick peas are indigenous to Arabian cooking, going back to the ancient Sumerians and Egyptians. For centuries they provided calories and proteins for the daily diets when meats were too difficult or too expensive to procure.

Lentils appear in spicy appetizers, as vegetable accompaniments and as a *tagine* on their own.

Chick peas – used in country-style recipes of chicken, beef, lamb and sheep's feet or calf's feet, and as the basis for a heart-warming soup – are a necessity in all North African cooking, featuring in recipes for *couscous* in Algeria, Tunisia and Morocco.

POUNDED GREEN PEPPER APPETIZER

Serve with Arab bread which you dip into the bowl.

900g/2lb green peppers, grilled (broiled or barbecued) and skinned (see page 105)
salt and freshly ground black pepper
4 tablespoons chopped flat-leafed (Italian) parsley
2–4 cloves garlic, peeled and finely chopped
2 tablespoons lemon juice
4 tablespoons olive oil

1 Drain the skinned, rinsed green peppers, remove core and seeds, and cut into small dice.

2 Place diced pepper in a mortar and pound slightly, being careful not to pound into a purée. Season with salt and freshly ground black pepper to taste and mix well. Chill.

3 When ready to serve, sprinkle with chopped parsley and garlic, and moisten with lemon juice and olive oil.

Serves 4

DICED LEMON, ONION AND PARSLEY SALAD

This deliciously tart, fresh-tasting salad is an unusual addition to the Moroccan Appetiser Salad section. I find it particularly delightful as a taste-tingling addition to marinated fresh sardines dressed in olive oil or as an accompaniment to grilled fish.

4 large ripe lemons (thin skinned, if possible), washed
1 large Spanish onion, peeled
1–1½ bunches flat-leafed (Italian) parsley, washed
salt

1 Peel and dice the lemons. Cut the onion in 6mm/¼ inch slices, then into even-sized dice. Chop flat-leafed (Italian) parsley very coarsely.

2 Toss these three ingredients in a bowl until well mixed, and add salt to taste.

Serves 4–6

GRATED CARROT SALAD WITH ORANGE

450g/1lb carrots, peeled and coarsely grated (4 cups grated carrots)
juice of 1 orange
juice of ½ lemon
¼ teaspoon salt
¼–½ teaspoon icing (confectioners') sugar
1–2 tablespoons orange-flower water

Mix all ingredients together, toss, and chill.

Serves 4–6

GRATED LONG RADISH SALAD WITH ORANGE

450g/1lb long radishes, washed, trimmed and grated (4 cups grated long radishes)
juice of ½ orange
juice of ½ lemon
1 tablespoon olive oil
¼ teaspoon salt
¼ teaspoon icing (confectioners') sugar
1–2 tablespoons orange-flower water

Mix all ingredients together, toss and chill.

Serves 4–6

RED RADISH SALAD WITH ORANGE

Use normal round, red-skinned radishes instead of long radishes as above. Wash and trim, then slice vertically into thin rounds. Prepare exactly as above thereafter.

GRATED CUCUMBER SALAD WITH ORANGE

450g/1lb cucumbers, washed and trimmed
4 tablespoons lemon juice
1 tablespoon olive oil
¼ teaspoon salt
¼ teaspoon icing (confectioners') sugar
1 tablespoon orange-flower water

1 Peel cucumbers, cut in half and remove seeds.

2 Grate cucumber, then mix with all the remaining ingredients, toss and chill.

Serves 4–6

COOKED TOMATO AND GREEN PEPPER SALAD

This salad is excellent as an accompaniment for fish.

6 tablespoons olive oil
6 large thin green peppers (or 3 green bell peppers, halved)
6 large ripe tomatoes
1 clove garlic, peeled and finely chopped
¼–½ teaspoon powdered cumin
⅛ teaspoon hot red pepper
salt and freshly ground black pepper
juice of ½ lemon

1 Heat olive oil in a large iron frying pan (skillet). Sauté the whole green peppers (or halved bell peppers) until soft and just beginning to change colour.

2 Cut tomatoes in half and gently squeeze out liquids and seeds. Place tomatoes, cut sides up, in pan and continue to cook, shaking pan from time to time (and turning green peppers occasionally) until tomatoes are cooked through.

3 Transfer tomatoes and peppers to a serving dish.

4 Pour off half the olive oil left in the frying pan (skillet), and return pan to heat. Add the garlic and sauté for 1 minute over a high heat.

5 Remove pan from heat and season oil in pan with cumin and hot red pepper, adding salt and freshly ground black pepper to taste. Add lemon juice and spoon this sauce over tomatoes and green peppers. Serve warm or cold.

Serves 4–6

COURGETTE (ZUCCHINI) SALAD

700g/1½lb small courgettes (zucchini), washed
4 tablespoons olive oil
¼ teaspoon each hot red pepper, powdered cumin and freshly ground black pepper
salt
4 tablespoons chopped flat-leafed (Italian) parsley

DRESSING
1 tablespoon vinegar
3–4 tablespoons olive oil

1 Trim ends from courgettes and cut into 6mm/¼ inch thick slices.

2 Combine the slices in a small saucepan with 150ml/¼ pint (⅔ cup) water, olive oil, hot red pepper, cumin and black pepper, and salt to taste. Cook for 5 minutes, or until just crisp-tender. Cool and chill.

3 When ready to serve, drain the courgettes (zucchini). Combine salad dressing ingredients, adding salt and pepper to taste, and add to courgettes (zucchini). Toss well, garnish with chopped parsley, and serve immediately.

Serves 4

LA TAMU'S AUBERGINE SALAD.

AUBERGINE (EGGPLANT) SALAD

2 aubergines (eggplant), about 450g/1lb each
salt
olive oil, for frying
3–4 cloves garlic, peeled and finely chopped
1–2 teaspoons sweet red pepper
¼–½ teaspoon hot red pepper
1 teaspoon powdered cumin

DRESSING
2–4 tablespoons olive oil
2–4 tablespoons lemon juice
freshly ground black pepper

GARNISH
coarsely chopped flat-leafed (Italian) parsley or fresh coriander
half lemon slices (or strips of preserved lemon), and/or black (ripe) olives

1 Remove vertical strips of skin from each aubergine (eggplant) with a cannulator or scorer, leaving 2.5 cm/1 inch wide strips of skin all round. Cut in slices 2.5cm/1 inch thick. Salt the slices and leave to drain in a colander for 30 minutes. Rinse well under running water, squeeze gently to remove excess water then pat slices dry with kitchen paper (paper towels).

2 Heat olive oil in a thick-bottomed frying pan (skillet) and fry the aubergine (eggplant) slices, a few at a time, over high heat until they are golden brown on both sides. Drain off excess oil. Chop aubergine (eggplant) slices coarsely then mix with garlic and spices. Return to frying pan (skillet) and continue to fry in pan until all excess liquid evaporates. Transfer roughly chopped aubergine (eggplant) pulp to a salad bowl, sprinkle with olive oil and lemon juice, and add salt and freshly ground black pepper to taste. Allow to cool.

3 Just before serving, toss the cooked aubergine (eggplant) salad. Correct seasoning, sprinkle with flat-leafed (Italian) parsley or fresh coriander and surround with half lemon slices (or strips of preserved lemon) and/or black (ripe) olives.

Serves 4–6

AUBERGINE (EGGPLANT) SALAD LA TAMU

4–6 small aubergines (eggplant), sliced
salt
2–3 tablespoons olive oil
¼ teaspoon freshly ground black pepper
½ teaspoon sweet red pepper
1 teaspoon vinegar (or lemon juice)
½ teaspoon finely chopped garlic
1 tablespoon finely chopped flat-leafed (Italian) parsley
2 large ripe tomatoes, skinned and coarsely grated (see page 105)
lemon quarters

1 Salt aubergine (eggplant) slices generously and leave to drain in a colander for 30 minutes. Rinse well under running water, squeeze gently to remove excess moisture, then pat dry on kitchen paper (paper towels).

2 Sauté aubergines (eggplant) in olive oil until just golden. Add salt to taste, freshly ground black pepper and sweet red peppers, vinegar (or lemon juice), garlic, parsley and tomatoes, and continue to cook, mashing mixture gently, for 10–12 minutes, or until excess liquids have evaporated. Correct seasoning, adding more salt, pepper, sweet red pepper and vinegar (or lemon juice) if desired.

3 Allow mixture to cool before serving, with lemon quarters.

Serves 4–6

SLICED AUBERGINE (EGGPLANT) SALAD

4 medium-sized aubergines (eggplant), about 225g/½lb each, or 8 small
salt
olive oil, for frying
2 cloves garlic, peeled and finely chopped

DRESSING
3–4 tablespoons olive oil
2 tablespoons lemon juice
½ teaspoon sweet red pepper
¼ teaspoon hot red pepper
freshly ground black pepper

GARNISH
2 tablespoons finely chopped flat-leafed (Italian) parsley
sprigs of flat-leafed (Italian) parsley or fresh green coriander
half lemon slices
black (ripe) olives

1 Remove vertical strips of skin from each aubergine (eggplant) with a cannulator or scorer, leaving 6mm/¼ inch wide strips of skin all round aubergine (eggplant).

2 Cut aubergines (eggplant) crossways into slices 6mm/¼ inch thick. Salt the slices generously and leave to drain in a colander for 30 minutes. Rinse well under running water, squeeze gently to remove excess water, and pat slices dry with kitchen paper (paper towels).

3 Heat olive oil in a thick-bottomed frying pan (skillet), add the garlic and fry the aubergine (eggplant), a few slices at a time, over a high heat until golden brown on all sides. Drain off excess oil.

4 Mix all the dressing ingredients together, adding salt and freshly ground black pepper to taste. Toss aubergine (eggplant) slices in the dressing and arrange on a serving dish. Sprinkle with finely chopped parsley and garnish dish with sprigs of parsley or coriander, half lemon slices and black (ripe) olives.

Serves 4–6

BEETROOT APPETIZER SALAD I
(BEET APPETIZER SALAD I)

900g/2lb beetroot (beets)
salt
½ Spanish onion, peeled and diced
4 tomatoes, skinned, seeded and diced (see page 105)
2 cloves garlic, peeled and finely chopped
4 tablespoons finely chopped flat-leafed (Italian) parsley
4 tablespoons finely chopped fresh green coriander
4 medium-sized potatoes, scrubbed and boiled

DRESSING
2–3 tablespoons vinegar
8 tablespoons olive oil
salt and freshly ground black pepper
hot red pepper

GARNISH
black (ripe) olives

1 Cut off ends of beetroot (beets). Wash well and cook in boiling salted water until tender. Drain and remove skins under cold running water. Cut beetroot (beets) into dice, or short stubby 'fingers'.

2 Mix the dressing ingredients together, adding salt, freshly ground black pepper and hot red peppers to taste.

3 Combine prepared beetroot (beets) in a salad bowl with diced onion and tomato, garlic, parsley and coriander. Pour over half the salad dressing, toss gently and chill for 30 minutes.

4 Peel and slice boiled potatoes, place in a shallow bowl and add remaining salad dressing. Chill.

5 When ready to assemble salad, arrange beetroot (beets), tomato and onion in the centre of a shallow bowl or serving dish and arrange potato slices in a ring around them. Garnish with black (ripe) olives.

Serves 4–6

BEETROOT APPETIZER SALAD II
(BEET APPETIZER SALAD II)

900g/2lb beetroot (beets)
salt
½ Spanish onion, peeled and finely chopped
2 cloves garlic, peeled and finely chopped
4 ripe tomatoes, thinly sliced

DRESSING
2–3 tablespoons vinegar
8 tablespoons olive oil
salt and freshly ground black pepper
hot red pepper

GARNISH
4 anchovy fillets, diced
black (ripe) olives
2 tablespoons each chopped flat-leafed (Italian) parsley and fresh green coriander

1 Prepare, cook and skin beetroot (beets) as above. Cut into thin slices.

2 Mix the dressing ingredients together, adding salt, freshly ground black pepper and hot red peppers to taste.

3 Combine beetroot (beets) in a salad bowl with finely chopped onion and garlic. Pour over half the salad dressing and toss gently. Chill. Toss thinly sliced tomatoes in remaining dressing. Chill again.

4 When ready to assemble salad, arrange beetroot (beets) and onion in the centre of a shallow bowl or serving dish and arrange sliced tomatoes in a ring around them. Garnish with diced anchovies, black (ripe) olives and a scattering of chopped parsley and coriander.

Serves 4–6

BEETROOT APPETIZER SALAD III
(BEET APPETIZER SALAD III)

900g/2 lb beetroot (beets)
salt
¼ Spanish onion, peeled and finely chopped
2 teaspoons finely chopped flat-leafed (Italian) parsley
6 tablespoons olive oil
2 tablespoons lemon juice
salt and freshly ground black pepper
hot red pepper

1 Prepare, cook and skin beetroot (beets) as on page 111. Cut into small dice.

2 Combine diced beetroot (beets) in a salad bowl with finely chopped onion and parsley, olive oil, lemon juice, and salt, freshly ground black pepper and hot red peppers, to taste. Toss and chill.

Serves 4–6

CRISP COOKED VEGETABLE APPETIZER

4 small green peppers, grilled (broiled or barbecued) skinned, and rinsed (see page 105)
4 tomatoes, skinned and seeded (see page 105)
½ large Spanish onion, peeled
2 small aubergines (eggplant), trimmed
4 small courgettes (zucchini), trimmed
olive oil
2 cloves garlic, peeled and finely chopped
1–2 teaspoons sweet red pepper
salt and freshly ground black pepper
2 small hot red peppers, thinly sliced

TO SERVE
olive oil
lemon juice
lettuce leaves
2 tablespoons finely chopped flat-leafed (Italian) parsley

1 Drain the skinned, rinsed peppers, and remove core and seeds. Cut peppers, tomatoes and onion into 1cm/½ inch cubes.

2 When ready to cook, cut unpeeled aubergines (eggplant) and courgettes (zucchini) into 1cm/½ inch cubes. Wash, drain and sauté in 6 tablespoons olive oil with the garlic, sweet red pepper, and salt and freshly ground black pepper to taste, until slightly softened.

3 Add green peppers and onion – and a little more oil, if necessary – then stir well and continue to cook over a low heat until vegetables are tender but still crisp, and the liquids have evaporated from pan. Add tomatoes and thinly sliced hot red peppers, toss once, then remove pan from heat. Allow to cool.

4 When ready to serve, sprinkle salad with olive oil and lemon juice to taste. Correct seasoning and pile high on lettuce leaves. Sprinkle each portion with a little finely chopped fresh parsley.

Serves 4–6

CRISP-COOKED VEGETABLE APPETIZER:
a medley of fresh colour and flavour.

LA TAMU'S BAKED STUFFED VEGETABLE APPETIZER

6 long thin green peppers
3 large ripe tomatoes
3 medium-sized onions
olive oil

AROMATIC STUFFING
1–2 teaspoons finely chopped garlic
4 tablespoons chopped flat-leafed (Italian) parsley
2 tablespoons chopped fresh green coriander
6–8 tablespoons olive oil
2–3 tablespoons vinegar
salt and freshly ground black pepper
hot red pepper
freshly grated breadcrumbs

1 Prepare the vegetables. Wash green peppers, slice off caps and remove seeds. Cut tomatoes in half, squeeze out seeds and scoop out pulp with a spoon, reserve pulp. Peel onions and cut in half. Place onion halves in cold water to cover, and bring gently to the boil. Scoop out interiors of onion with a spoon. Reserve onion pulp.

2 For the stuffing, chop tomato and onion pulp coarsely. Add the garlic, parsley, coriander, olive oil, vinegar, and salt, freshly ground black pepper and hot red peppers to taste. Add enough freshly grated breadcrumbs to fill vegetables loosely. Correct seasoning and mix well.

3 Fill vegetables with aromatic stuffing and place in a baking tin. Moisten with a little olive oil and bake in a preheated oven (350°F/180°C/Gas 4) for 30 minutes, or until vegetables are just tender. Serve at room temperature.

Serves 6

LA TAMU'S COLD STUFFED VEGETABLE APPETIZER

3 large ripe tomatoes
6 artichoke hearts
olive oil
salt and freshly ground black pepper
6–8 tablespoons chopped onion
6–8 tablespoons chopped cooked beetroot (beets)
2–3 hard-boiled eggs, shelled and chopped
6 tablespoons chopped flat-leafed (Italian) parsley
3 tablespoons chopped fresh green coriander
lemon juice
150ml/¼ pint (⅔ cup) mayonnaise, flavoured with sweet and hot red peppers

1 Cut tomatoes in half, squeeze out seeds and excess moisture, and scoop out pulp with a spoon. Chop tomato pulp and place in a bowl. Add chopped onion, beetroot (beets) and eggs to tomato pulp with parsley and coriander. Add 6 tablespoons olive oil, and lemon juice, salt and black pepper to taste.

2 Brush artichoke hearts and insides of tomatoes with olive oil, and season generously with salt and freshly ground black pepper.

3 Fill artichoke hearts and tomato halves with the stuffing and top with a teaspoon or two of seasoned mayonnaise.

Serves 6

LA TAMU'S COOKED AND RAW VEGETABLE APPETIZERS *photographed in Abdeslam and Sacha's attractive* riad.

MOROCCAN POTATO SALAD

900g/2lb potatoes, scrubbed
salt
groundnut (peanut) oil

DRESSING
6 tablespoons olive oil
2 tablespoons vinegar
2 tablespoons finely grated onion
2 tablespoons finely chopped flat-leafed (Italian) parsley
$\frac{1}{4}$ teaspoon sweet red pepper
$\frac{1}{8}$ teaspoon hot red pepper
freshly ground black pepper

1 Cook potatoes in their skins in boiling salted water until just tender. Drain and peel while still hot. Brush with groundnut (peanut) oil and allow to cool. When cold, cut into finger shapes, or dice.

2 To make the dressing, combine all the ingredients in a small bowl with salt and freshly ground black pepper to taste.

3 Toss the potatoes in the dressing. Chill.

Serves 4–6

POTATO SALAD MIMOSA

To make Potato Salad Mimosa, scatter the salad just before serving with the grated yolks and whites of 2–3 hard-boiled eggs.

MOROCCAN GLAZED CARROTS

Serve these glazed carrots hot as a vegetable, or cold as an appetizer or accompanying vegetable salad.

900g/2lb carrots, peeled
salt
4 tablespoons olive oil
2 tablespoons sugar
2 tablespoons lemon juice
1–2 tablespoons chopped fresh green coriander
hot red pepper, to taste
sweet red pepper, to taste

1 Cut out cores of carrots if necessary and cut into thinnish slices (6mm/$\frac{1}{4}$ inch thick) lengthwise. Cut slices into 2cm/$\frac{3}{4}$ inch lengths. Cook carrot segments in boiling salted water until tender, then drain.

2 Toss in saucepan with remaining ingredients.

Serves 4

GLAZED CARROT SALAD

This salad is also delicious when served hot as a vegetable accompaniment to *tagines* of lamb or beef. In this case, double recipe to serve four generously.

700g/1$\frac{1}{2}$lb carrots, peeled
salt

1 tablespoon olive oil
½ teaspoon vinegar
juice of 1 large lemon
½ teaspoon finely chopped garlic
½ teaspoon finely chopped flat-leafed (Italian) parsley
½ teaspoon salt
⅛ teaspoon each freshly ground black pepper and sweet red pepper

GARNISH
strips of preserved lemon peel (see page 64)

1 Cut out cores of carrots and cut into thinnish slices lengthways.

2 Cook carrot segments in boiling salted water until tender, then drain.

3 Combine drained carrot segments in a serving dish with all the remaining ingredients, adding ½ teaspoon salt. Mix well and cool. Garnish with strips of preserved lemon.

Serves 4–6

COOKED GRATED CARROT SALAD

700g/1½lb carrots, peeled
salt
2 tablespoons olive oil
½ teaspoon vinegar
lemon juice (optional)

AROMATICS
¼ teaspoon salt
¼ teaspoon finely chopped garlic
½ teaspoon finely chopped flat-leafed (Italian) parsley
½ teaspoon each powdered cumin and sweet red pepper

1 Cook carrots in boiling salted water until tender. Drain, then grate coarsely.

2 Place grated carrots in a small saucepan with the aromatics. Add olive oil and vinegar and simmer gently for 10 minutes, stirring constantly. Correct seasoning, adding more salt, cumin, sweet red pepper and a squeeze of lemon juice, if desired. Allow to cool.

Serves 4–6

MOROCCAN LIVER SALAD
KIBBDHA

450g/1lb calf's liver, trimmed
flour (or fine semolina or cornmeal)
groundnut (peanut) oil
4–6 tablespoons olive oil
1–2 tablespoons lemon juice
salt
powdered cumin
hot red pepper

CHERMOULA
1 clove garlic, peeled and finely chopped
2 tablespoons finely chopped flat-leafed (Italian) parsley
1 tablespoon finely chopped fresh green coriander
½ teaspoon each salt and sweet red pepper
¼ teaspoon hot red pepper
4 tablespoons olive oil
2 tablespoons lemon juice

1 Ask your butcher to cut the liver into slices about 8mm/⅓ inch thick. Cut slices into 8mm/⅓ inch cubes (or into 'fingers' 8mm × 3cm/⅓ × 1⅓ inches). Place half the liver pieces into a large colander and pour boiling water over to blanch them. Repeat with remaining liver segments. Drain both portions well.

2 Place blanched liver in a large flat bowl and pour over the *chermoula*. Toss well and leave to marinate for at least 2 hours.

3 When ready to cook, drain liver pieces well and dredge with flour (or fine semolina or cornmeal). Heat 1cm/½ inch groundnut (peanut) oil in a large thick-bottomed frying pan (skillet) and sauté one-third of the seasoned liver, stirring constantly, until liver is golden brown on all sides but still rare in the middle. Remove liver pieces from pan. Repeat with remaining liver pieces, cooking them in two further batches. Drain well.

4 Add olive oil and lemon juice to taste to the remaining *chermoula* juices and pour over liver pieces. Toss well, then sprinkle with salt, cumin and hot red pepper, to taste. Serve at room temperature.

Serves 4–6

MOROCCAN BRAIN SALAD
MUHKT

550g/1¼ lb calf's brains (or lamb's brains, if you can get them)
juice of 1 lemon
2–3 cloves garlic, peeled and finely chopped
4 tablespoons chopped flat-leafed (Italian) parsley
2 tablespoons chopped fresh green coriander
4–6 tablespoons olive oil
½ teaspoon sweet red pepper
¼ teaspoon each hot red pepper and powdered cumin
4 large ripe tomatoes, skinned, seeded and diced (see page 105)
salt and freshly ground black pepper

1 Wash the brains under cold running water, removing membranes and blood, then soak in cold water with juice of half the lemon for at least 1 hour. Drain.

2 Place the prepared brains in a medium-sized casserole with garlic, parsley and coriander. Add olive oil, sweet and hot red peppers and cumin and toss over a medium heat, stirring constantly, until brains begin to stiffen (about 5 minutes).

3 Remove casserole from heat, add diced tomatoes and just enough water to cover, and simmer, the pan partially covered, for 20–30 minutes, or until brains are tender.

4 Season with the remaining lemon juice, and salt and freshly ground black pepper to taste. Cool, not chill, before serving. A little more olive oil and chopped flat-leafed (Italian) parsley may be added if desired.

Serves 4–6

LENTILS AND PUMPKIN WITH KHLII

450g/1lb (2⅓ cups) dried lentils, soaked overnight
900g/2lb pumpkin, peeled
2 Spanish onions, peeled and cut in quarters
225g/½lb khlii (see page 68), cut into strips 7.5cm/3 inches long
2 tablespoons fat from khlii
1 teaspoon sweet red pepper
¼ teaspoon hot red pepper
½ teaspoon powdered cumin
salt
1–2 small hot green peppers, thinly sliced
4 tomatoes, skinned, seeded and chopped (see page 105)
2 tablespoons tomato concentrate (purée)
4 tablespoons butter

ABOVE: TAGINE OF LENTILS AND PUMPKIN
WITH KHLII.

BELOW: *A cross-section of richly coloured,
highly flavoured Moroccan pumpkins called
courge rouge in the local markets.*

1 Drain the lentils, and cut the pumpkin flesh into thick slices.

2 In a medium-sized flameproof casserole, cook quartered onions, strips of *khlii*,
fat from *khlii*, sweet and hot red peppers, cumin, and salt to taste, and cook
until onion is transparent. Then add thinly sliced hot green pepper, tomato and
tomato concentrate (purée). Add water to cover and cook for 30 minutes, or
until meat is tender. Remove meat and reserve.

3 Add drained lentils to casserole, then pour in 1.2 litres/2 pints (5 cups) cold
water. Bring to the boil, skim, lower heat and continue to cook 30–40 minutes
until lentils are tender.

4 In the meantime, in a medium-sized saucepan, cook the pumpkin in boiling
salted water until tender, about 20 minutes. Add pieces of *khlii* to lentils and
continue to cook until meat is warmed through.

5 When ready to serve, drain the pumpkin and heat through in butter. Serve
lentils garnished with pieces of cooked pumpkin and *khlii*.

Serves 4–6

MOROCCAN APPETIZER SALAD
TRANSATLANTIQUE.

MOROCCAN APPETIZER SALAD TRANSATLANTIQUE

The Transatlantique Hotel in Meknes serves a delicious Moroccan appetizer salad made up of various cooked and raw vegetable salads: beetroot, glazed carrots, aubergine, pepper, tomato and cucumber salad garnished with black olives, hard-boiled eggs and strips of Moroccan preserved lemon.

½ recipe Beetroot (Beet) Appetizer Salad (I, II or III)
½ recipe Diced Pepper, Tomato and Onion Salad
½ recipe Aubergine (Eggplant) Salad
½ recipe Glazed Carrot Salad
½ recipe Potato Salad

GARNISH
thin strips of preserved lemon peel (see page 64)
black (ripe) olives
3–4 hard-boiled eggs, quartered
lettuce hearts

1 Prepare all the salads according to directions, then chill.

2 Arrange a small mound of each salad decoratively on a salad plate.

3 Garnish the Aubergine (Eggplant) Salad and Glazed Carrot Salad with strips of preserved lemon peel, and each dish with olives, hard-boiled egg quarters, and a heart or two of lettuce.

Serves 4–6

FATIMA'S TIERED SALAD

This is a very visual appetizer salad which Fatima serves as the first course of a light supper, to be followed by brochettes of lamb in a savoury *chermoula* marinade accompanied by rice or rice-shaped pasta tossed in aromatic butter.

    The dish is most attractive if all the vegetable slices are equal in diameter or, better yet, if each successive tier, starting with the tomato base, is slightly smaller than the one under it.

    To serve four you will need twelve slices of each vegetable. There is thus a lot of wastage in this salad, but Fatima dices all the remaining sliced vegetables left over, adds a little diced preserved lemon peel (see page 64) and serves it as a flavoursome accompaniment to the brochettes.

4 ripe tomatoes (12 fat slices)
2 Spanish onions, peeled and very thinly sliced (12 very thin slices)
4 boiled potatoes, peeled and thickly sliced (12 fat slices)
2 beetroots (beets), thinly sliced (12 thin slices)
½ cucumber, peeled and thinly sliced (12 thin slices)
1 long thin green pepper, thinly sliced (12 thin rings)
6 hard-boiled eggs, shelled and cut in thirds crossways

FATIMA'S SALAD DRESSING
150ml/¼ pint (⅔ cup) olive oil
3 tablespoons vinegar
1 tablespoon finely chopped garlic
3 tablespoons finely chopped flat-leafed (Italian) parsley
1 tablespoon finely chopped fresh green coriander
¼ teaspoon each sweet red pepper and powdered cumin
salt and freshly ground black pepper

1 Mix all the dressing ingredients together, adding salt and pepper to taste. The trick is to drizzle a little dressing over each layer of the salad as you build up the layered 'towers' of raw and cooked vegetables.

2 To assemble the salad, arrange the fat slices of tomato on a large round serving dish. Top each with a thin slice of onion (slightly smaller in circumference than the tomato). Add a slice of cooked potato (slightly smaller) to each onion slice, then place a thin round of cooked beetroot (beets) on each slice of potato, and place a slice of cucumber on top. Centre a small ring of thinly sliced green pepper on each slice of cucumber and finish each 'tower' with an end slice of hard-boiled egg.

Serves 4

POMMES FRITES

450–700g/1–1½lb potatoes
oil for deep frying
salt and freshly ground black pepper

1 Peel the potatoes and cut them 6mm/¼ inch square by 7.5cm/3 inches long. Rinse in cold water to remove any excess starch and drain thoroughly. Dry well on paper towels.

2 Heat the oil in a deep-fat fryer to 375°F/190°C.

3 Fill the frying basket half to two-thirds full of potatoes and immerse it gently in the hot oil. Shake the basket from time to time while frying to keep the potatoes from sticking together. Continue to fry until the potatoes are nearly tender but only slightly coloured. Drain them well and spread on a baking tray lined with paper towels to soak up the excess oil while you fry the remaining potatoes in the same way.

4 Reheat the oil to 375°F/190°C and fry potatoes again in small quantities until golden brown. Drain on paper towels.

5 Sprinkle with salt and freshly ground black pepper and serve immediately.

Serves 4

TAGINE OF CHICK PEAS WITH AROMATICS

900g/2lb (4 cups) chick peas, soaked overnight
salt
1 Spanish onion, peeled and coarsely grated
3 large ripe tomatoes, skinned, seeded and diced (see page 105)
6 sprigs flat-leafed (Italian) parsley, chopped
4 sprigs fresh green coriander, chopped
¼ teaspoon each hot and sweet red peppers, powdered cinnamon, saffron, cumin and ginger
freshly ground black pepper
6 tablespoons olive oil

1 Drain chick peas and cook in boiling salted water until tender. Strain. Peel the chick peas, and combine them with grated onion in a *tagine* (or shallow casserole). Add diced tomatoes, chopped herbs, spices, and salt and freshly ground black pepper to taste. Mix well.

2 When ready to cook, add olive oil and simmer over a low heat for 15 minutes, or until the chick peas are well impregnated with aromatic flavours.

Serves 4–6

AUBERGINE (EGGPLANT) FRITES

4–6 small ripe aubergines (eggplant)
salt
olive oil, for deep-frying
seasoned flour (salt, hot and sweet red peppers)

GARNISH
1 tomato, or red pepper

1 Wipe the aubergines (eggplant) clean with a damp cloth and trim off the stem ends. Cut into thin slices, crossways or lengthways, depending on shape of the aubergines (eggplant). Sprinkle with salt and leave to drain in a colander for at least 30 minutes, to allow the salt to draw out the bitter juices.

2 Heat the oil in a deep-fat fryer to 375°F/190°C. At this temperature a 1cm/$\frac{1}{2}$ inch cube of day-old bread will take 50 seconds to turn crisp and golden brown.

3 Rinse the aubergine slices thoroughly. Pat them dry with paper towels, pressing firmly to get rid of as much moisture as possible. Dust lightly with seasoned flour.

4 Deep-fry the slices in four batches, for 4–5 minutes, or until crisp and golden brown. Drain thoroughly on paper towels and keep warm.

5 Arrange aubergine (eggplant) slices on a heated serving dish. To garnish, cut the tomato (or red pepper) into six wedges, leaving them joined at the stalk end. Remove the seeds, and arrange in a flower shape at one end of the dish. The slices will go limp very quickly, so serve them immediately.

Serves 4

STUFFED AUBERGINES (EGGPLANT)

Serve hot as a vegetable, cold as an appetizer.

4 medium-sized aubergines (eggplant)
salt
olive oil
2 Spanish onions, peeled and sliced
2 cloves garlic, peeled and finely chopped
2 tablespoons finely chopped flat-leafed (Italian) parsley
$\frac{1}{4}$–$\frac{1}{2}$ teaspoon sweet red pepper
$\frac{1}{8}$–$\frac{1}{4}$ teaspoon hot red pepper
$\frac{1}{4}$ teaspoon powdered cumin
6 ripe tomatoes, seeded and chopped

GARNISH
4 whole tomatoes
sugar
salt and freshly ground black pepper

1 Trim the aubergines (eggplant). Cut in half lengthways and scoop out some of the flesh, leaving a shell about 6mm/$\frac{1}{4}$ inch thick. Make four incisions lengthways in each half, being careful not to cut through skin. Salt aubergine (eggplant) halves, making sure salt goes into incisions and leave for 20 minutes. Wash aubergines (eggplant), squeeze dry, and sauté in olive oil on both sides until soft and pliable. Reserve oil.

2 In another frying pan (skillet), sauté the sliced onions in fresh olive oil until transparent. Add garlic, parsley, sweet and hot red peppers, cumin and tomatoes, and sauté for a few minutes more, stirring from time to time. Allow to cool.

3 Place sautéed aubergines (eggplant) cut side up in a fairly deep ovenproof dish or shallow casserole. Stuff with onion and tomato mixture, spooning any left over around aubergines (eggplant).

4 Slice the 4 whole garnish tomatoes and place slices on top of stuffing; sprinkle with a little sugar, salt and freshly ground black pepper to taste.

5 Pour over the reserved aubergine (eggplant) oil, add a little water to baking dish and cook in a low oven (325°F/160°C/Gas 3) for 1 hour.

Serves 4–6

MOROCCAN AUBERGINE (EGGPLANT) FLOWERS

Aubergines (eggplant) can be really small in Morocco, some only 6cm/2½ inches in length, so use eight of those for four people, or less if using larger ones. Serve with a 'dipping' tomato sauce (see page 143) if you like, hot as a vegetable or cold as an appetizer.

8 small aubergines (eggplant)
4 tablespoons olive oil
salt and freshly ground black pepper
a pinch of hot red pepper
8 sprigs flat-leafed (Italian) parsley

1 Wash aubergines (eggplant) and cut each in quarters to stem end, leaving stem end uncut, to represent petals of a 'flower'. Brush with a little olive oil. Season generously with salt and pepper and leave to shed excess liquids for a minimum of 2 hours. Rinse aubergines (eggplant) well and squeeze dry.

2 Bring a saucepan of water to the boil, add aubergines (eggplant) and cook for 20 minutes, or until tender. Drain and squeeze out excess moisture.

3 Season remaining olive oil with salt, freshly ground black pepper and hot red peppers to taste, and brush 'flowers' with this highly seasoned mixture.

4 To serve, arrange aubergines (eggplant) on a serving dish and garnish each 'flower' with a sprig of flat-leafed (Italian) parsley for a 'leaf'.

Serves 4 or 8 (depending on size of aubergines/eggplant)

BROAD (FAVA) BEAN SALAD WITH CUMIN

900g/2lb/4½ cups fresh broad (fava) beans
4–6 tablespoons olive oil
1 teaspoon powdered cumin
salt
4 tablespoons chopped flat-leafed (Italian) parsley
2 cloves garlic, peeled and finely chopped
juice of ½ lemon

1 Shell the beans and cook (with three or four pods) about 20 minutes until tender in the top of a steamer. Drain, then peel the beans.

2 While still warm, add olive oil, cumin, and salt to taste. Toss well and chill.

3 Serve with parsley and garlic, a little more oil if necessary, and the lemon juice.

Serves 4–6

SPICY GREEN BEANS

900g/2lb green beans, topped and tailed
6 tablespoons groundnut (peanut) oil
2 cloves garlic, peeled and finely chopped
1 Spanish onion, peeled and finely chopped
6 tomatoes, skinned, seeded and chopped (see page 105)
1 small fresh hot red pepper, finely chopped

1 Wash the beans and drain carefully. Reserve.

2 Heat oil in *tagine* or large frying pan (skillet). Add garlic and onion, and sauté until vegetables are transparent. Add the tomatoes and pepper and continue to sauté for 1–2 minutes more. Finally add the green beans, and stir over a high heat for 3 minutes.

3 Add 8 tablespoons water and simmer about 15–20 minutes, until beans are just tender. Serve hot.

Serves 4

COURGETTE (ZUCCHINI) STRIPS WITH CHERMOULA

900g/2lb courgettes (zucchini), washed and trimmed
olive oil

CHERMOULA
1 Spanish onion, peeled and grated
2 fat cloves garlic, peeled and finely chopped
¼ teaspoon hot red pepper
½ teaspoon sweet red pepper
¼ teaspoon cracked black pepper
½ teaspoon powdered cumin
½ teaspoon salt
6 tablespoons olive oil
6 tablespoons water

GARNISH
2 tablespoons chopped flat-leafed (Italian) parsley
2 tablespoons chopped fresh green coriander
· lemon juice

1 To make *chermoula*, combine the first seven ingredients in a bowl. Add olive oil and water and mix well.

2 Cut courgettes (zucchini) into eighths lengthways and place strips in a large shallow casserole. Spoon over the chermoula mixture and add a little more olive oil and water, if pan seems too dry. Cook over a medium heat until courgettes (zucchini) are tender, about 20 minutes.

3 Just before serving, sprinkle with chopped parsley and coriander and heighten flavours with a hint of lemon juice.

Serves 6

MEZGALDI OF ONIONS

900g/2lb Spanish onions, peeled and sliced (6½ cups peeled and sliced Spanish onions)
150ml/¼ pint/⅔ cup olive oil
¼ teaspoon powdered saffron
1 teaspoon powdered ginger
1 teaspoon crushed black pepper
4 tablespoons powdered cinnamon
2 tablespoons sugar
2 celery stalks

1 Arrange onions in layers in a large shallow bowl.

2 Combine olive oil, saffron, ginger, pepper and half the powdered cinnamon and sugar in another bowl. Pour over onions, then add just enough water to cover the onions. Mix well, and leave onions to marinate in this mixture for 2 hours.

3 When ready to cook, place the celery stalks crossways on the bottom of a large *tagine* or flameproof casserole, to protect the onions from scorching. Arrange sliced flavoured onions in overlapping layers and pour marinade juices over them. Sprinkle with remaining cinnamon and sugar and place *tagine* (or casserole) over a medium heat.

4 Over *tagine* (or casserole) put an upturned saucepan lid large enough to cover it or cover *tagine* base with a larger *tagine*. Pile with hot charcoal, and cook for 30–40 minutes, making sure you shake contents of *tagine* (or casserole) carefully from time to time as it cooks. (In more modern terms, cook this recipe in the oven (325°F/160°C/Gas 3) and then brown under the grill (broiler) just before serving.) The onions should be meltingly tender, highly flavoured and slightly caramelized.

Serves 4–6

12

HARIRA
AND OTHER
MOROCCAN SOUPS

Ramadan is the Arab Lent, a whole month in the Islamic year when good Moslems fast all day, abstaining from food, drink and tobacco, and even medicines and sex, during daylight.

Ramadan begins officially with seven volleys of cannon sounded at first sight of the tiniest sliver of the new moon. And at the first light of the following dawn the day's fast begins, to be broken only at the setting of the sun. For thirty days, Moroccans live to this exciting new rhythm: calm and sleepy during the day, rustling with activity at night. Ramadan is not a complete fast at all, but a strict discipline between the hours of sun-up and sun-down: at night there is feasting.

For a week before Ramadan, there is a feeling of excitement in the streets of Marrakech. For weeks the women have been buying dried pulse vegetables for *harira* and stocks of honey, dates and almonds for the delicious honey-dipped sweetmeats that are such an important part of the festivities.

The Moslem year is ten days shorter than our year, so Ramadan – like the other religious events of the calendar – creeps slowly throughout the seasons. It is when the holy month of Ramadan falls in the full African summer that the men of the villages rarely leave their homes before evening, because the heat and long drawn-out fast makes them irritable and of sombre humour.

The day's fast ends at the setting of the sun and the voice of prayer issues forth simultaneously from *minaret* and radio. Suddenly the streets are magically deserted; the Moslems are all at home waiting for the moment when they can sip a glass of lemonade, a bowl of *café au lait* or a steaming hot bowl of *harira*, the traditional 'break fast' soup of Ramadan, and take up again all the pleasures of the Moroccan night.

ABOVE: *Morocco at night during Ramadan.*

OPPOSITE: HARIRA *is a delicious soup of many flavours and many textures. Sweet titbits traditionally accompany the soup at Ramadan – deep-fried pastries, dates, figs and hard-boiled eggs.*

124

Harira

Harira – a subtle mix of lamb broth, diced lamb, lentils, chick peas, chopped tomatoes, onion, garlic, fresh herbs and spices, thickened at the last minute with fresh (compressed) yeast or flour and beaten eggs – is the traditional 'break fast' soup of Ramadan, warming, fortifying and inexpensive. In Morocco, it is often served as a much loved first course for evening meals – or as a supper on its own with a squeeze of fresh lemon juice added by each guest to his own portion at the table.

During Ramadan, this wonderfully fortifying soup is served the minute the *muezzin* sounds and the family rushes back to the household for their first meal of the day. The whole house is filled with the wonderful aromas of the soup as it cooks, and the family happily sits down to bowls of the hot soup traditionally served with a series of sweet and savoury tidbits: fresh dates, dried figs, hard-boiled eggs and sweet cakes and triangles of fried flaky pastry stuffed with almonds, lamb or chicken. *Harira* is traditionally served from a large covered bowl surrounded with little earthenware bowls and specially carved soup spoons fashioned of lemon wood.

In Fez, during the hot days of summer, a special diet version of *harira* is served spiced with *carvi, gomme mastique* and *ambroisie* as a light summer supper designed to clear the stomach

The aroma of HARIRA soup, amber-tinted and thickened with yeast or flour, made with chick peas, lentils, onion, tomatoes, garlic and coriander, perfumes the houses of rich and poor alike. This recipe includes KEFTA (finely minced, highly flavoured lamb) for its unique flavour.

and liver of impurities. In Meknes I enjoyed *harira* with chopped watercress leaves or chopped flat leaves of lemon-scented purslane, a pleasing variation.

Enjoy your first taste of *harira* in one of the little street restaurants – open booths really – around the square in Marrakech, or the Grande Rue de Fes el Jadin or the Place Boujeloud in Fez. It will be an experience.

In *Moorish Recipes*, compiled by John, Fourth Marquis of Bute, there is a recipe for *kufta*, a fragrant, spice-laden version of *harira* that combines pieces of mutton the 'size of a date' with saffron, pepper, ginger, *smen* and finely chopped onion and three pieces of cinnamon bark. At the last minute, finely chopped parsley and chervil are stirred in with 4 tablespoons of raw *kefta* (see page 49) and simmered for a few minutes more.

MOROCCAN HARIRA

450g/1lb lamb, cut into 1cm/½ inch cubes
chicken giblets and trimmings, if available
1 large Spanish onion, peeled and finely chopped
100g/¼lb (generous ½ cup) lentils, soaked overnight and drained
100g/¼lb (½ cup) chick peas, soaked overnight and drained
1 teaspoon turmeric
½ teaspoon powdered cinnamon
¼ teaspoon each powdered ginger, saffron stamens and sweet red pepper
water
salt and freshly ground black pepper
4 tablespoons butter
100g/¼lb (generous ½ cup) rice
1 tablespoon dried (active dry) yeast
2 tablespoons chopped fresh green coriander
4 tablespoons chopped flat-leafed (Italian) parsley
4 large, ripe tomatoes, skinned, seeded and chopped (see page 105)
lemon quarters

1 To prepare broth, in a large saucepan or casserole place all the ingredients, up to and including 1.5 litres/2½ pints (6¼ cups) water. Add salt and freshly ground black pepper to taste.

2 Bring to the boil, skimming all froth from the surface as water begins to bubble, then add half the butter. Turn down heat and simmer soup, covered, for 1½–2 hours, adding a little more water, from time to time, as necessary.

3 To prepare the rice, bring 900ml/1½ pints (3¾ cups) water to the boil in a saucepan, add rice, remaining butter, and salt to taste. Cook rice in the usual manner until tender, but not mushy. Drain rice, reserving liquid, and add cooked rice to soup.

4 To finish soup, dilute yeast in a little of the reserved rice liquid in a small saucepan. Stir in coriander, parsley, and tomatoes, and simmer, stirring from time to time, for 15 minutes, then add to soup. Correct seasoning and serve immediately with lemon quarters. Guests squeeze a little lemon juice to taste into each serving.

Serves 6–8

There are many variations of HARIRA. One of the most soothing to the tired is what the simple food shops reckon to be their Ramadan soup – the dish with which the day's fasting is traditionally broken at nightfall. Usually based upon lamb flavoured with cumin and coriander and laced with lemon it is creamy textured and very digestible.

MUSTAPHA'S HARIRA WITH KEFTA

350g/¾lb minced (ground) lamb
salt and freshly ground black pepper
hot red pepper
1–2 spring onions (scallions), trimmed and cut into 6mm/¼ inch segments
1 celery stalk, with leaves, cut into 6mm/¼ inch segments
1 Spanish onion, peeled and coarsely grated
175g/6oz (scant 1 cup) lentils, soaked overnight and drained
100g/¼lb (½ cup) chick peas, soaked overnight and drained
175g/6oz dried broad (fava) beans, soaked overnight and drained
2 packets (heaped 1 teaspoon) powdered saffron
water
6 tablespoons salad oil
2 tablespoons olive oil
50g/2oz (generous ⅓ cup) rice
4 tablespoons flour, mixed to a smooth paste with water
3 tablespoons each chopped fresh green coriander and flat-leafed (Italian) parsley
4 large, ripe tomatoes, skinned and coarsely grated (see page 105)
½ preserved lemon (see page 64), peel only, diced
lemon quarters

1 To prepare *kefta* balls, season minced (ground) lamb with salt, freshly ground black pepper and hot red pepper, to taste. Roll lamb into small balls 1cm/½ inch in diameter.

2 To prepare broth, in a large saucepan or casserole combine *kefta* balls and all the ingredients up to and including 1.5 litres/2½ pints (6¼ cups) water. Add salt and freshly ground black pepper to taste.

3 Bring to the boil, skimming all froth from the surface as water begins to bubble, then add the oils. Turn down heat and simmer soup, covered, for 1½ hours, adding a little more water, as necessary.

4 To prepare rice, bring 900ml/1½ pints (3¾ cups) water to the boil in a saucepan, add rice, and salt to taste. Cook rice in the usual manner until tender, but not mushy. Drain rice, reserving liquid, and add cooked rice to soup.

5 To finish soup, dilute flour and water mixture in a little of the reserved rice liquid, then pour into a small saucepan. Stir in coriander, parsley, tomatoes and preserved lemon peel. Simmer, stirring from time to time, for 15 minutes, then add to the soup. Correct seasoning and serve immediately with lemon quarters. Guests squeeze a little lemon juice, to taste, into each serving.

Serves 6–8

FATIMA'S HARIRA IN THE MODERN MANNER

350g/¾lb lamb, cut into 6mm/¼ inch pieces
1 Spanish onion, peeled and coarsely grated
1 medium can tomato purée
225g/½lb (generous 1 cup) lentils, soaked overnight and drained
225g/½lb (1 cup) chick peas, soaked overnight and drained
1 teaspoon freshly ground black pepper
½ teaspoon powdered ginger
¼–½ teaspoon powdered cinnamon
1 packet (heaped ½ teaspoon) powdered saffron
1 chicken stock cube (2 chicken bouillon cubes), crumbled

water
100g/¼lb (generous ½ cup) rice
salt
50g/2oz flour (4 tablespoons), mixed to a smooth paste with water
3 tablespoons chopped fresh green coriander
3 tablespoons chopped flat-leafed (Italian) parsley
2 eggs, beaten
lemon quarters

1 To prepare broth, in a large saucepan or casserole combine all the ingredients, up to and including 1.5 litres/2½ pints (6¼ cups) water.

2 Bring to the boil, skimming all froth from the surface as water begins to bubble, then turn down heat and simmer soup, covered, for 1½–2 hours, adding a little more water from time to time, as necessary.

3 To prepare rice, bring 900ml/1½ pints (3¾ cups) water to the boil in a saucepan; add rice, and salt to taste. Cook rice in the usual manner until tender but not mushy. Drain rice, reserving liquid, and add cooked rice to soup.

4 To finish soup, dilute flour paste with a little of the reserved rice liquid in a small saucepan, and stir in coriander and parsley. Simmer, stirring from time to time, for 15 minutes, then add to soup. Whisk in beaten eggs, correct seasoning, and serve immediately with lemon quarters. Guests squeeze a little lemon juice, to taste, into each serving.

Serves 6–8

COUSCOUS SOUP WITH SUN-DRIED MEAT

100g/¼lb khlii (see page 68), diced
4 tablespoons olive oil
1 tablespoon tomato concentrate (purée)
1–2 teaspoons harissa (see pages 65–66)
1 Spanish onion, peeled and finely chopped
2 cloves garlic, peeled and finely chopped
½ teaspoon each powdered cumin and sweet red pepper
water
100g/¼lb (scant 1 cup) raw couscous
1–2 tablespoons dried powdered mint
salt and freshly ground black pepper

TO SERVE
lemon juice
olive oil
chopped flat-leafed (Italian) parsley and garlic

1 Heat olive oil in a saucepan and add diced dried meat, tomato concentrate (purée), *harissa*, onion, garlic, cumin and sweet red pepper. Mix well, cover with water, and simmer until meat is tender.

2 Add 1.5 litres/2½ pints (6¼ cups) water, bring gently to the boil, then add *couscous* gradually, stirring until well mixed. Add mint, and salt and freshly ground black pepper to taste, and simmer for 15–20 minutes.

3 Serve hot accompanied by a small pitcher or bowl each of lemon juice and olive oil, and a small bowl of chopped parsley and garlic. Guests add their own seasonings to this country soup.

Serves 4–6

CHICKEN SOUP WITH VERMICELLI

1 roasting (broiler/fryer) chicken
coarse salt
2 tablespoons olive oil
2 tablespoons butter (or smen)
1½ Spanish onions, peeled and coarsely grated
¼ teaspoon each cracked black pepper and powdered cinnamon
⅛–¼ teaspoon hot red pepper
100g/¼lb (½ cup) chick peas, soaked overnight and drained
water
100g/¼lb vermicelli noodles
2 egg yolks, beaten
½ bunch flat-leafed (Italian) parsley, chopped
½ bunch fresh green coriander, chopped
juice of 1 lemon

1 To prepare chicken, rinse well under running water and remove any pin feathers with a pair of tweezers. Rub chicken well with coarse salt inside and out. Rinse, and cut it into sixteen to twenty small pieces.

2 In a large flameproof casserole, combine olive oil and butter (or *smen*) then add chicken pieces, onion, black pepper, cinnamon, hot red pepper and 2 teaspoons salt. Cook over a medium heat, stirring constantly, until chicken pieces stiffen and onion becomes transparent.

3 Add 1.5 litres/2½ pints (6¼ cups) water and bring gently to the boil. Skim. Add chick peas to casserole, cover, and simmer for 1–1½ hours, or until chicken and chick peas are tender and bouillon is well flavoured. Add a little more water, from time to time, as necessary.

4 About 15 minutes before serving, stir in vermicelli noodles and cook until tender, stirring once or twice.

5 Place beaten egg yolks in a small bowl, whisk in a ladle of the hot bouillon until well blended, then add parsley, coriander and lemon juice and mix well.

6 Just before serving, pour egg yolk mixture into soup and mix well. Correct seasoning, adding a little more salt, black pepper, hot red pepper, cinnamon or lemon juice, and serve immediately.

Serves 6–8

MOROCCAN LENTIL SOUP

450g/1lb shin of veal, meat and bones
100g/¼lb (generous ½ cup) lentils
2 tablespoons olive oil
2 tablespoons butter (or smen)
1½ Spanish onions, peeled and coarsely grated
¼ teaspoon each crushed black pepper and hot red pepper
2 teaspoons coarse salt
water
2 large potatoes, peeled and diced
2 large carrots, peeled and diced
1 bunch fresh green coriander, coarsely chopped
lemon juice

1 Pour boiling water over lentils, allow to soak for 15 minutes, then drain.

2 In the meantime, combine olive oil and butter (or *smen*) in a large flameproof casserole. Add veal, onion, black pepper, hot red pepper and salt and cook, stirring constantly, until onion is transparent.

3 Add 1.5 litres/2½ pints (6¼ cups) water and bring gently to the boil. Skim and add drained lentils. Cook for 1½ hours or until meat and lentils are tender, adding a little more water, from time to time, as necessary.

4 About 20 minutes before the end of cooking time, add diced potatoes and carrots and continue to simmer until vegetables are tender.

5 Just before serving, stir in chopped coriander, and lemon juice to taste, and serve immediately.

Serves 6–8

MOROCCAN VEGETABLE SOUP

225g/½lb shoulder of lamb
450g/1lb ripe tomatoes, skinned and seeded (see page 105)
2 potatoes, peeled
2 large carrots, peeled
2 courgettes (zucchini), trimmed
2 celery stalks, trimmed
2 tablespoons olive oil
2 tablespoons butter (or smen)
1½ Spanish onions, peeled and coarsely grated
¼ teaspoon each crushed black pepper, powdered cinnamon and hot red pepper
½ teaspoon sweet red pepper
¼–½ teaspoon powdered saffron
2 teaspoons salt
water
100g/¼lb (½ cup) chick peas, soaked overnight and drained
1 bunch fresh green coriander, chopped
100g/¼lb vermicelli
lemon juice

1 Trim the lamb and cut it, tomatoes, potatoes and carrots into dice. Cut the courgettes and celery into thin slices.

2 In a large heatproof casserole, combine olive oil and butter (or *smen*). Add lamb, onion and tomato, and sauté, stirring constantly, for 3 minutes. Add black pepper, cinnamon, hot and sweet red peppers, saffron and salt and continue to cook, stirring constantly, for 5 minutes more. Then add 1.5 litres/2½ pints (6¼ cups) water and bring gently to the boil. Skim.

3 Add pre-soaked chick peas to the bouillon and cook for 1 hour. Then add diced potatoes and carrots, sliced courgettes (zucchini) and celery and half the coarsely chopped coriander. Cover casserole and allow meat and vegetables to simmer gently for 30 minutes, or until both are tender, adding a little more water from time to time, if necessary.

4 About 15 minutes before serving, add vermicelli and remainder of coarsely chopped coriander and cook until vermicelli is tender.

5 Just before serving, correct seasoning, adding a little lemon juice, salt, crushed black pepper and hot red pepper to taste. Serve immediately.

Serves 6–8

HOT SOUP WITH HARISSA

350g/¾lb lamb, cut into tiny dice
2 tablespoons olive oil
2 tablespoons butter (or smen)
light stock (broth) or water
100g/¼lb (½ cup) chick peas, soaked overnight and drained
2 courgettes (zucchini), trimmed and diced
2 carrots, peeled and diced
1 potato, peeled and diced

HARISSA MIXTURE
1 Spanish onion, peeled and chopped
2–4 cloves garlic (according to size), peeled and chopped
½ teaspoon hot red pepper
1 teaspoon salt
1–2 teaspoons harissa (see pages 65–66)

1 In a large saucepan, combine diced lamb, olive oil and butter (or *smen*).

2 To prepare *harissa* mixture, combine ingredients in a mortar and pound until a smooth paste is formed. Add 6 tablespoons of the light stock (broth) or water, and mix well. Add to meat in saucepan.

3 Cook meat and spices over a medium heat, stirring constantly, until meat starts to stiffen. Add 1.5 litres/2½ pints (6¼ cups) light stock (broth) or water and the chick peas, and bring gently to the boil. Skim, lower heat, cover and simmer for 1 hour.

4 Add diced courgettes (zucchini), carrots and potato and continue to cook until meat and vegetables are tender, about 15–20 minutes.

Serves 6–8

MOROCCAN SOUP WITH BROAD (FAVA) BEANS

225g/½lb lamb, diced
225 g/½lb (1⅓ cups) dried broad (fava) beans, soaked overnight and drained
4 tablespoons olive oil
1½ Spanish onions, peeled and coarsely grated
4 large tomatoes, skinned, seeded and diced (see page 105)
2 tablespoons tomato concentrate (purée)
¼ teaspoon crushed black pepper
1 teaspoon hot red pepper
salt
water
1 bunch fresh green coriander, chopped

1 In a large flameproof casserole, combine olive oil, onion, tomato and tomato concentrate (purée). Add crushed black pepper and crushed hot red pepper, and salt to taste, and sauté, stirring constantly, until onion is transparent.

2 Add 1.5 litres/2½ pints (6¼ cups) cold water, bring to the boil, and skim. Add diced meat and broad (fava) beans, cover and simmer for 1½ hours or until meat and beans are tender, adding a little more water, from time to time, as necessary.

3 Immediately before serving, add chopped coriander, and correct seasoning.

Serves 6–8

BESSARA

A thick purée of broad (fava) beans – a speciality of the Rif – is usually served as a dip. I prefer it, with a little more liquid added, as a delicious hot soup. The trick is to garnish it with powdered cumin, sweet red pepper and chopped spring onion (scallion), with a dribble of fruity olive oil to add to the flavour.

450g/1lb (2⅔ cups) dried broad (fava) beans, soaked overnight
water
6 cloves garlic, peeled
salt
150ml/¼ pint (⅔ cup) olive oil
1 tablespoon each powdered cumin and sweet red pepper

GARNISH
powdered cumin
sweet red pepper
chopped green of 1 spring onion (scallion), or chives (optional)
olive oil
lemon juice

1 Drain the beans and remove skins.

2 Bring 1.5 litres/2½ pints (6¼ cups) water to the boil in a large flameproof casserole or stock pot. Add skinned broad (fava) beans and garlic. Bring slowly back to the boil, skimming froth from surface from time to time. Cook until beans are very tender, adding a little more water if necessary.

3 Pass beans, garlic and liquid through a fine sieve.

4 Return to a clean saucepan and place over a low heat. Stir in salt to taste, olive oil, cumin and sweet red pepper. Continue to cook over low heat until smooth and well flavoured.

5 Just before serving, pour into soup bowls and decorate with ribbons of cumin and sweet red pepper and, if desired, chopped green of spring onion (scallion), or chives. Sprinkle with a little more olive oil and some lemon juice, and serve immediately.

Serves 4–6

Simple porridges, gruels and other plain foods based mainly on grains, cracked wheat or fava beans, sometimes enriched with pieces of meat and vegetables (forerunners of today's national dish, couscous), abound in the culinary history of Morocco. I particularly enjoy BESSARA, *an earthy purée of broad (fava) beans, when served with chopped parsley, coriander and garlic, a mix of hot and sweet red pepper and a sprinkling of Moroccan olive oil.*

13

MOROCCAN FISH

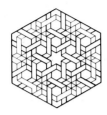

Morocco's coastal cities – the ancient Carthaginian and Portuguese settlements of El Jadida, Essaouira, Safi and Azemmour – have very different culinary traditions. This beautiful strip of coast, cut off from the rest of Morocco by the mountain ranges behind, is well worth a visit on its own to taste the different seafood specialities of each region.

Each port has developed its own variations on the regional recipes, and these have not altered much over half a dozen centuries. The rigidity of such patterns, once formed, is demonstrated by one of the chief differences between the food of the coastal region and that of the interior – the richness of seafood on the coast, its virtual non-existence just behind it. This was natural enough in the days when no means existed to keep fresh fish from spoiling in a climate that never produced natural ice, and when transport was not fast enough to move perishable goods very far before they spoiled. It makes no sense today, when fish from the coast can not only be packed in artificially made ice or dry ice, but can also be moved from, say, Safi or Agadir to Marrakech, in less than 2 hours.

Travelling the coast to enjoy the local specialities is a constant pleasure: oysters, mussels and sea urchins at Oulidia; shad from the Oum er Rbia river at Azemmour; crevettes, sardines and tiny fried soles at Safi and Essaouira; and *palomete* and tiny shrimps and *calamaris* at Agadir. At Essaouira, especially – a delightful little town that used to be a quiet hideaway off the main travel routes but has now become something of a summer attraction for tourists and Moroccans alike – the freshly caught fish sold from the fleet of small boats in the old port make for wonderful eating. Fresh sardines, and the occasional sea bass or lobster, are grilled over open charcoal braziers and consumed on trestle tables right in the open port. Nothing could be more delicious than six freshly grilled sardines, flavoured with salt, hot red pepper and a squeeze of the little green *limoun* so loved

ABOVE: *The fish market at Casablanca is renowned throughout Morocco for the freshness and variety of the seafood on sale. This plateful shows off the shellfish available on my last visit to the market.*

OPPOSITE: *The coastlines of Morocco are teeming with magnificent fish, tiny red mullet, sards, pageot, sea bream and sardines. These are grilled over charcoal, baked, poached or cooked in* tagines. *Here, a fresh catch in the wine-red nets of the fishing port of Essaouira on the Atlantic coast.*

by the Moroccans, and eaten with crusty rounds of Moroccan bread and a salad of chopped tomatoes, onion and preserved lemon peel. Bring your own wine (and corkscrew) though, and maybe a few tangerines, or better yet, *cornes de gazelle* to munch with sweetened mint tea for dessert.

Chermoula

One of the most delicious fish dishes I ever tasted was a fresh salmon trout, rubbed with an aromatic mixture of chopped onion and garlic, fresh green coriander and parsley, flavoured with undertones of saffron, turmeric, sweet and hot red peppers, and salt. The fish was allowed to 'marinate' in this fragrant mixture for 2 hours, then was wrapped loosely in foil and baked in the oven until it was just cooked, its natural taste rounded out by its supporting seasonings to give it an outstanding depth of flavour. This was my first introduction to how wonderfully well the rich flavours of an intrinsically Moroccan cooking technique could work in a western kitchen, with western ingredients and a western cooking method.

The mixture used was a Moroccan dry marinade called *chermoula* (or, occasionally, *tchermila*) which is particularly well suited for use with fish and poultry – each marinade a subtly different means of adding excitement and flavour in the grilled, poached, baked or braised food. But lamb, too, whether *en brochette* or cooked in a *tagine*, benefits greatly from an acquaintance with this fascinating blend of flavours. I like, too, the earthier, spicier version I first tasted in Ouarzazate on the edge of the pre-Sahara, used to flavour an enormous *tagine* of baby pigeons cooked with onions, raisins and almonds. This version used onion, garlic, parsley, salt and sweet and hot red peppers with added cinnamon, honey and raisins to achieve its magic.

The object of the *chermoula* seasoning is not to mask the natural taste of the food, but enhance it. As the seasonings dissolve in the evaporating liquid of a *tagine*, for instance, during the long, slow cooking time, they blend intimately with the food as it cooks. The pan juices are then reduced over a high heat to complete the blending of flavours and oils, and spooned lovingly over the food to be served. Here, for fish, the marinade is rubbed well into fish steaks or pieces – or whole slashed fish – and left to impart its flavours for at least 2 hours or, preferably, overnight.

The recipes for *chermoula* vary from family to family, from cook to cook. Almost all of them feature chopped parsley, coriander and onion and an assortment of spices. This first is my favourite.

CHERMOULA FOR FISH I

This fragrant seasoning mix is equally good with fish or poultry – and (minus the saffron) makes an excellent seasoning for lamb and beef. Then, just remove the chopped fresh coriander, add cinnamon to taste, and you will have an aromatic 'flavourer' for pigeon and game in the Moroccan manner.

1 large sweet onion, peeled and finely chopped
4 small cloves garlic, peeled and finely chopped (or 2 large cloves)
½ teaspoon powdered cumin
¼ teaspoon sweet red pepper
⅛ teaspoon hot red pepper
1 packet (heaped ½ teaspoon) powdered saffron
6 tablespoons each chopped fresh green coriander and flat-leafed (Italian) parsley
6 tablespoons olive oil
juice of ½ lemon
salt, to taste

Combine all the ingredients in a small bowl.

CHERMOULA FOR FISH II

2–3 cloves garlic, peeled and finely chopped
½ teaspoon each sweet red pepper and powdered cumin
¼ teaspoon hot red pepper
4–6 tablespoons olive oil
2 tablespoons each vinegar and water

Mix all the ingredients together.

The cooks of Morocco season fish before cooking with a dry marinade called CHERMOULA, a highly seasoned mixture of chopped garlic and onion, flat-leafed parsley, green coriander and spices – saffron, turmeric, cumin, hot and sweet red pepper. Often a little olive oil and vinegar, water or lemon juice is added to distribute the flavours. Left overnight in this bath of fragrances, the fish is baked in the oven with sliced tomatoes, green peppers and sliced preserved lemon. Alternatively, it can be patted dry, dusted with seasoned flour and shallow fried in bubbling olive oil.

. One might think that so flavourful a condiment would banish all other taste than its own. On the contrary, it brings out brilliantly the diverse flavours of what is being cooked with it.

CHERMOULA WITH MOROCCAN PRESERVED LEMON

2–3 cloves garlic, peeled and finely chopped
1 preserved lemon (see page 64), peel only, finely diced
1 bunch fresh green coriander, chopped
1 bunch flat-leafed (Italian) parsley, chopped
1 packet (heaped ½ teaspoon) powdered saffron
½ teaspoon sweet red pepper
¼–½ teaspoon hot red pepper
4–6 tablespoons olive oil
2 tablespoons each lemon juice and water

Mix all the ingredients together.

FRIED FISH STEAKS WITH CHERMOULA

Use the *chermoula* below or one of those in the preceding pages.

A whole fish is often marinated and fried in exactly the same way. Wash it thoroughly as below, then score it diagonally on each side and rub well with the *chermoula*.

1 sea bream, about 1.25 kg/2½ lb, or 2 sea bass
salt
flour, sifted
oil for frying
lemon quarters

CHERMOULA
½ bunch fresh green coriander, finely chopped
3 cloves garlic, peeled and crushed
2 teaspoons coarse salt
1½ teaspoons each powdered cumin and sweet red pepper
¼ teaspoon hot red pepper
½ teaspoon powdered saffron
4–6 tablespoons olive oil
2 tablespoons lemon juice

1 To prepare *chermoula*, combine all the ingredients.

2 Scale, clean and wash the fish carefully in salted water, inside and out, then pat dry. Cut fish into steaks 4cm/1½ inches thick, and rub well with *chermoula*. Allow fish to marinate in this mixture for at least 2 hours, or overnight.

3 When ready to cook, pat fish dry with paper towels and dredge well with sifted flour.

4 Heat oil in a large frying pan (skillet) or shallow flameproof casserole large enough to hold fish comfortably. Fry in hot oil (375°F/190°C/Gas 5) until golden brown. Serve with lemon quarters.

Serves 4–6

POISSON À LA MAROCAINE

POISSON À LA MAROCAINE *as cooked in Fez.*

1 large daurade or pageot, or 2 sea bass
1 recipe chermoula (see page 137)
1.5kg/3lb tomatoes, skinned, seeded and sliced (9 cups skinned and seeded tomato slices) (see page 105)
6 tablespoons groundnut (peanut) oil
¼ teaspoon each powdered ginger and hot red pepper
½ teaspoon each powdered saffron and sweet red pepper
1–2 cloves garlic, peeled and finely chopped
1 preserved lemon (see page 64), peel only, cut into fine dice
4–6 tablespoons chopped flat-leafed (Italian) parsley
4–6 celery stalks, trimmed
1 preserved lemon, peel only, cut into thin strips
24 green or violet olives, cracked

1 Scale, clean and wash the fish, then pat dry. Rub *chermoula* mixture well into whole slashed fish (or fish steaks) and leave to absorb flavours overnight.

2 In a large saucepan, combine tomatoes, peanut oil, spices, garlic, and 4 tablespoons *chermoula* mixture from fish. Cook over a medium heat, stirring constantly, until the liquids have evaporated and the tomatoes are reduced to a highly flavoured purée. Remove from the heat and add the peel of 1 preserved lemon, finely diced, and the chopped parsley.

3 Place celery stalks on the bottom of a *tagine* (or oval flameproof casserole). Place fish on top, and spoon over remaining *chermoula* and the tomato purée.

4 Decorate fish with the peel of the second preserved lemon, cut into strips, and the olives. Cover *tagine* (or casserole), heat through on top of stove, then transfer to a preheated oven (375°F/190°C/Gas 5). Cook for 30–40 minutes.

Serves 4–6

MOROCCAN BAKED FISH

1 whole sea bream, pageot or 2 sea bass, cleaned (about 1.75kg/4lb)
12 fresh artichoke hearts, blanched
2–3 Spanish onions, peeled and thinly sliced
3–6 large tomatoes, thickly sliced
4 tablespoons chopped flat-leafed (Italian) parsley
2 tablespoons chopped fresh green coriander
1 tablespoon fresh thyme or 1 teaspoon dried thyme
salt and freshly ground black pepper
olive oil
water
1 packet (heaped ½ teaspoon) powdered saffron
¼ teaspoon each sweet and hot red peppers
3 lemon slices, halved
black (ripe) olives

GARNISH
6 strips green or red pepper, sautéed in oil
3–6 strips preserved lemon peel (optional, see page 64)

CHERMOULA
6 tablespoons finely chopped onion
2 cloves garlic, peeled and finely chopped
4 tablespoons chopped flat-leafed (Italian) parsley
2 tablespoons chopped fresh green coriander
½ teaspoon each sweet red pepper and powdered saffron
¼ teaspoon hot red pepper
4 tablespoons each olive oil and water
2 tablespoons lemon juice
salt and freshly ground black pepper

1 Scale, clean and wash fish, then pat dry. Cut three slits about 5cm/2 inches long on both sides of fish.

2 Combine all the ingredients for *chermoula*, including salt and pepper to taste.

3 Place fish in a large flat porcelain, earthenware or stainless steel dish large enough to hold it comfortably, and pour over the *chermoula*. Rub well into fish, inside and out, and leave to marinate, turning the fish from time to time, for at least 2 hours, or overnight.

4 In a large shallow, heatproof serving dish or roasting pan (large enough to hold fish comfortably), arrange alternate slices of blanched artichoke hearts, onion and tomatoes. Season with the parsley, coriander, thyme, and salt and pepper to taste.

5 In a bowl, combine 6 tablespoons each of the *chermoula* (from fish), olive oil and water. Add saffron, sweet and hot red peppers, and more salt and freshly ground black pepper to taste. Mix well, then pour over the vegetables. Add just enough water to cover them. Cover the dish with foil and bake in preheated oven (375°F/190°C/Gas 5) for 30 minutes. Reduce the oven temperature to 325°F/160°C/Gas 3.

6 Place halved lemon slices in the incisions you have made in fish. Place fish on top of the vegetables, brush with 2 tablespoons olive oil, and scrape any remaining *chermoula* mixture over fish. Add black (ripe) olives and return to the oven uncovered. Cook for 30 minutes, or until the fish flakes easily at the touch of a fork. Baste fish two or three times during cooking.

7 Serve immediately, garnished with strips of sautéed green or red pepper and preserved lemon.

Serves 6

TAGINE OF FISH WITH HONEY AND RAISINS

SEA BASS WITH RAISINS AND HONEY.

2 sea bass
175g/6oz (1 cup) raisins
olive oil
350g/¾lb Spanish onions, peeled and diced (3 cups peeled and diced Spanish onions)
2 tablespoons chopped flat-leafed (Italian) parsley
¼ teaspoon each hot red pepper, crushed black pepper and powdered cinnamon
4 tablespoons each liquid honey and vinegar
salt

CHERMOULA
4 tablespoons each olive oil and water
¼ teaspoon each ground cinnamon, hot red pepper and crushed black pepper
½ teaspoon mixed (apple pie) spice (or ras el hanout, see page 49)

1 Scale, clean and wash fish well, then pat dry. Cut it into 4cm/1½ inch steaks. Soak raisins in 150ml/¼ pint (⅔ cup) hot water.

2 To prepare the *chermoula*, combine all the ingredients together and rub over fish. Leave for 2 hours to allow fish to absorb flavours.

3 To cook fish, pour marinade juices into a large frying pan (skillet) or shallow flameproof casserole, add 4 tablespoons olive oil to pan and place over a medium heat. When oil is hot, add fish steaks and sauté on each side until golden. Remove fish from pan with a fish slice and reserve.

4 Add diced onions to pan, with a little more olive oil if necessary, and sauté, stirring constantly, until onions just begin to turn gold. On no account allow them to burn, or they will taste bitter. Season with parsley and spices. Add honey, vinegar and drained raisins to pan. Turn heat down to low, and simmer sauce for 15 minutes. Season with salt to taste.

5 When ready to serve, place fish steaks in a *tagine* or flameproof dish, pour over sauce and raisins, cover and continue cooking for another 10 minutes. Serve immediately.

Serves 4–6

MOROCCAN FISH BROCHETTES

700g/1½lb white fish (daurade, monkfish, pageot, etc.)
½–1 Spanish onion, peeled and finely chopped
1 clove garlic, peeled and finely chopped
2 tablespoons chopped fresh green coriander
4 tablespoons chopped flat-leafed (Italian) parsley
1 packet (heaped ½ teaspoon) powdered saffron
1 teaspoon salt
½ teaspoon sweet red pepper
¼ teaspoon hot red pepper
4 tablespoons olive oil
2 tablespoons lemon juice

1 Cut fish across the grain into 2.5cm/1 inch steaks, then cut each steak into 2.5cm/1 inch squares. Combine remaining ingredients and spoon over fish cubes. Mix well, and leave to marinate for at least 2 hours, or overnight.

2 To grill fish, place fish cubes on metal skewers and grill over charcoal, turning skewers until fish is lightly browned on all sides.

3 Serve the fish brochettes with small bowls of sweet red pepper, hot red pepper and salt.

Serves 4

BEIGNETS DE SARDINES À LA MAROCAINE

FRIED SARDINE 'SANDWICHES'

36 fresh sardines
lemon juice
flour, sifted
oil, for deep-frying
lemon segments
tomato segments

CHERMOULA STUFFING MIXTURE
1 Spanish onion, peeled and grated
1 bunch flat-leafed (Italian) parsley, chopped
½ bunch fresh green coriander, chopped
¼ teaspoon each crushed black pepper, hot and sweet red peppers, and powdered cinnamon
½ teaspoon powdered cumin
salt

1 Clean the sardines, and remove backbones and heads. Flatten out each sardine, and sprinkle inside of each with a little lemon juice.

2 To make *chermoula* stuffing mixture combine all the ingredients well, including salt to taste.

3 To assemble *beignets*, place one opened sardine, skin side down, on work surface. Spread with *chermoula* stuffing mixture and cover with another sardine, skin side up. Press together and continue with other sardines.

4 Just before frying, dredge sardine 'sandwiches' with flour and deep-fry in hot oil until crisp and golden. Drain and serve immediately with segments of lemon and tomato.

Serves 6

BOULETTES OF FISH WITH TOMATO SAUCE

900g/2lb fillet of cod, codling or whiting
1 egg, beaten
¼ teaspoon powdered saffron, dissolved in 4 tablespoons water
salt and freshly ground black pepper
2 tablespoons chopped chives or flat-leafed (Italian) parsley

TOMATO SAUCE
4 large ripe tomatoes, skinned, seeded and chopped (see page 105)
2 Spanish onions, peeled and coarsely grated
2 cloves garlic, peeled and finely chopped
1 teaspoon sweet red pepper
¼ teaspoon each hot red pepper and powdered cumin
6 tablespoons olive oil
150ml/¼ pint (⅔ cup) water

1 To prepare fish, cut fish fillets into strips and combine in the food processor with beaten egg, saffron and water, and season with salt and black pepper to taste. Process in short bursts until smooth. Form into *boulettes* (small balls) about the size of a walnut.

2 To make tomato sauce, combine all the ingredients in a shallow casserole, adding salt and pepper to taste, and bring to the boil. Skim, add *boulettes* and simmer in sauce for 15–20 minutes, turning them from time to time.

3 To serve, transfer *boulettes* to a heated serving dish, then reduce sauce over a high heat. Strain over fish balls, and garnish with chopped chives or flat-leafed (Italian) parsley.

Serves 4–6

MOROCCAN FISH BROCHETTES *are not like French fish brochettes or Turkish fish kebabs with their square chunks of fish threaded alternately on skewers with pieces of onion, tomato, courgette or mushroom. Here the fish is the thing – sliced 2.5 cm (1-inch) thick and then cut into 2.5 cm (1-inch) cubes. The fish is marinated in a dry Moroccan marinade (using a* chermoula *spice mixture) for at least two hours before being threaded on metal skewers* (LEFT) *and grilled over charcoal* (BELOW). *The result is tender and quite delicious.*

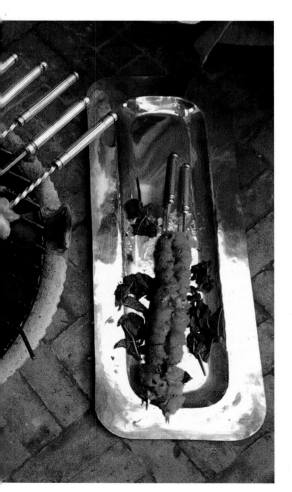

FRESH TOMATO SAUCE FOR FISH

This uncooked sauce is excellent as an accompaniment for saffron-flavoured fried or grilled (broiled or barbecued) fish. Try it, too, with cold poached fish.

4 large tomatoes, skinned, seeded and diced (see page 105)
2 hot red peppers, thinly sliced
3 spring onions (scallions), green parts only, sliced
½ bunch fresh green coriander, chopped
125–150ml/4–5fl.oz (½ cup – 10 tablespoons) olive oil
salt and freshly ground black pepper
lemon juice (optional)
finely chopped onion (optional)

1 Combine first four ingredients in a bowl, and add olive oil, salt and freshly ground black pepper, to taste. A squeeze of lemon juice and a little finely chopped onion is often added.

2 Chill until ready to use.

Makes 300 ml/½ pint (1¼ cups)

BARBECUED STEAMED FISH WITH MOROCCAN MARINADE

These packets of fish can be prepared ahead of time and stored in the refrigerator until ready to use.

4 large fillets sea bass, daurade, sar or pageot (175–225g/6–8oz each), or 8 fillets smaller fish
1 preserved lemon (see page 64)
4 tablespoons thinly sliced spring onion (scallion) (green parts only)
2 small cloves garlic, peeled and finely chopped
2 tablespoons each chopped fresh green coriander and flat-leafed (Italian) parsley
4 tablespoons olive oil
2 tablespoons lemon juice
4 pinches each hot red pepper and powdered saffron
salt and freshly ground black pepper

1 Place fillets of fish on individual sheets of aluminium foil. If using eight smaller fillets, put two together on one sheet.

2 Cut preserved lemon into eight thin wedges. With a small sharp knife, remove lemon flesh. Place two wedges of peel on each fillet and sprinkle with spring onion (scallion), garlic, coriander and parsley.

3 In a small bowl, combine olive oil, lemon juice, hot red pepper and saffron and drizzle over fish fillets. Season with salt and black pepper to taste.

4 Fold foil and seal securely. Place packets on grid of charcoal grill (15–20cm/6–8 inches from the heat) or in the oven heated to 350°F/180°C/Gas 4. Cook for 20 minutes, then serve immediately.

Serves 4

SOLES FRITES 'EN OMELETTE'

4–8 small lemon sole, according to size
salt and freshly ground black pepper
4 eggs
2 tablespoons coarsely chopped flat-leafed (Italian) parsley
⅛ teaspoon hot red pepper
¼ teaspoon each sweet red pepper and powdered cumin
flour, sifted
olive oil
sprigs of flat-leafed (Italian) parsley
lemon wedges

1 Trim and clean sole, rinse well and pat dry. Season generously with salt and freshly ground black pepper.

2 In a small bowl, beat eggs as for an omelette. Add chopped parsley, spices, and salt and pepper to taste.

3 Brush sole with omelette mixture then dredge with flour. Dip again in omelette mixture, dredge with flour, and fry in very hot olive oil until crisp and golden. Drain well.

4 Serve immediately with sprigs of parsley and lemon wedges.

Serves 4

POISSONS FRITS EN PLEIN AIR

1–1.25kg/2–2½lb fish
salt
150ml/¼ pint (⅔ cup) olive oil
4 small cloves garlic, peeled and finely chopped
4 tablespoons finely chopped fresh green coriander
½ teaspoon each hot red pepper, powdered cumin and crushed black pepper
juice of 1 lemon
flour

1 Scale and clean fish, then wash several times in salted water. Pat dry and cut into steaks of about 4cm/1½ inches.

2 Combine in a bowl half the olive oil with garlic, coriander, hot red pepper, cumin, black pepper, lemon juice, and salt to taste. Rub this into fish pieces and leave for 1–2 hours to allow flavours to develop.

3 Pat fish dry with a paper towel then roll in flour.

4 Heat remaining olive oil in a large frying pan (skillet). Add fish steaks and sauté until golden on both sides. Add salt to taste and serve immediately.

Serves 4–6

POISSONS GRILLÉS EN PLEIN AIR

1–1.25kg/2–2½lb fish
½ teaspoon each hot red pepper and powdered cumin
150ml/¼ pint (⅔ cup) olive oil
salt and freshly ground black pepper

1 Scale, clean and wash the fish, then pat dry. Cut three diagonal slashes on each side of each fish. Combine hot red pepper, cumin and olive oil, and add salt and black pepper to taste. Rub this well into the fish, inside and out. Leave for 1–2 hours, to absorb flavours.

2 When ready to grill fish, place on a grill 15cm/6 inches from charcoal fire and grill until fish flakes easily with a fork, turning fish once during cooking time. Brush fish from time to time with marinade mixture.

Serves 4–6

Freshly-caught fish from the sea ports of Agadir, Safi and Essaouira set against a Moroccan blue door.

14
THE FEAST OF THE LAMB

Morocco is a country where the past and present live together in close harmony; where a still very much alive yesterday lends added lustre to living today. Nowhere is this more apparent than in the way Moroccans love to take part in the rituals of their past, in the observance of their great religious festivals, for example. The starting point is *Achoura*, a once dark pagan rite, now known as the Festival of the Children, celebrated with particular zest in Marrakech. *Mouloud* marks the Festival of the Birthday of the Prophet. *Ramadan*, the month-long fast when religious fervour is at its height, is followed by the climax of the Moslem year, the *Aid el Kebir*, the Great Festival which commemorates the Prophet Abraham's sacrifice of a sheep in place of his son.

Aid el Kebir is held fifty days after *Ramadan*, and every family kills a head of livestock. This is normally a sheep which is kept in the patio or on the roof-top terrace of each house in the *medina*. You can hear the bleating coming from every direction during the ten to fifteen days before the feast. Some families even buy their animals as much as a month ahead of time, to be able to fatten them properly for the sacrifice. The children parade their family's potential sacrifice through the streets to see who has the biggest and the best. For poor families, the prospect of having no sheep at all can be a social disgrace of enormous proportion.

On the great day there is a palpable feeling of excitement in the streets as it approaches ten or eleven o'clock in the morning. And then, suddenly, it is quiet, and throughout the country the head of each household – rich or poor – slaughters a sheep and unites his prayers with the millions of devout Moslems around the world.

Moroccan lanterns shed exotic candlelight on a dinner picnic arranged in the grand manner to celebrate Aid el Kebir (The Great Feast). *A braised shoulder of lamb surrounded by stuffed vegetables provides the centrepiece of the evening meal. Musicians play gently in the background.*

147

This great festival lasts for four magic days, and on each day special dishes are made from the slaughtered lamb. It is a time of feasting and of prayer; a happy time when sons and daughters who live away from home come back to stay with their families; a time when every member of the household likes to share with his friends the generosity and bounty of the family table.

Lamb, more than any other meat, is the cornerstone of Moroccan cooking and nowhere is this more apparent than during *Aid el Kebir*. It appears as brochettes, as minced stuffings for vegetables, as grills, as the main ingredient for countless highly flavoured *tagines* with fruits (quinces, pears, prunes, dates, raisins and apples) and vegetables (artichoke hearts, courgettes (zucchini), cardoons, okra, broad (fava) beans and chick peas), and as one of the prime ingredients of the most famous Moroccan dish of all, *couscous*. Every part of the lamb is used, including the feet, innards and head.

The festivities start off with *boulfaf*, brochettes of fresh lamb's liver wrapped in lacy sheep's caul and grilled over the open fire (see page 51). Other dishes of the four-day feast are *douara*, lamb's tripe and innards simmered in a hot spicy sauce (see page 154) and *t'dlla*, lamb's shoulder marinated in onion, garlic, parsley and spices and then cooked in a casserole over charcoal, with more charcoal piled on the lid (see page 157). This great dish is sometimes served surrounded by lamb-stuffed Moroccan vegetables, green peppers, tomatoes, aubergines (eggplant), courgettes (zucchini) and onions (see page 162) – a veritable 'Feast of the Lamb'.

Couscous à la tête de mouton – steamed *couscous* with sheep's head – is a great speciality of the festival as is *Couscous au khlii*. One of the most ancient of the great feast dishes, *mrouzia*, is a *tagine* of mahogany-hued lamb simmered slowly in honey with raisins and almonds, nutmeg and thyme, lavender and myrtle, garlic, mint and the roots of strapwort, all generously sprinkled with sweet and hot red peppers. And *hergma*, a *tagine* of lamb's trotters simmered with chick peas and cracked wheat (one of my favourite country-style dishes) is always served at this time of the year, and is reputed to be one of the dishes served daily at the royal breakfasts of His Majesty King Hassan II.

One of the best lamb dishes I ever had during this great feast was in a little beach town below Ifni, called Aglou Plage, on the Atlantic coast. Here, in front of her beaming master, a black cook from the Sudan served us individual *tagines* of lamb – tender cutlets from the breast, simmered in a clear broth with bits of diced onion, tomato, turnip and cardoon. A few stewed, pitted prunes and raisins were added to lend sweetness to the meat, and the broth itself was flavoured with a hint of saffron, cinnamon, sugar, and just a touch of hot red pepper (as much

The slaughtered sheep hanging in the riad *ready to take its part in the festivities. The main dish – T'DLLA, shoulder of lamb in a dry marinade of chopped sweet onion, garlic, parsley and spices – is cooked* à l'étouffée *in a casserole over charcoal and with charcoal piled on the lid. This wonderful dish is surrounded by lamb-stuffed vegetables, courgettes, green peppers, aubergines, tomatoes and onions and served with Moroccan salads to refresh the palate during the meal.*

as could be picked up on the point of a knife) to give depth of flavour. It was perfection: so unexpected, with its touch of mediaeval sweetness backed up by the earthier tones of saffron and hot red pepper. I still remember this dish today, more than twenty years later!

The most interesting and famous of Moroccan lamb dishes, though, is the Berber *m'choui*, the great dish of the nomadic desert Bedouin who travels the grazing lands with his family and his flock. On one of my periodic forays into the Sahara below Erfoud, I had the good fortune to be invited to one of these great desert feasts and watched with great attention the ritual preparation that preceded the meal. First of all, the lamb was carefully chosen, not too young, yet big enough to feed the company, fine and fat. It was led away from the flock to be bled, washed and quickly skinned, much as we would skin a rabbit or a hare, leaving the feet and horned head untouched.

The lamb was then hung up on a tree so that it could be emptied and cleaned. The liver, heart and caul were given to the women to wash and hang to dry in the sun; the tripes were carefully scrubbed and washed, given their final rinsing and hung too, to dry. In the meantime, the men dug the pit for the fire: 1.25 metres/4 feet long, 50cm/nearly 2 feet wide and 40cm/16 inches deep. A sturdy forked stick was hammered into the earth at each end of the pit and a wood fire was built in the depression. A second fire, smaller than the first, was built nearby and water was set to boil for repeated pots of fresh mint tea, which provided the only refreshment during the 3–4 hours it took to roast the lamb.

Many of the lamb dishes popular in Moroccan cooking today were developed in Morocco centuries ago and exported all over the Mediterranean basin. Others were inspired by Greek, Roman and Persian recipes of old, or were brought back to Morocco from Andalusian Spain in the sixteenth century. All of them use exotic spices and the earthy tones of chopped onion, garlic, flat-leafed parsley and coriander to work their magic.

149

When the fire was reduced to glowing embers, covered by light grey ash, it was time for the men to pierce the lamb through with a pointed stick long enough to rest comfortably on the two forks of wood placed at each end of the fire pit. The lamb was brushed all over, inside and out, with melted butter flavoured with coarse salt, crushed black pepper, powdered cumin and ground sweet and hot red peppers, and set over the ashes to begin its long slow cooking with a few more hot embers from the second fire added from time to time to revive the dying fire.

The most important part of the ritual was to keep turning the lamb and brushing it with flavoured butter every 10–15 minutes, so that it was evenly cooked, uniformly crisp and golden on the outside, and yet meltingly moist and tender under its crisp highly-flavoured crust.

Towards the end of the cooking time, the heart and liver were cut into pieces about $1 \times 5cm/\frac{1}{2} \times 2$ inches and blanched for a minute or so in simmering water on the second fire. They were then drained, patted dry, seasoned with ground cumin and salt and wrapped in a thin sheet of prepared *crépinette* (sheep's caul) before being fixed, one by one, with alternate cubes of lamb fat, on long metal brochettes, ready to grill at the last minute to accompany the great roast in the traditional manner.

Now the beast was ready to be served on a great brass platter in all its glory; its skin golden and shiny and as crisp as a lacquered shell, not charred in any part. The meat as moist and tender as could be wished, its flavour like no other lamb I had ever tasted. Bowls of coarse salt, crushed pepper, crushed cumin seed and hot red pepper surrounded the beast, and field flowers, gathered by the children from the neighbouring scrub, were scattered in tribute over the brass platter.

Moroccans use other animals for *m'choui* and similar celebratory dishes – wild mountain sheep, gazelle and very young camel – and I have included a few recipes, although these will probably be of academic interest only in other countries. In the Moroccan countryside, the whole beasts (or forequarters, saddles or haunches) are barbecued over open pits as described above. In the city, *m'choui* is often cooked at the local baker's, or in one of the special *m'choui* stalls in the market where the lamb is roasted in deep oven pits. Or, more simply, the lamb is quartered and steamed over bouillon or oven-roasted at home.

PIT-ROASTED M'CHOUI OF LAMB

1 fine fat lamb (or forequarter or haunch)

MELTED BUTTER MARINADE
450g/1lb (2 cups) butter
50g/2oz black peppercorns, crushed
50g/2oz powdered cumin
25g/1oz sweet red pepper
15g/½oz hot red pepper
salt

1 Rub the prepared whole lamb (or forequarter or haunch) with the highly flavoured melted butter marinade, and leave to marinate while the pit is being dug (see above); prepare the liver and heart and wrap in *crépinette* (sheep's caul) as above; light a fire and allow to die down to ashes.

2 Pierce the lamb from end to end as above, and place over embers. If there are any aromatic plants nearby, throw them on the fire as the lamb cooks. Turn the spit and brush the lamb with the butter marinade every 15 minutes until it is tender.

3 Cook the liver and heart at the last minute as above.

4 When cooked, arrange the lamb in the centre of a large brass platter and garnish. Serve immediately so that the fat does not coagulate. In Morocco, each guest takes a portion on his plate, choosing and eating with the fingers. Small bowls of coarse salt, powdered cumin and hot red pepper are served with the lamb. To eat in Western style, place the lamb on a cutting board and cut immediately into serving portions, again so that the fat contained in the crisp skin does not coagulate. Hot plates are an absolute necessity, and provide bowls of seasonings as above, with knives and forks.

Moroccans often serve steamed *couscous* (or cracked wheat) with sautéed chick peas or almonds as an accompaniment.

OVEN-ROASTED M'CHOUI

1 forequarter lamb, about 4.5kg/10lb, or 1 saddle lamb
450g/1lb (2 cups) butter
2–4 cloves garlic, peeled and finely chopped
2 teaspoons coarse salt
2 teaspoons powdered cumin
1 teaspoon sweet red pepper
¼–½ teaspoon hot red pepper

1 Carefully trim extraneous fat from lamb. Cut each leg behind knuckle and bend leg back at knuckle, fastening it in position with kitchen string. Then, with a sharp knife, cut shallow diagonal incisions along upper leg and breast of lamb.

2 Blend softened butter, garlic, salt, cumin, sweet and hot red peppers into a paste and rub well into meat. Set aside for at least 2 hours, or overnight, to allow meat to absorb flavours before roasting.

3 Preheat oven to 450°F/230°C/Gas 8.

4 Place the lamb, fat side up, on a large baking tray that will just fit into the oven. Roast in preheated oven for 15–20 minutes, then reduce oven heat to 350°F/180°C/Gas 4 and continue to roast – basting with melted flavoured butter every 15 minutes – until lamb comes easily away from the bone with your fingers, or with the prongs of a fork, about 2½–3 hours.

5 To serve, place lamb on a large heatproof tray or board and garnish board with sprigs of fresh mint, coriander and watercress. Place *m'choui* in the centre of the table and surround with small bowls of coarse salt, ground cumin and hot red pepper, so that guests may season their own lamb as they eat it with their fingers.

M'CHOUI OF YOUNG CAMEL

The camel was introduced into the Sahara at the beginning of the Christian era. For centuries before that, men were accustomed to move about the desert with oxen, in horse-drawn chariots, or on horseback (*vide* cave drawings in the Sahara).

In North Africa, gigots of camel (dromedary) are sold for minced (ground) meat for *kefta*; fat from the hump (a delicacy in the desert) is sliced into huge 'petals' for the preparation of *khlii* (see page 68). The heart, liver and tripe are also much savoured by the desert nomads, both heart and liver considered delicious when diced, wrapped in caul and grilled over charcoal (see *boulfaf*, page 51), or served in a savoury stew highly spiced with hot and sweet red peppers (see *douara*, page 154).

1 forequarter or haunch of young camel

CHERMOULA FOR CAMEL (OR GAZELLE)
2 large Spanish onions, peeled and coarsely grated
2–3 cloves garlic, peeled and finely chopped
1 bunch flat-leafed (Italian) parsley, chopped
½ bunch fresh green coriander, chopped
1–1½ teaspoons powdered cumin
½ teaspoon each powdered cinnamon, ginger and saffron, sweet and hot red peppers
150ml/¼ pint (⅔ cup) olive oil
6 tablespoons liquid honey
4 tablespoons lemon juice
225g/½lb (1⅓ cups) black raisins

1 Mix all the *chermoula* ingredients together and rub over the meat. Leave to marinate for 4–6 hours, or overnight.

2 Skin, spit and cook the camel over an open fire as in the *m'choui* of lamb recipe until tender, basting every 10 minutes with the *chermoula*.

3 Serve in a similar fashion to the lamb above.

M'CHOUI OF GAZELLE

Skin gazelle as you would a whole lamb, and marinate in *chermoula* as above if you like before spit-roasting, or merely baste with melted butter marinade as in pit-roasted *m'choui* of lamb.

CUISSE DE CHAMEAU (OU GAZELLE) AUX PATATES DOUCES
HAUNCH OF CAMEL (OR GAZELLE) WITH SWEET POTATOES

1 haunch of young camel (or gazelle)
6 tablespoons melted camel fat, smen or olive oil
1 recipe chermoula for camel (or gazelle), as opposite

TO SERVE
flat-leafed parsley, chopped
900g/2lb boiled sweet potatoes, peeled and quartered
coarse salt
powdered cumin

1 Score meat of camel (or gazelle) lightly at 7.5cm/3 inch intervals.

2 Combine *chermoula* ingredients in a roasting pan, and mix well. Place camel (or gazelle) in pan and rub it well with the *chermoula* on all sides, rubbing it into the slits in surface of meat. Allow meat to absorb the flavour of the marinade for 4–6 hours, or overnight.

3 When ready to cook, in a large casserole or roasting pan (large enough to hold meat comfortably) sauté camel (or gazelle) on all sides in melted fat, *smen* or olive oil. Add *chermoula* and enough water to come one-third way up meat. Bring to the boil, skim off impurities, then simmer gently for 3–4 hours.

4 To serve, sprinkle with parsley and serve with boiled sweet potatoes. Serve accompanied by small bowls of coarse salt and powdered cumin.

TAGINE OF CAMEL (OR GAZELLE) WITH SWEET POTATOES

If you have no casserole large enough to hold haunch of young camel (or gazelle), cut meat off bones into 4cm/1½ inch cubes and proceed as in recipe above. Cook until tender. To serve, transfer meat to a heated dish, and garnish with boiled sweet potatoes and chopped flat-leafed parsley.

MOROCCAN BUTTERFLIED LEG OF LAMB

1 leg of lamb, about 2.25kg/5lb
1 recipe Chermoula Mixture (see page 152)
1 tablespoon chopped za'atar (wild thyme very popular in Morocco: substitute thyme, or rosemary)

1 To butterfly a leg of lamb, turn over leg to expose its bottom, or less fatty side, and cut a slash down from the wide to the thin end of the leg, cutting right down to the bone. Then carefully cut around the bone and remove it. At this point, the meat will open out into a rough 'butterfly' shape.

2 Gently pound meat of the lamb to approximately 2.5cm/1 inch thick. Rub the chermoula mixture well into both sides of the lamb and marinate for 2 hours at room temperature, or overnight in the refrigerator. Grill (broil) the lamb 15cm/6 inches from the source of heat for 15–20 minutes per side for pink meat. Or, in the more traditional manner, grill the lamb over charcoal, basting every 10 minutes with the chermoula, until the lamb is done to your liking.

DOUARA – *a long-simmered* tagine *of sheep's tripe with aromatics – is one of the famous dishes of* Aid el Kebir *(The Great Feast) when every part of the sacrificial lamb is used in imaginative and delicious ways.*

DOUARA

This richly flavoured country-style *tagine* uses the tripe, heart and liver of a freshly killed sheep. If these are not readily available, use partially cooked beef tripe with 175g/6oz each diced beef heart and liver.

450g/1lb sheep's tripe, partly cooked
2 tablespoons vinegar
6 tablespoons olive oil
1 sheep's heart, cut into 1cm/½ inch cubes
1 sheep's liver, cut into 1cm/½ inch cubes
2–3 tomatoes, skinned, seeded and chopped (see page 105)
1½ Spanish onions, peeled and chopped
2–3 cloves garlic, peeled and finely chopped
1–1½ teaspoons sweet red pepper
¼–½ teaspoon hot red pepper
½ teaspoon powdered cumin
salt and freshly ground black pepper

1 Cut tripe into 2.5cm/1 inch dice and soak in a mixture of vinegar and oil for about 1 hour to tenderize, turning from time to time. Drain, reserving marinade. Place diced heart and liver in marinade and soak until ready to add them to the casserole.

2 In a large *tagine* (or flameproof casserole), place the pieces of marinated tripe, the tomatoes, onion and garlic. Season with the spices, and salt and freshly ground black pepper to taste. Add water to cover, and cook in a moderate oven (350°F/180°C/Gas 4) for 45–50 minutes, adding a little more water from time to time, if necessary.

3 Add diced liver and heart with marinade juices and continue to cook for 10 minutes more. Transfer tripe, liver and heart to a heated serving dish (or *tagine*) and keep warm while you reduce sauce, stirring constantly, over a high heat. Correct seasoning. Pour sauce over meats and serve immediately.

Serves 4

BARBECUED LAMB SHANKS

4 young lamb shanks
salt and freshly ground black pepper

CHERMOULA MIXTURE
1 medium onion, peeled and grated
1 clove garlic, peeled and finely chopped
4 tablespoons chopped flat-leafed (Italian) parsley
4 tablespoons chopped fresh green coriander
¼ teaspoon powdered saffron
½ teaspoon powdered cumin
¼ teaspoon sweet red pepper
¼ teaspoon hot red pepper
6 tablespoons olive oil
2 tablespoons lemon juice

1 Season the lamb shanks generously with salt and freshly ground black pepper, and place in a saucepan with just enough water to cover. Bring gently to the boil, then skim. Lower heat and simmer the meat until it is almost tender, about 1 hour. Remove the lamb from the water and cool.

2 Place the lamb shanks in a shallow bowl, rub well with chermoula mixture, and leave to marinate for at least 2 hours, or overnight. Drain.

3 Grill the lamb shanks 15cm/6 inches above hot coals for 20–30 minutes, turning the lamb shanks every 5–10 minutes.

4 Serve the lamb shanks with grilled (broiled or barbecued) aubergine slices, and steamed *couscous*, boiled rice or boiled cracked wheat into which you have stirred equal quantities of chopped coriander, chopped flat-leafed (Italian) parsley and chopped raw onion to taste (about 4 tablespoons of each).

KEBAB MACHDOUR WITH EGGS

1.4kg/3lb leg of lamb, cut into 2.5cm/1 inch cubes
6 eggs

CHERMOULA
1 Spanish onion, peeled and coarsely grated
2 cloves garlic, peeled and finely chopped
½ teaspoon sweet red pepper
¼ teaspoon hot red pepper
salt and freshly ground black pepper
4 tablespoons each chopped flat-leafed (Italian) parsley and fresh green coriander
4 tablespoons olive oil

GARNISH
thin strips preserved lemon peel (see page 64)

1 Place cubed lamb in a large bowl. Combine the *chermoula* ingredients, pour over lamb and mix well. Leave meat to absorb flavours for at least 2 hours, or overnight.

2 When ready to cook, transfer lamb and *chermoula* to a casserole, and sauté meat, stirring constantly, for 5 minutes. Add water to just cover meat and bring to the boil. Lower heat, cover casserole, and simmer until just tender, about 1 hour.

3 To serve, transfer meat to a *tagine slaoui* and keep warm. Cook sauce over a high heat until reduced to half its original volume.

4 Pour reduced sauce over meat and return to *tagine* to heat until sauce is bubbling.

5 Break eggs gently into sauce and continue to cook, covered, until whites of eggs have set. Garnish with the strips of peel.

Serves 6

MROUZIA

Mrouzia is best when served with one or two other, lighter, *tagines* to complement its richness. You can reduce the amount of butter used in the recipe if you wish, but if you are planning to keep the meat (it will keep for 2–3 weeks in the refrigerator without any problem), you will need the full amount.

1.5kg/3¼lb neck or shoulder of lamb, cut into pieces about 150g/5oz each
1 tablespoon ras el hanout (see page 49)
1 teaspoon each freshly ground black pepper and powdered ginger
¼ teaspoon powdered saffron
175g/6oz (¾ cup) butter
2 Spanish onions, peeled and coarsely grated
2 cloves garlic, peeled and finely chopped
2 cinnamon sticks
salt
225g/½lb (1⅓ cups) raisins
225g/½lb (1⅓ cups) blanched almonds
150ml/¼ pint (⅔ cup) dark liquid honey
1 teaspoon powdered cinnamon

1 Put meat in a bowl, and combine *ras el hanout*, black pepper, ginger and saffron with 4–6 tablespoons water. Rub half this mixture well into the pieces of meat. Leave to marinate for at least 2 hours, or preferably overnight.

2 Put spiced meat in an earthenware *tagine*, or large shallow flameproof casserole, and add butter, onions, garlic, cinnamon sticks, and salt to taste.

3 Add just enough water to cover meat and bring gently to the boil. Skim, reduce heat to a simmer, and cover. Simmer for 1½ hours, stirring occasionally, and adding a little more water from time to time, as necessary.

4 In the meantime, place raisins in a small bowl and pour over boiling water to cover. Add the remaining *ras el hanout* mixture, and let raisins marinate in this until ready to use.

5 When meat is almost cooked add spiced raisins, almonds, honey and powdered cinnamon, and cook for 30–60 minutes more, or until meat comes easily off the bones and the sauce is thick and well flavoured.

6 Serve meat on a heated round platter, garnish with raisins and almonds, and pour sauce over. Serve immediately.

Serves 6

TAGINE OF LAMB M'KFOUL

6 slices lamb shank, 5cm/2 inches thick (about 225g/½lb each)
6 tablespoons olive oil
salt and freshly ground black pepper
1 Spanish onion, peeled and coarsely grated
900ml/1½ pints (3¾ cups) water
3 large ripe tomatoes, skinned, seeded and halved (see page 105)
sugar
1 tablespoon tomato concentrate (purée)
1 teaspoon powdered cinnamon

CHERMOULA
½ teaspoon each powdered ginger and cumin
1 teaspoon powdered cinnamon
6 sprigs flat-leafed (Italian) parsley, chopped
6 sprigs fresh green coriander, chopped

1 Place lamb pieces in an earthenware, glass or porcelain bowl. Combine *chermoula* ingredients and add to lamb. Toss well and marinate for 2 hours.

2 Transfer lamb pieces and *chermoula* to a *tagine* or large flameproof casserole. Add olive oil and sauté until the lamb is well browned on all sides. Season generously with salt and freshly ground black pepper to taste.

3 Cover meat with coarsely grated onion and add water. Bring gently to the boil, then lower heat and simmer for 2 hours, or until lamb is meltingly tender. (You could also cook in a very low oven at 225–250°F/110–120°C/Gas ¼–½.)

4 About 20 minutes before the end of cooking time, remove casserole from heat and arrange a tomato half, cut side down, over each onion-topped lamb shank. Sprinkle with sugar.

5 In a small bowl, combine 6 tablespoons of the hot lamb sauce with the tomato concentrate (purée), cinnamon and 3 tablespoons sugar. Mix well and drizzle over tomatoes and onions. Cover casserole and cook for the final 20 minutes.

Serves 6

BRAISED LAMB WITH AROMATIC HERBS
T'DLLA

One of the great dishes of the *Aid el Kebir*, it is simmered in a casserole over charcoal, with additional charcoal piled on top of the lid. If you are used to cooking in this manner, or would like to experiment, this is the traditional way. Otherwise, it works well when cooked in a moderate oven as here.

1 shoulder of lamb, or forequarter (shoulder and cutlets)
175g/6oz (¾ cup) softened butter
freshly ground black pepper

SPICE MIX
1 large Spanish onion, peeled and finely chopped
2 cloves garlic, peeled and finely chopped
½ teaspoon powdered cumin
¼ teaspoon each powdered cinnamon and ginger
⅛ teaspoon hot red pepper
¼ teaspoon saffron pounded with 1 teaspoon salt
4–6 tablespoons olive oil

1 Rub lamb with half the softened butter and season generously with black pepper.

2 To make spice mix, combine onion and garlic in a small bowl with the spices, then add olive oil and 4–6 tablespoons water. Mix well.

3 Pat half this aromatic mixture gently over the buttered lamb. Place remaining mixture in the bottom of a large casserole (big enough to hold lamb comfortably in one piece). Place seasoned lamb on this bed of aromatics, and sauté on all sides over a high heat until meat is evenly browned.

4 Add just enough hot water to come half way up the joint, and continue to cook until water comes to the boil. Add remaining butter to casserole, cover and cook in a preheated moderate oven (375°F/190°C/Gas 5) for 2 hours or until lamb pulls easily away from the bone and the water is totally evaporated. Brown lamb in fat remaining in casserole until meat is crisp and golden.

5 Serve lamb in a large *tagine slaoui* or large, shallow, round serving dish, surrounded by colourful Moroccan stuffed vegetables (see page 113). To eat this delicious dish in the traditional Moroccan manner, rub the highly seasoned lamb with a small piece of Moroccan bread which you then dip into the sauce, for a first taste of the bread drenched with the aromatic sauce. Then detach a piece of meat delicately with your fingers or with a small piece of bread if the meat is still too hot to handle or, failing that, with a tablespoon.

BRAISED LAMB STUFFED WITH COUSCOUS, ALMONDS AND RAISINS
T'DLLA FARCI AUX AMANDES, SEMOULE ET RAISINS SECS

This is a grander version of the *t'dlla* recipe above.

1 forequarter of lamb (shoulder and cutlets), boned
175g/6oz (¾ cup) softened butter (or smen)
3 cloves garlic, peeled and finely chopped
1 large Spanish onion, peeled and finely chopped
1 teaspoon salt
½ teaspoon each powdered ginger and saffron

STUFFING
175g/6oz (generous 1 cup) uncooked couscous (see page 182)
75g/3oz (½ cup) seedless raisins
4 tablespoons butter (or smen)
75g/3oz (½ cup) peeled almonds, coarsely chopped
¼ teaspoon each powdered cinnamon, sweet red pepper and ras el hanout (see page 49)
1 teaspoon sugar

GARNISH
sprigs of fresh mint, fresh green coriander or flat-leafed (Italian) parsley

1 To make the stuffing, wash the *couscous* as described on page 184 (stage one, steps 1, 2 and 3), then combine with the raisins and steam over simmering water for 30 minutes.

2 Rub in butter, or *smen*, and add all the remaining stuffing ingredients. Mix well.

3 To prepare the lamb, rub it with a third of the softened butter (or *smen*) over a flat baking tray. Combine garlic, onion, salt, ginger and saffron, and rub lamb with this mixture.

4 Stuff seasoned lamb with stuffing mixture. Sew up.

5 Place lamb in a flameproof casserole large enough to hold it comfortably, and add any of the aromatic mixture which has fallen on to the baking tray. Sauté lamb in half the remaining butter (or *smen*) until evenly browned on all sides.

6 Add just enough hot water to come half way up the joint, and continue to cook until water comes to the boil. Add remaining butter to casserole, cover and cook in a moderate oven (375°F/190°C/Gas 5) for 2 hours or until lamb pulls easily away from the bone and the water is totally evaporated.

7 Brown lamb in fat remaining in casserole until meat is crisp and golden.

8 Serve lamb as in the previous recipe, garnished with sprigs of fresh mint and fresh green coriander or flat-leafed (Italian) parsley.

T'DLLA – shoulder of lamb stuffed in this case with couscous, raisins and almonds – is one of the great dishes of Moroccan cuisine. BELOW: *Cooks preparing t'dlla for the wedding feast;* BOTTOM LEFT: *Stuffing the shoulder of lamb with couscous, raisins and almonds;* BOTTOM RIGHT: *The finished dish.*

MUSTAPHA'S TANGIA MARRAKSHIA
MUSTAPHA'S *TANGIA*, MARRAKECH VERSION

Tangia is known as a 'bachelor's' dish in Marrakech, for with a *tangia* – a two-handled amphora-shaped earthenware vessel, glazed on the inside – the cook has no need of a kitchen or stove. Tradition has it that the *tangia* is taken to the *hammam* (steam bath) where it is numbered and baked in the ashes for 8 hours, or overnight. But both my friends, Mustapha and Abdeslam, assure me that 2½ hours to 3 hours is long enough – and proved it.

There are no real cooking directions for *tangia*. Just put all the ingredients into the well-cleaned *tangia*, and cover the opening with parchment paper. Tie it securely with string and take it to the *hammam* to cook for the desired number of hours.

Tangias can also be made with beef or veal as in one of the *tangia* recipes following.

Abdeslam bringing TANGIA *back from the* hammam *where it has been cooking for hours in the hot embers of the* hammam *fire.*

1.6kg/3½lb lamb (shoulder and/or breast), cut into 100g/¼lb pieces
100g/¼lb (½ cup) smen (or butter)
4 tablespoons olive oil
2 Spanish onions, peeled and coarsely grated
2–3 tablespoons finely chopped garlic
½ bunch fresh green coriander, finely chopped
½ bunch flat-leafed (Italian) parsley, finely chopped
1½ preserved lemons (see page 64), peel only
1 tablespoon coarse salt
½ teaspoon each powdered ginger and ras el hanout (see page 49)
2 large tomatoes, skinned, seeded and grated (see page 105)
300ml/½ pint (1¼ cups) water

To cook, place ingredients in a flameproof casserole, cover and place in a preheated, very slow oven (275–300°F/140–150°C/Gas 1–2), and cook for 2½–3 hours.

Serves 6

ABDESLAM'S TANGIA FASSIA
ABDESLAM'S TANGIA, FEZ VERSION

1.6kg/3½lb leg or shoulder of lamb, cut into cubes
100g/¼lb (½ cup) smen (or butter)
6 tablespoons olive oil
3 Spanish onions, peeled and coarsely grated
6 cloves garlic, peeled and finely chopped
1 tablespoon each powdered ginger and sweet red pepper
2 teaspoons each ground coriander seed and coarse salt
4 large tomatoes, skinned, seeded and coarsely grated (see page 105)
½ packet (heaped ¼ teaspoon) powdered saffron
900ml/1½ pints ((3¾ cups) water

Cook as above.

Serves 6

ALAMI'S TANGIA DE BOEUF AUX HERBES
ALAMI'S TANGIA OF SHIN OF BEEF OR OXTAIL WITH HERBS

1.6kg/3½lb shin of beef cut into segments 2.5cm/1 inch thick (or 1 oxtail, cut into 7.5cm/3 inch pieces)
100g/¼lb (½ cup) smen (or butter)
3 Spanish onions, peeled and coarsely grated
4–6 cloves garlic, peeled and finely chopped
1 teaspoon each powdered ginger, coarse salt and sweet red pepper
¼ teaspoon powdered cumin
½ packet (heaped ⅓ teaspoon) powdered saffron
1 bunch fresh green coriander, chopped
1 bunch flat-leafed parsley (Italian), chopped
600ml/1 pint (2½ cups) water
4 tablespoons lemon juice

Cook as Mustapha's *Tangia*, opposite.

Serves 6

Pouring out the deliciously scented TANGIA *from its cooking pot of the same name.*

STEAMED LAMB

1.25–1.4kg/2½–3lb lamb (shoulder and/or breast)
3 tablespoons olive oil
1 tablespoon coarse salt
½ teaspoon powdered cumin
¼ teaspoon each powdered saffron and hot red pepper
freshly ground black pepper
4 tablespoons butter or smen (optional)

GARNISH
coarse salt
powdered cumin

1 Combine olive oil, salt, cumin, saffron and hot red pepper and rub lamb with this mixture. Season with freshly ground black pepper to taste.

2 Wrap meat in a piece of muslin (cheesecloth), or a clean tea towel and place in the top section of a large steamer over boiling water. The bottom section of the steamer should be three-quarters full of bubbling water.

3 Cover steamer hermetically with damp tea towels and the lid and steam lamb over a medium heat for 1½–2 hours without uncovering. The meat should come away easily from the bone.

4 Serve lamb just as it is, with accompanying bowls of coarse salt and powdered cumin. Or, if you prefer, sauté lamb on all sides in butter or *smen* until golden before serving. Delicious accompaniments are boiled rice or steamed new potatoes.

Serves 4–6

STEAMED LAMB WITH GARLIC AND CORIANDER PASTE

1.25–1.4kg/2½–3lb lamb (shoulder and/or breast)
1 tablespoon coarse salt
4 fat cloves garlic (or 8 tiny cloves, according to size), peeled and chopped
8 sprigs fresh green coriander, chopped
1 tablespoon powdered cumin
3–4 tablespoons olive oil
freshly ground black pepper

1 Combine salt, garlic, coriander and cumin in a mortar and pound until mixture begins to amalgamate. Add olive oil and pound again until smooth.

2 Rub lamb with this mixture, then season with freshly ground black pepper to taste. Cook as in steps 2 and 3 above. Serve as in previous recipe.

Serves 4–6

LAMB-STUFFED VEGETABLES

4 small aubergines (eggplant)
4 courgettes (zucchini)
4 medium onions
4 small green peppers, or 2 bell peppers, halved lengthways
salt
4 small tomatoes
olive oil

LAMB STUFFING
225g/½lb minced (ground) lamb
50g/2oz minced lamb fat (½ cup ground lamb fat)
½ large Spanish onion, peeled and finely chopped
1–2 cloves garlic, peeled and finely chopped
olive oil
2 slices white bread, crusts removed, soaked in a little water
4 tablespoons each chopped flat-leafed (Italian) parsley and fresh green coriander
¼ teaspoon each powdered cumin, cinnamon and sweet red pepper
salt and freshly ground black pepper
1 egg, beaten

1 To prepare the vegetable 'cases', poach aubergines (eggplant), courgettes (zucchini), onions and green peppers for 2–3 minutes in boiling salted water. Drain. Cut tops off tomatoes, aubergines (eggplant), courgettes (zucchini), green peppers and onions. Remove seeds from green peppers. Scoop out interiors of remaining vegetables, leaving a shell of about 6mm/¼ inch thick. Chop pulp of aubergines (eggplant), courgettes (zucchini) and tomatoes coarsely and reserve for stuffing.

2 To make the stuffing, sauté lamb and lamb fat with onion and garlic in 4 tablespoons olive oil until vegetables are transparent.

3 Squeeze bread dry and shred it. Add to meat and onion mixture with parsley, coriander and the reserved chopped courgette (zucchini), aubergine (eggplant) and tomato. Season with spices, and salt and black pepper to taste. Mix well.

4 Sauté mixture for a few minutes more, stirring continuously, then allow to cool a little and mix in the beaten egg. Stuff vegetables with the mixture. Place the stuffed vegetables in an oiled ovenproof baking dish. Sprinkle a little olive oil on each vegetable and bake in a moderate oven (375°F/190°C/Gas 5) for 30 minutes, or until vegetables are tender.

Serves 4–6

TAGINE DE VIANDE AUX COINGS
MEAT TAGINE WITH QUINCES

You can substitute peeled and cored pears for the quinces or add 450g/1lb okra cooked separately in a little of the juice.

1.4kg/3lb shoulder of lamb
4 tablespoons butter
1 cinnamon stick
1 teaspoon each powdered ginger and saffron
salt
900g/2lb quinces, washed
3 tablespoons honey
1 teaspoon powdered cinnamon

1 Cut the meat into eight or twelve pieces so that you can serve two pieces per person. Place in a flameproof casserole with butter, cinnamon stick, ginger and saffron, and add salt to taste. Cover with water and cook over a low heat, stirring from time to time, adding more water if necessary.

2 When meat is tender, after about 45–50 minutes, remove it from the casserole and reserve. Remove cinnamon stick.

3 Cut quinces in half, and remove and discard cores and pips. Add to the casserole with honey and powdered cinnamon. Add enough water, if necessary, to half cover quinces. Mix well and allow to simmer until quinces are tender.

4 Just before serving, return meat to casserole and reheat.

Serves 4–6

TAGINE OF LAMB WITH POTATOES AND OLIVES

1.25–1.4kg/2½–3lb leg or shoulder of lamb, cut into cubes
2 large Spanish onions, peeled and coarsely grated
2 cloves garlic, peeled and finely chopped
6 tablespoons chopped flat-leafed (Italian) parsley
6 tablespoons chopped fresh green coriander
½–1 teaspoon each powdered ginger and cumin
¼–½ teaspoon sweet red pepper
6 tablespoons olive oil
salt
350g/¾lb (2⅓ cups) cured green olives
700g/1½lb potatoes, peeled and cut into eighths (4 cups peeled potatoes cut into eighths)
½ teaspoon powdered saffron
2 tablespoons butter

1 Place cubed lamb in an earthenware bowl and add onion, garlic, parsley, coriander, spices, olive oil, and salt, to taste. Mix well and leave to marinate for at least 2 hours, or overnight.

2 When ready to cook, transfer lamb with marinade juices to a *tagine* or shallow flameproof casserole. Add water to just cover meat, and cook over a low heat for 45 minutes.

3 Add olives and cook for another 15 minutes.

4 In the meantime, cook potatoes in boiling salted water with powdered saffron until just tender. Drain, toss with butter and keep warm.

5 To serve, arrange meat on a heated serving dish and keep warm. Rapidly reduce sauce until it is thick, strain over meat, and garnish with olives and saffron potatoes.

Serves 4–6

TAGINE SLAOUI – *a delicious dish of* kefta *(little balls of seasoned minced lamb) simmered in a well-flavoured sauce of tomatoes, onion, garlic, flat-leafed parsley, fresh coriander and spices – is one of my favourite everyday* tagines. *Try it, too, with eggs poached in the delicious sauce just before serving.*

TAGINE SLAOUI
TAGINE OF MOROCCAN MEATBALLS

700g/1½lb lamb from the leg, cubed
225g/½lb lamb fat, or less, made up to this amount with beef suet, cubed
½ Spanish onion, peeled and chopped
6 sprigs flat-leafed (Italian) parsley, finely chopped
salt and freshly ground black pepper
¼ teaspoon each powdered cumin, hot and sweet red peppers
1 generous pinch of 2 of the following: powdered cinnamon, ginger and cardamom
fresh breadcrumbs (optional)

KEFTA BUTTER SAUCE
450g/1lb tomatoes, skinned, seeded and coarsely chopped (generous 3 cups skinned, seeded, and coarsely chopped tomatoes) (see page 105)
1 Spanish onion, peeled and coarsely grated
4 tablespoons chopped flat-leafed (Italian) parsley
4 tablespoons chopped fresh green coriander
1 clove garlic, peeled and finely chopped
4 tablespoons olive oil
300ml/½ pint (1¼ cups) water
1 teaspoon sweet red pepper
½ teaspoon each hot red pepper, powdered cumin, ginger and saffron

1 To make sauce, combine ingredients and simmer for 30 minutes, uncovered.

2 To make *kefta*, put cubed lamb, lamb fat and onion through the finest blade of your mincer three times. Combine in a large mixing bowl with parsley, salt and pepper to taste, and spices. Mix well. The *kefta* mixture should be very highly flavoured. (I sometimes add fresh breadcrumbs to make *kefta* more tender.)

3 Form into little balls the size of a marble and poach gently in water for 10 minutes. Then sauté gently in butter until lightly browned.

4 Finally, simmer the *kefta* in the sauce for at least 10 minutes before serving. Serve in sauce in a *tagine slaoui* or heated serving dish.

Serves 6

TAGINE SLAOUI WITH EGGS
TAGINE OF MOROCCAN MEATBALLS WITH POACHED EGGS

1 recipe Tagine Slaoui (see above)
6–12 eggs

Make as above, but when ready to serve, carefully break the eggs into the sauce. Cover *tagine* and cook until whites of eggs are set. Serve immediately.

Serves 6

HERGMA
CALF'S FEET, CHICK PEAS AND BARLEY

In Morocco they often cook *hergma* in a sealed container overnight in the banked fires of the *hammam* (steam bath). You could do the same in the oven of your Aga.

This recipe should use sheep's feet, which are rarely available, but if you do find them, buy eight.

4 cleaned calf's feet, each cut into 4 pieces across the bone
225g/½lb (1 cup) chick peas, soaked overnight
100g/¼lb (generous ½ cup) barley
6 Spanish onions, peeled and coarsely grated
6 tablespoons olive oil
1 tablespoon salt
¼ teaspoon each powdered ginger and sweet red pepper
⅛ teaspoon hot red pepper

1 Wash calf's feet segments. Drain chick peas and remove skins. Soak barley in water for 30 minutes, then drain.

2 Place calf's feet segments in a *tagine* or large flameproof casserole. Add grated onions, drained chick peas and barley.

3 Sprinkle over olive oil, salt and spices. Add enough water to barely cover and simmer over a very low heat for at least 2 hours, or until calf's feet are meltingly tender, adding a little more water from time to time, as necessary.
Serves 6–8

HERGMA, *Marrakshi-fashion, simmers calf's feet or sheep's trotters with chick peas and black raisins for a truly magnificent country-style dish.*

HERGMA II (MARRAKSHI VERSION)
CALF'S FEET WITH CHICK PEAS AND RAISINS

4 cleaned calf's feet, each cut into 4 pieces across the bone
450g/1lb (2 cups) chick peas, soaked overnight
225g/½lb (1⅓cups) black raisins
4–6 cloves garlic, peeled
2–3 large Spanish onions, peeled and coarsely grated
1 tablespoon each salt and powdered cumin
¼–½ teaspoon hot red pepper
2 packets (heaped 1 teaspoon) powdered saffron
150ml/¼ pint (⅔ cup) olive oil

1 Wash calf's feet segments. Drain chick peas and remove skins. Wash raisins and place in a bowl just large enough to hold them. Add boiling water to just cover them, and leave for about 15 minutes.

2 Place calf's feet segments in a *tagine* or large flameproof casserole with chick peas, plumped-up raisins, whole garlic cloves, and all the remaining ingredients. Add just enough water to cover.

3 Bring to the boil, skim, then lower heat. Cover *tagine* (or casserole) and simmer over a very low heat for 2 hours or until calf's feet are meltingly tender, adding a little more water from time to time, as necessary.

Serves 4–6

15

TAGINES AND OTHER MAIN COURSE DISHES

The wonderfully aromatic meat or poultry stews of Moroccan cooking are called *tagines* after their cooking pot – much as daubes and casseroles are named similarly in French cooking.

If there was a competition for the greatest cooking pot in the world – the Chinese *wok*, the New England fish kettle, the French enamelled iron casserole, the English griddle pan – Morocco's age-old *tagine* would deserve a star rating on its own. These round dishes with pointed, conical lids, made of brown half-glazed earthenware, are available for less than £1 ($1.60) in the open markets of any town or village in Morocco. There is a choice of sizes available – from an individual serving to one of mammoth proportions, enough to serve sixteen to twenty guests.

It was just such a dish – but one with its lid embossed with deep-cut stylized patterns – that sent me on an odyssey around each of the potting villages of Morocco to find the craftsman who had received the King's warrant to produce this unique model with deep-set moulded pomegranate, pineapple and palm leaf indentations.

I was advised to take two friends with me – one Berber and one Arab – as it was almost certain that the head potter would speak no French. We travelled the length and breadth of Morocco for over two weeks in our search and finally, in the flatlands behind Salé, the seventeenth-century pirates' city across the river from Rabat, we found the most picturesque pottery works I have ever seen where the head potter – an artist craftsman of great talent – had trained his family to produce the regally decorated *tagines* in nine sizes. I bought one in every size imaginable from 13cm/5 inches to 60cm/2 feet in diameter, the latter a most noble dish which is a decoration on its own in my English country kitchen.

ABOVE: CHICKEN MQUALLI *served on a bed of fried aubergine (eggplant) slices and pommes frites (French-fried potatoes) in Casablanca.*

OPPOSITE: TAGINE OF CHICKEN WITH TOMATOES AND PRESERVED LEMONS *as served at the Hotel Taroudant.*

The *tagine* is specially well adapted to eating in the Moroccan manner where the main dish is put in the centre of a low, round table and everyone eats from the central dish. They are useful for other things too. I like to use the lower part to present dessert fruits or as an attractively rustic container for colourful raw vegetables as a table centrepiece. It is used extensively in Moroccan homes to keep bread fresh; and I use it to keep ice cool for outdoor entertaining. Something about the high conical lid (could it be the pyramid factor?) keeps the ice 'iced' for hours.

But the *tagine* really comes into its own as an admirably efficient 'casserole' for cooking on top of individual charcoal braziers. These earthenware braziers are available in street markets for only a few *dirhams*. Often this inexpensive source of heat is the only stove available in a traditional Moroccan kitchen, and is used at floor level in what seems to us to be uncomfortable circumstances. In my own kitchen in Marrakech, I have installed a waist-high barbecue grill similar to the ones found in Mediterranean kitchens. All to no avail. I'm the only one who uses it. My cook, Bacha, prefers her own floor-level *mishmihr* to all the more sophisticated cookers in the world.

Luckily for western cooks, however, the *tagine* – once 'matured' – is equally at home over a low gas flame or in the oven. And even Bacha concedes that. For extra protection, however, use a heat-diffusing mat if on direct heat.

How to mature a new Moroccan tagine

Moroccan glazed earthenware *tagines* are 'matured' and 'flavoured' at a low temperature in the oven with aromatics before using, to (1) remove any earthenware flavour from the new *tagine*; (2) impregnate the *tagine* with aromatic flavours; (3) ensure the new *tagine* is introduced gently to heat before being used over charcoal (in the Moroccan manner) or (protected by an asbestos heat diffuser) on top of the stove.

In the bottom part of *tagine*, combine 1 peeled and sliced onion, 4 sliced carrots, 2 cloves peeled garlic and 1 bay leaf with 1.1 litre/2 pints (5 cups) water and 4 tablespoons olive oil. Cover with conical lid of *tagine* and cook in a preheated cool oven (275–300°F/140–150°C/Gas 1–2) for 30–40 minutes, or until vegetables are tender. Remove *tagine* from oven and allow to cool gradually at room temperature before removing ingredients and washing *tagine*.

TFAIA
TAGINE OF LAMB WITH HARD-BOILED EGGS AND ALMONDS

1 shoulder of lamb, about 1.25kg/2½lb, cut in serving pieces
6 tablespoons butter
4 tablespoons olive oil
1½ large Spanish onions, peeled and coarsely grated
¼ teaspoon powdered saffron
2 teaspoons powdered ginger
½ teaspoon crushed black pepper
salt
1 bunch fresh green coriander, coarsely chopped

GARNISH
4 hard-boiled eggs
225g/½lb (1⅓ cups) blanched almonds, sautéed in groundnut (peanut) oil
salt

1 Melt butter and olive oil together in a large *tagine* or flameproof casserole, then add onion, saffron, ginger, black pepper, and salt to taste. Stir over a medium heat until onions are transparent. Add meat pieces and stir well over heat for 2–3 minutes.

2 Add just enough water to cover meat, and bring gently to the boil. Lower heat, cover and simmer until meat is tender, about 1½–2 hours, adding more water from time to time, as necessary. About 20 minutes before the end of cooking time, add the chopped coriander.

3 To prepare the garnish, shell hard-boiled eggs, cut them in half lengthways, and reserve. Drain the almonds when crisp and golden brown, season with salt to taste, and reserve.

4 When ready to serve, transfer meat to a heated serving platter. Reduce sauce over a high heat, then spoon sauce over meat and garnish dish with halved hard-boiled eggs and golden almonds which you have reheated for an instant in a little hot oil.

Serves 6

TAGINE DE MOUTON AUX DATTES
TAGINE OF LAMB WITH DATES

1.4kg/3lb lamb (shoulder and/or cutlets), cut into 100g/¼lb pieces
½ teaspoon freshly ground black pepper
¼–½ teaspoon powdered saffron
2 Spanish onions, peeled and coarsely grated
100g/¼lb (½ cup) butter
salt
2 tablespoons thick honey
½–1 teaspoon powdered cinnamon
lemon juice (optional)
450g/1lb (3 cups) fresh dates
225g/½lb (1⅓ cups) blanched almonds, sautéed in oil
1 tablespoon toasted sesame seeds (optional)

1 Place lamb pieces in a *tagine* or flameproof casserole, and add pepper, saffron, onion, butter, and salt to taste. Cover with water, and bring gently to the boil. Skim, reduce heat, cover and simmer for 1½–2 hours.

2 Towards the end of the cooking time – when lamb is just tender – add honey and cinnamon. Turn the meat in this sauce until it is well impregnated with sweet and spicy flavours.

3 Remove meat from sauce with a slotted spoon and keep warm. Correct sauce seasoning adding more salt and pepper and, if desired, a squeeze of lemon juice.

4 Rinse dates under running water. Drain and add to sauce in pan and allow to simmer for 10 minutes. Return meat to pan.

5 Transfer pieces of meat to a heated serving dish, and garnish with dates. Spoon sauce over and garnish with almonds, and toasted sesame seeds if desired.

Serves 6

TAGINE OF LAMB WITH COMPOTE OF SWEETENED TOMATOES AND ALMONDS *simmers the lamb in* smen *(or butter or oil) with tomato juice, grated onion, garlic, cinnamon, ginger and saffron until tender. Chopped tomatoes are then cooked in the reserved pan juices with honey and cinnamon until thick and well-flavoured.*

OPPOSITE: *The* tagine *of lamb known as* TFAIA *simmers lamb in butter and oil with grated onion, saffron, ginger, black pepper and salt. The dish is garnished with sautéed almonds and halved hard-boiled eggs just before serving.*

TAGINE OF LAMB WITH COMPOTE OF SWEETENED TOMATOES AND ALMONDS

1.4kg/3lb lamb (shoulder and/or cutlets)
6 tablespoons butter, smen or olive oil
1½ Spanish onions, peeled and coarsely grated
2 cloves garlic, peeled and finely chopped
1 cinnamon stick
1 teaspoon powdered ginger
1 packet (heaped ½ teaspoon) powdered saffron
salt and freshly ground black pepper
1.4kg/3lb large, ripe tomatoes, skinned, seeded and chopped (9 cups skinned, seeded and chopped tomatoes) (see page 105)
2 tablespoons tomato concentrate (purée)
4 tablespoons liquid honey
1 teaspoon powdered cinnamon
225g/½lb (1⅓ cups) blanched almonds, sautéed in butter

1 Cut the meat into eight or twelve pieces so that you can serve two per person. Place meat in a *tagine* or flameproof casserole with butter (*smen* or olive oil), onion, garlic, cinnamon stick, ginger and saffron. Add salt and black pepper to taste.

2 Strain the juice from the chopped tomatoes, and mix with the tomato concentrate (purée). Add this and enough water to just cover meat to the casserole, and cook over a low heat, stirring from time to time, until meat is tender, adding a little more water, if necessary.

3 When the meat is tender, after about 1–1¼ hours, remove it from the casserole and reserve. Remove cinnamon stick. Add chopped tomatoes and let them cook down in the sauce in the casserole over a high heat, stirring from time to time until most of the liquid has reduced. Then continue cooking, stirring constantly to avoid scorching, as the last of the liquid evaporates and only the oils and meat juices are left in the casserole. At this point, add the honey and powdered cinnamon and cook for a few minutes more.

4 Reheat the lamb in the sauce, tossing to coat the pieces evenly. Then transfer the pieces of lamb to a heated serving dish, or *tagine*, and sprinkle with sautéed almonds. Serve immediately.

Serves 4–6

TAGINE OF LAMB WITH VEGETABLES

1.25kg/2½lb leg of lamb, cut into 2.5cm/1 inch cubes
2 large Spanish onions, peeled and coarsely grated
2 cloves garlic, peeled and finely chopped
6–8 tablespoons each chopped flat-leafed (Italian) parsley and fresh green coriander
1 teaspoon each powdered ginger and cumin
1 packet (heaped ½ teaspoon) powdered saffron
coarse salt
8 tablespoons olive oil
700g/1½lb ripe tomatoes, skinned, seeded and cut into eighths (4½ cups skinned and seeded tomatoes cut into eighths) (see page 105)
700g/1½lb haricots verts (French green beans) or okra, trimmed
2 tablespoons butter

1 Place cubed lamb in an earthenware bowl and add onion, garlic, parsley, coriander, spices, 1 teaspoon salt, and olive oil. Mix well and leave to marinate for at least 2 hours, or overnight.

2 When ready to cook, transfer meat and marinade juices to a *tagine*, or shallow flameproof casserole. Add enough water to cover the meat, and cook over a low heat for 45 minutes. Add tomato segments and cook for another 5–10 minutes.

3 In the meantime, cook *haricots verts* (French green beans or okra) in boiling salted water until just tender. Drain and reserve.

4 Just before serving, sauté *haricots verts* (French green beans or okra) in butter until heated through.

5 To serve, arrange vegetables in a ring on a heated round serving dish. Pile cubed cooked lamb in the centre and decorate vegetable ring with tomato sections.

Serves 4–6

TAGINE OF LAMB WITH GREEN PEAS AND PRESERVED LEMONS

This tagine can be made with beef as well. Use shin of beef.

1.25–1.4kg/2½–3lb leg of lamb, cut into 2.5cm/1 inch cubes
2 large Spanish onions, peeled and chopped
2 cloves garlic, peeled and chopped
6 tablespoons each chopped flat-leafed (Italian) parsley and fresh green coriander
½–1 teaspoon each powdered ginger and cumin
¼ teaspoon powdered saffron
salt
8 tablespoons olive oil
2 preserved lemons (see page 64), cut into quarters, pulp removed
700g/1½lb (4 cups) shelled green peas
2–4 tablespoons butter

1 Place cubed lamb in an earthenware bowl and add onions, garlic, parsley, coriander, spices, and salt to taste. Add olive oil, mix well and leave to marinate for at least 2 hours, or overnight.

2 When ready to cook, transfer meat and marinade juices to a *tagine* or shallow flameproof casserole. Add enough water to just cover meat, and cook over a low heat for 45 minutes.

3 Add preserved lemon peel and cook for another 15 minutes.

4 In the meantime, simmer peas in boiling salted water until just tender. Drain, toss with butter and keep warm.

5 To serve, arrange meat on a heated serving dish and keep warm. Rapidly reduce sauce until it is thick and strain it over meat. Garnish with cooked peas and arrange the preserved lemon pieces on top.

Serves 4–6

TAGINE OF BEEF WITH PRUNES AND ALMONDS

1.25–1.4kg/2½–3lb beef, cut into 4cm/1½ inch cubes
2 large Spanish onions, peeled and coarsely grated
2 tablespoons olive oil
1 teaspoon salt
½ teaspoon each freshly ground black pepper and powdered saffron
1 teaspoon powdered cinnamon
¼ teaspoon powdered ginger
100g/¼lb (½ cup) butter
450g/1lb (generous 2 cups) dried prunes
4 tablespoons sugar
1 strip of lemon peel
2–3 short cinnamon sticks
225g/½lb (1½ cups) blanched almonds, sautéed in butter
sprigs of fresh mint or watercress

TAGINE OF BEEF WITH PRUNES AND ALMONDS *combines the sweetness of cinnamon- and lemon-flavoured prunes and the crispness of sautéed almonds with cubes of beef cooked in a highly flavoured sauce.*

1 Put the meat cubes and onion into a large bowl along with the olive oil, salt, black pepper and spices. Mix well, rubbing aromatics into each piece of meat with your fingers.

2 When ready to cook, transfer prepared meat to a *tagine* or thick-bottomed flameproof casserole and add butter and enough water to just cover meat. Cook over a medium heat, covered, until meat is tender, about 45–60 minutes.

3 In the meantime, prepare the prunes. Cover with boiling water, allow to infuse for 20 minutes, then drain. Remove 2 ladles of sauce from the casserole, put in a small saucepan and skim off all fat. Add half the sugar, the lemon peel and cinnamon sticks. Cook prunes in this sauce for 20 minutes, or until prunes are soft and swollen.

4 Add remaining sugar to casserole with meat, and stir well.

5 To serve, transfer meat to a heated serving dish and garnish with prunes and their sauce. Reduce sauce remaining in casserole to half its original volume over a high heat, then pour over meat and prunes. Sprinkle with sautéed almonds, and garnish dish with sprigs of fresh mint or watercress. Serve immediately.

Serves 4

POULET AUX TOMATES ET CITRONS CONFITS – HOTEL TAROUDANT

1 small roasting (broiler/fryer) chicken, cut into 6 serving portions (breasts reserved for another use)
1 Spanish onion, peeled and coarsely grated
1–2 cloves garlic, peeled and finely chopped
¼ teaspoon each powdered saffron and sweet red pepper
⅛ teaspoon each hot red pepper and powdered cumin
salt and freshly ground black pepper
4 tablespoons butter
4 tablespoons olive oil
1 preserved lemon (see page 64), peel only, cut into 6 segments
3 large, ripe tomatoes, skinned, seeded and halved (see page 105)
light chicken stock (broth)
2 tablespoons chopped flat-leafed (Italian) parsley
1 tablespoon chopped fresh green coriander

1 Season chicken pieces generously with onion, garlic and spices, with salt and black pepper to taste, rubbing mixture well into chicken pieces. Add 6 tablespoons water, mix well and leave to marinate for at least 2 hours, or overnight.

2 Melt butter and olive oil in a large frying pan (skillet) or shallow flameproof casserole and sauté chicken pieces until golden.

3 Add lemon peel segments and tomato halves and enough light chicken stock (broth) to cover, and simmer gently for 1 hour, or until chicken is tender.

4 Transfer meat and vegetables to a *tagine* and keep warm. Reduce sauce over a high heat until half its original volume. Just before serving, pour sauce over chicken and garnish with chopped parsley and fresh coriander.

Serves 2–3

Bacha adds an extra packet of saffron to her multiple chicken version of CHICKEN M'HAMMAR.

BACHA'S CHICKEN M'HAMMAR

1 roasting (broiler/fryer) chicken with giblets
coarse salt
225g/½lb (generous 1½ cups) green olives, cracked
150ml/¼ pint (⅔ cup) water

BACHA'S CHERMOULA
½ bunch flat-leafed (Italian) parsley, chopped
½ bunch fresh green coriander, chopped
2 garlic cloves, peeled and finely chopped
½ large Spanish onion, peeled and coarsely grated
1 packet (heaped ½ teaspoon) powdered saffron
¼ teaspoon salt
½ teaspoon freshly ground black pepper
1 preserved lemon (see page 64), peel only, cut into thin slices (3mm/⅛ inch thick)
1 tablespoon powdered cumin
6 tablespoons olive oil

1 Wash chicken well inside and out with salt, removing any pin feathers with tweezers. Leave for 1 hour, then rinse well.

2 Combine all the *chermoula* ingredients and rub over and inside chicken and giblets. Leave for a minimum of 2 hours, or overnight preferably, so chicken can absorb flavours.

3 To prepare the olives, place them in a small saucepan, add enough water to just cover and bring gently to the boil. Drain and rinse under cold water to remove bitterness.

4 When ready to cook, place chicken, giblets and marinade juices in a *tagine* (or flameproof casserole). Add measured water and simmer for 30 minutes. Then add olives and simmer for 15 minutes more.

5 To serve, remove chicken giblets and cut gizzard, liver and heart into tiny dice and add to sauce. Reduce sauce. Place chicken on a heated serving dish. Spoon over reduced sauce and serve immediately.

Serves 4

DOUBLE-COOKED CHICKEN M'HAMMAR

2 roasting (broiler/fryer) chickens about 1.4kg/3lb each
coarse salt
3 large Spanish onions, peeled and grated
2 cloves garlic, peeled and finely chopped
$\frac{1}{2}$ teaspoon each of freshly ground black pepper and powdered saffron
$\frac{1}{4}$–$\frac{1}{2}$ teaspoon powdered ginger
salt
100g/$\frac{1}{4}$lb ($\frac{1}{2}$ cup) butter
120ml/4fl.oz ($\frac{1}{2}$ cup) groundnut (peanut) oil

1 Wash chickens carefully, removing any pin feathers with tweezers. Rub inside and out with salt and water and leave for 1 hour. Rinse well, then place in a large casserole. Add onion, garlic, black pepper, saffron, ginger, and salt to taste, with 300ml/$\frac{1}{2}$ pint (1$\frac{1}{4}$ cups) water.

2 Cover the casserole, and cook over a medium heat for 1–1$\frac{1}{4}$ hours, turning chickens in the sauce from time to time, and adding a little hot water, from time to time, if necessary.

3 When chickens are tender, remove them from casserole and keep warm. Reduce the sauce until it is thick and well flavoured.

4 About 20 minutes before you are ready to serve the chickens, heat butter and oil in a large frying pan (skillet) or flameproof casserole and sauté chickens until they are golden brown on all sides.

Double-cooked CHICKEN M'HAMMAR *cooking in a combination of butter and oil.*

5 To serve, arrange double-cooked chickens on a heated serving dish and keep warm. Reheat sauce and spoon over chickens. Serve immediately.

Serves 6

MOROCCAN CHICKEN WITH CHICK PEAS AND RICE

1 roasting (broiler/fryer) chicken about 1.5–1.75kg/3$\frac{1}{2}$–4lb
$\frac{1}{4}$ teaspoon each sweet red pepper and powdered cumin
salt and freshly ground black pepper
75g/3oz (6 tablespoons) butter
olive oil
350g/$\frac{3}{4}$lb Spanish onions, peeled and thinly sliced (scant 2$\frac{1}{2}$ cups thinly sliced Spanish onions)

¼–½ teaspoon powdered saffron
100g/¼lb (½ cup) chick peas, soaked overnight and drained
well-flavoured chicken stock (broth)
4 tablespoons each chopped flat-leafed (Italian) parsley and fresh green coriander
175g/6oz (scant 1 cup) rice
lemon juice

1 Wash, salt and rinse chicken, then cut into serving pieces, season generously with sweet red pepper, cumin, and salt and freshly ground black pepper to taste. Leave to marinate for at least 2 hours.

2 Melt butter and 2 tablespoons olive oil in a large frying pan (skillet) or shallow flameproof casserole, and sauté chicken pieces with onions until golden.

3 Sprinkle with powdered saffron. Add the skinned chick peas with enough well-flavoured chicken stock (broth) to cover, and simmer gently for 1 hour, or until chicken is tender. Just before serving, add chopped parsley and coriander.

4 In the meantime, cook rice in boiling salted water until tender. Drain and keep warm over simmering water.

5 To serve, spoon half the cooked rice on to a heated serving dish. Place chicken pieces on top, cover with the saffron sauce and add remaining rice. Sprinkle with lemon juice to taste.

Serves 4–6

GRILLED BABY CHICKENS WITH MOROCCAN SPICES
(BARBECUED OR BROILED BABY CHICKENS WITH MOROCCAN SPICES)

2 baby chickens, cleaned and cut into quarters
6–8 tablespoons butter
1 teaspoon sweet red pepper
⅛ teaspoon hot red pepper
¼ teaspoon powdered cumin
1 clove garlic, peeled and finely chopped
salt and freshly ground black pepper

GARNISH
sprigs of watercress
lemon wedges
hot red pepper
coarse salt
powdered cumin

1 Melt butter in a small saucepan with all the remaining ingredients, adding salt and black pepper to taste. Allow to cool. Rub chicken quarters with seasoned butter and leave to absorb flavours for at least 2 hours, or in the refrigerator overnight, before grilling (barbecuing or broiling).

2 Remove chickens from refrigerator at least 2 hours before grilling.

3 To cook chicken, grill over charcoal, or under grill (broiler), for 25–30 minutes, turning the birds occasionally, and basting frequently with melted seasoned butter.

4 Serve very hot, garnished with watercress and lemon wedges. Guests season their own serving from bowls of hot red pepper, coarse salt and powdered cumin, if desired.

Serves 4

CHICKEN MEFENNED WITH OMELETTES

1 roasting (broiler/fryer) chicken, cooked as in Chicken M'hammar (page 175),
but halving the flavouring ingredients
4 tablespoons butter
4 tablespoons fat from Chicken M'hammar (see page 175)

PARSLEY OMELETTES
8 eggs
4 tablespoons chopped flat-leafed (Italian) parsley
½ teaspoon sweet red pepper
¼ teaspoon powdered cumin
½ teaspoon salt
¼ teaspoon cracked black pepper

CHICKEN MEFENNED WITH OMELETTES
– an unusual and imposing chicken dish
which is quite easy to do. The paper-thin
omelettes with their parsley, sweet red pepper
and powdered cumin accents are pan-fried
separately and draped over the chicken just
before serving.

1 Prepare and cook chicken as in Chicken M'hammar (page 175), up to and including step 4. Moisten with a little of the sauce and keep warm in oven while you make omelettes.

2 To make parsley omelettes, whisk eggs in bowl until well mixed. Add the remaining ingredients and whisk again.

3 Combine butter and fat in a 23cm/9 inch frying pan (skillet). Pour in 1 small ladle (3–4 tablespoons) of omelette mixture, swirl mixture around pan and cook a thin omelette on one side only, without letting omelette colour. Place omelette in a dish, and keep warm. Continue to make omelettes as above until all the mixture has been used.

4 When ready to serve, place chicken on a heated serving dish, and top with several omelettes. Arrange remaining omelettes around the dish, moisten omelettes with a little of the sauce, and pour remaining sauce around bird.

This dish may also be served with the chicken cut into serving pieces either before or after cooking. In this case, the chicken pieces are warmed through in the sauce and arranged on a heated serving dish. A folded omelette is arranged over each piece. A little of the hot sauce is spooned over each omelette and the remaining sauce poured around the chicken pieces.

Serves 4–6

CHICKEN K'DRA WITH CHICK PEAS

1 roasting (broiler/fryer) chicken, 1.6kg/3½lb, or 2 × 1.25–1.5kg/2¼–3lb chickens
coarse salt
100g/¼lb (½ cup) softened butter (or smen)
¼–½ teaspoon freshly ground black pepper
½ teaspoon powdered saffron
100g/¼lb (½ cup) chick peas, soaked overnight, drained and peeled
4 Spanish onions, peeled and thinly sliced
4–6 tablespoons chopped flat-leafed (Italian) parsley

1 Wash chicken (or chickens) carefully, removing any pin feathers with tweezers. Rub inside and out with coarse salt and water and allow to absorb flavours for 1 hour. Rinse well, inside and out.

2 Cut chicken (or chickens) into serving pieces, pat dry and rub with half the softened butter (or *smen*), flavoured with black pepper and saffron.

3 Place chicken pieces in a flameproof casserole, pour over 300ml/½ pint (1¼ cups) water, and add remaining seasoned butter (or *smen*), chick peas, and onions. Cook over a medium heat until tender, about 60 minutes, turning chicken pieces in sauce from time to time, adding a little more water if necessary. About 10 minutes before end of cooking time, correct seasoning and add parsley.

4 To serve, arrange chicken pieces on a heated serving dish, or *tagine*, and keep warm. Reduce sauce over high heat and pour chick peas and sauce over the chicken.

Serves 4–6

PIGEONS K'DRA WITH ALMONDS

6 pigeons
coarse salt
¼ teaspoon freshly ground black pepper
½ teaspoon powdered saffron
100g/¼lb (½ cup) butter
6 large Spanish onions, peeled and thinly sliced
4 tablespoons chopped flat-leafed (Italian) parsley
2 tablespoons chopped fresh green coriander
100g/¼lb (⅔ cup) shelled almonds
sprigs of flat-leafed (Italian) parsley

1 Wash pigeons, carefully removing any pin feathers with tweezers. Wash with salt, and rinse and dry well.

2 Place pigeons in a flameproof casserole just large enough to hold them in one layer. Add 1 teaspoon salt, black pepper, saffron, half the butter and half the onions. Add 250ml/8fl.oz (1 cup) water, cover and cook over a medium heat, for about 45 minutes, or until tender, turning pigeons from time to time in the sauce and adding a little more water, if necessary.

3 Remove pigeons from casserole and keep warm. Add remaining onions to the sauce with parsley and coriander and cook until the onions are tender. In the meantime, sauté almonds in remaining butter until golden.

4 To serve, arrange the pigeons in a heated round serving dish. Spoon the sauce over them, and garnish with sautéed almonds and sprigs of parsley. Serve immediately.

Serves 6

STEAMED STUFFED CHICKEN I WITH TOMATOES, RICE AND PARSLEY

1 roasting (broiler/fryer) chicken
coarse salt

STUFFING
900g/2lb ripe tomatoes, skinned, seeded and cut into segments (6 cups skinned and seeded tomatoes cut into segments)
2 bunches flat-leafed (Italian) parsley, chopped
50g/2oz rice, cooked
¼ teaspoon each freshly ground black pepper, hot and sweet red peppers
4–6 tablespoons melted butter (or smen)

GARNISH
sprigs of flat-leafed (Italian) parsley, fresh green coriander and mint
tomato quarters
powdered cumin
coarse salt

1 Rub the chicken with salt inside and out, and leave for an hour. Rinse well and pat dry, removing any pin feathers with tweezers.

2 In a large bowl, mix all the stuffing ingredients, adding salt to taste.

3 Stuff chicken loosely and fasten vents with string or wooden skewers.

4 Fill a *couscoussier* (or steamer) three-quarters full with water and bring to the boil. Place stuffed chicken in the top and cover with a piece of moistened muslin (cheesecloth) and the lid. Steam over a medium heat for 1¼–1½ hours.

5 To serve chicken, place on a heated serving dish and garnish with parsley, coriander and mint sprigs and quartered tomatoes. Serve immediately, accompanied by small bowls of powdered cumin and coarse salt.

Serves 4

STEAMED STUFFED CHICKEN II WITH COUSCOUS, ALMONDS AND RAISINS

1 roasting (broiler/fryer) chicken
coarse salt

STUFFING
100g/¼lb couscous, cooked (see page 184)
100g/¼lb (⅔ cup) raisins, soaked and drained
100g/¼lb (⅔ cup) almonds, sautéed in butter until golden
¼ teaspoon each freshly ground black pepper and sweet red pepper
½ teaspoon powdered cinnamon
4 tablespoons melted butter (or smen)
salt
sugar

GARNISH
sprigs of mint
sweet red pepper
coarse salt

1 Prepare chicken as in the previous recipe.

2 In a large bowl, mix all the stuffing ingredients together, adding salt and sugar to taste. The mixture should be slightly sweet.

3 Stuff and cook the chicken as in the previous recipe.

4 To serve chicken, place on a heated serving dish and garnish with sprigs of mint. Serve immediately, accompanied by small bowls of sweet red pepper and coarse salt.

Serves 4

L'KEBDA M'CHERMEL I
FRIED LIVER STRIPS WITH *CHERMOULA*

4 thin slices calf's liver, cut into strips 1cm/½ inch wide
flour
olive oil

CHERMOULA
1 tablespoon sweet red pepper
1 teaspoon powdered cumin
2 tablespoons vinegar
4 tablespoons water
4 tablespoons chopped fresh green coriander
6 tablespoons chopped onion

1 Place liver strips in a shallow bowl. Mix *chermoula* ingredients together and pour over liver. Leave to marinate for at least 2 hours.

2 When ready to fry, pat liver strips dry. Dredge with flour and sauté in olive oil until crisp and golden.

Serves 4

L'KEBDA M'CHERMEL II
MARINATED LIVER STRIPS IN OLIVE AND LEMON SAUCE

4 thin slices calf's liver, cut into strips as in previous recipe
flour
olive oil
Chermoula as in previous recipe

OLIVE AND LEMON SAUCE
8 green olives, cracked, rinsed, pitted and cut into thin strips
juice of 1 small lemon
½ preserved lemon (see page 64), peel only, cut into thin strips
4 tablespoons olive oil
4 tablespoons chopped flat-leafed (Italian) parsley
6–8 tablespoons water

1 Marinate liver strips in *chermoula* for at least 2 hours.

2 When ready to fry, pat liver strips dry and dredge with flour. Sauté in olive oil until golden. Remove liver strips from pan with a slotted spoon and cut into 1cm/½ inch squares.

3 Combine the sauce ingredients in a frying pan (skillet), and bring gently to a simmer. Add liver pieces and simmer in gently bubbling sauce for 2–3 minutes

Serves 4

CHICKEN MQUALLI WITH OLIVES AND PRESERVED LEMONS

1 roasting (broiler/fryer) chicken
coarse salt
6 tablespoons groundnut (peanut) oil
6 tablespoons butter
2 large Spanish onions, peeled and grated
2 cloves garlic, peeled and finely chopped
½ teaspoon powdered saffron
¼ teaspoon each powdered ginger, hot and sweet red peppers
1 preserved lemon (see page 64), peel only, cut into eighths
36 green or violet olives, cracked
1–2 tablespoons lemon juice
1–2 tablespoons finely chopped flat-leafed (Italian) parsley

1 Wash chicken carefully. Rub inside and out with salt and water and leave for 1 hour. Rinse well. In a casserole just large enough to hold chicken, heat oil and butter until sizzling. Add chicken and brown lightly on all sides. Then add onion, garlic, spices and 250ml/8fl.oz (1 cup) water.

2 Cover casserole and cook over a low heat, turning chicken in the sauce from time to time, until chicken is tender (1–1¼ hours). Add a little more hot water from time to time during cooking if necessary. About 10–15 minutes before the end of cooking, add preserved lemon peel pieces and olives. Taste sauce and correct seasoning, adding a little lemon juice and chopped parsley.

3 To serve, place chicken in the centre of a heated serving dish; garnish with preserved lemon peel and olives, and strain the reduced sauce over.

Serves 4

TAGINE DU PAUVRE

Tagine du pauvre – so-called because it requires only lentils, vegetables, spices and the leftover raw bone and trimmings of a leg of lamb used for making brochettes or *kefta* – is one of my favourite vegetable-based supper dishes.

450g/1 lb lentils
6 tablespoons olive oil
2 Spanish onions, peeled and coarsely grated
2 cloves garlic, peeled and finely chopped
4 tomatoes, peeled, seeded and diced
4 carrots, sliced
1 raw bone from leg of lamb (with a little meat adhering), cut into 10cm/4 inch segments
½ teaspoon each powdered cumin and cinnamon
¼ teaspoon each powdered ginger, sweet and hot red peppers
salt and freshly ground black pepper

1 Thoroughly wash the lentils until the water runs clear. Place the lentils in a large saucepan. Fill pan with water and bring gently to the boil. Remove saucepan from heat and let lentils soak in hot water for 1 hour.

2 Drain lentils, and combine in a large saucepan with all the remaining ingredients. Add water to cover, and bring to the boil. Skim, reduce heat to a simmer, and cover saucepan. Cook gently until the lentils are just tender.

3 Check seasoning, adding a little more salt, pepper and spices as desired.

Serves 4–6

CHICKEN MQUALLI *with olives and preserved lemons.*

16

COUSCOUS

ABOVE: COUSCOUS, *the national dish of the Maghreb, was introduced by the Berbers, whose influence has shaped the culinary heritage of Morocco. Here, the raw ingredients for* HADDA'S COUSCOUS WITH RABBIT.

OPPOSITE: *The variety of different recipes for* couscous *is legion. There are vegetarian* couscous *recipes, sweet* couscous *recipes, recipes that use dried meats, rabbit or game for their flavouring and even a recipe – unknown to many Moroccans – that features fish.*

No Moroccan *diffa* or feast is complete without a *couscous*, presented at the end of the meal after a bewildering array of sumptuous *tagines* served, one after the other, in a galaxy of exotic flavours and textures. Just when you think you can eat no more, comes a great platter piled high with fluffy grains of cream-coloured semolina steamed over a highly flavoured bouillon of meat and vegetables, hiding its rich cargo of simmered lamb or chicken, the top and sides beautifully garnished with jewel-bright vegetables and colourful trails of honey-simmered onions, boiled chick peas and plumped-up dark raisins decorating the top.

Couscous is one of the truly great dishes of the Maghreb – Tunisia, Algeria and Morocco – but is at its festive best, to my mind, as served in the Imperial cities of Rabat, Fez, Meknes and Marrakech.

The word *couscous* refers both to various cooked dishes (of Berber origin), and to the actual grains of semolina. These are made from strong or hard wheat, moistened with water, coated with a fine flour, then formed into tiny cream-coloured pellets. In the Maghreb the pellets are made by hand. Elsewhere, machine-produced *couscous* from France can be found in cardboard packets in most supermarkets and in specialist food shops, in medium or fine grain.

The traditional vessel for cooking *couscous* is called a *couscoussier*. Made of tin, aluminium or stainless steel (sometimes brass or pottery in Morocco), it consists of a large, deep stock pot, topped with a perforated steamer and cover. The *couscous* grains are steamed in the top part of the *couscoussier* which is first lined with a piece of thin muslin or cheesecloth. If you have no traditional *couscous* steamer, substitute a muslin (cheesecloth)-lined colander or steamer which fits closely over a large saucepan. This will work just as well, but if there is a gap, pack a damp tea towel between the steamer and the pan, so that no

A majestic lamb-based couscous *garnished with chick peas, raisins and vegetables, photographed in front of one of the great* tabia *palaces of the pre-Sahara.*

steam can escape, and top the colander/steamer with the lid of the saucepan.

Couscous is cooked in several stages.

1. Place the *couscous* grains in a large bowl, cover with cold water, then drain immediately. Stir once with a fork and let the grains rest for 15 minutes, or until they begin to swell.

2. Work the semolina grains lightly with your fingers to separate them, then, dribbling the grains through your fingers, turn half the *couscous* into the muslin (cheesecloth)-lined steamer or top of the *couscoussier*.

3. Place this over boiling seasoned water (or bouillon) and the meat and vegetables the grain is to accompany. When steam rises through the grains, add the remainder.

4. Steam the *couscous*, uncovered, for 30 minutes after you have added the second amount, occasionally drawing a fork through the grains to separate them and ensure that they do not stick together in lumps.

5. Remove the steamer from the heat, and turn the *couscous* on to a large flat dish. Sprinkle with a little lightly salted water, and separate the grains with your fingers.

6. Take a little *smen* (or butter) and mix it into the *couscous*, rubbing grains between the hands with a lightning movement to allow the air to get at it to remove any lumps. Take remaining *smen* (or butter) and gently rub it over the hot *couscous*, turning *couscous* over with the other hand as you do so. The addition of *smen* at this stage imparts an indescribably fragrant flavour and aroma to the *couscous* grains (much in the same manner that butter and freshly grated Parmesan cheese do to Italian pasta). See page 63 for ways in which to emulate the full-bodied flavour of *smen* at home.

7. To complete the cooking, once again dribble the *couscous* into the top of the *couscoussier* or strainer above the simmering stew or boiling water and steam for 20–30 minutes more, fluffing the grains occasionally with a fork.

Some packets of *couscous* provide instructions for cooking the *couscous* quickly by boiling: this method *does* save time, but the grains will not be as soft, fluffy and separate as they should.

North African recipes for the accompanying stew vary greatly. Each region has its own characteristic flavourings and the main ingredient can be lamb, chicken, fish, *kefta*, *merguez* (spicy sausages, see page 66), *khlii*, *tête de mouton* (steamed lamb's head) or, more simply, vegetables.

Moroccan cooks stuff pigeons, chickens and turkeys with a sweetened, spiced *couscous* with chick peas and raisins. I use leftover *couscous* – the grains and the meat and vegetables diced – to make a wonderfully savoury Eastern stuffing when roasting a young turkey or a brace of fat capons. I like, too, to serve the grain *couscous* (steamed on its own) as a vegetable accompaniment to dishes other than the traditional ones: try it with grilled lamb chops, for example, or a curry. And steamed *couscous* moistened with a well-flavoured vinaigrette dressing makes a good base for a sliced fish or diced raw vegetable (green and red pepper, diced tomato and black olive) appetizer salad.

For dessert, decorate steamed sweetened *couscous* with dates or plumped-up prunes and raisins, and sweeten further with decorative trails of powdered cinnamon and icing (confectioners') sugar. Serve with sweetened almond milk or buttermilk in the traditional manner, or with cream and yoghurt if desired.

COUSCOUS AUX SEPT LÉGUMES

700g/1½lb (scant 5 cups) couscous
900g/2lb lamb shanks, cut into 100g/¼lb pieces
900g/2lb lamb shoulder, cut into 100g/¼lb pieces
100g/¼lb (½ cup) smen (or butter)

BOUILLON
4 Spanish onions, peeled and quartered
2 cloves garlic, peeled and halved
2 cinnamon sticks
1 tablespoon coarse salt
1 teaspoon cracked black pepper
1–2 little hot red peppers
½ teaspoon each powdered saffron and sweet red pepper
6 tablespoons olive oil
100g/¼lb (½ cup) chick peas, soaked overnight and drained

VEGETABLES
8 small carrots, scraped
8 small turnips, scraped
8 small courgettes (zucchini), trimmed
4 small aubergines (eggplant), trimmed and halved lengthways
4 large ripe tomatoes, halved and seeded (see page 105)
4 tablespoons chopped flat-leafed (Italian) parsley
4 tablespoons chopped fresh green coriander
700g/1½lb pumpkin, peeled and cut into 4cm/1½ inch slices
salt

1 Place the prepared lamb pieces in the bottom of a *couscoussier* or steamer and add all the bouillon ingredients. Add 1.2L/2 pints (5 cups) water to cover and bring gently to the boil.

2 Skim off any impurities, reduce heat to a simmer, cover and simmer gently for 30 minutes.

3 To prepare the *couscous*, place *couscous* grains in a large flat bowl or *gsaa*. Cover with cold water, then drain off immediately. Stir once with a fork and let the grains rest for 15 minutes, or until they begin to swell.

4 Add carrots and turnips to bouillon.

5 Work the semolina grains lightly with your fingers to separate them, then, dribbling the grains through your fingers, turn half the *couscous* into the muslin (cheesecloth)-lined top of the *couscoussier* or steamer, and place it over the boiling flavoured bouillon, vegetables and lamb. Add a little more water if necessary.

6 When steam rises through the grains, add the remainder of the *couscous* and steam, uncovered, over the meat, vegetables and bouillon for 30 minutes, occasionally drawing a fork through the grains to separate them and ensure that they do not stick together in lumps.

7 Remove the steamer from the heat and transfer the *couscous* to a large flat dish. Sprinkle with a little lightly salted water, separate the grains with your fingers, and then mix in a little of the *smen* (or butter). Rub the grains between your hands with a lightning movement to allow the air to get at it and to remove any lumps.

8 Take the remaining lump of *smen* (or butter), and gently rub it over the hot *couscous*, turning *couscous* over with the other hand as you do so.

9 Add courgettes (zucchini), halved aubergines (eggplant) and tomatoes to the bouillon. Stir in flat-leafed (Italian) parsley and fresh green coriander. Replace top of *couscoussier* or steamer over the pan and continue to simmer for a further 30 minutes, or until lamb and vegetables are tender.

10 About 30 minutes before serving *couscous*, cook the sliced pumpkin in boiling salted water in a separate saucepan until tender.

11 To serve *couscous*, heap steamed *couscous* in an even ring around the outside of a large heated serving platter. Smooth grains with your hands into an attractive shape. With a perforated spoon, transfer the lamb and vegetables to the centre of the dish. Add the drained pumpkin slices and spoon over chick peas and as much of the bouillon as you wish. Serve the remaining bouillon separately, flavoured with a little *harissa* or additional spices (see page 189).

Serves 6–8

OPPOSITE: COUSCOUS AUX SEPT LEGUMES *photographed in the Minzah in Marrakech.*

SIMPLE STEAMED COUSCOUS (OR CRACKED WHEAT) WITH CHICK PEAS

700g/1½lb (scant 5 cups) couscous (or raw cracked wheat)
2 Spanish onions, peeled and quartered
½ teaspoon powdered cumin
1 sprig thyme
100g/¼lb (½ cup) chick peas, soaked overnight and drained
100g/¼lb (½ cup) butter (or smen), melted
2 tablespoons olive oil
salt and freshly ground black pepper
hot red pepper

1 Bring 1.2 litres/2 pints (5 cups) water to the boil in the bottom of the *couscoussier*. Add onions, cumin, thyme and drained chick peas, and bring back to the boil.

2 Place muslin (cheesecloth)-lined top of *couscoussier* in place over simmering water and add *couscous* (or cracked wheat). Cover and steam until *couscous* (or cracked wheat) and chick peas are tender, about 1 hour.

3 Transfer *couscous* (or cracked wheat) to a large, flat bowl and add melted butter (or *smen*) and olive oil. Toss well with a fork, season with salt, freshly ground black pepper and hot red pepper to taste, then toss again. Serve immediately.

Serves 6

SIMPLE STEAMED COUSCOUS (OR CRACKED WHEAT) WITH CHICK PEAS, KEFTA AND ONIONS

700g/1½lb (scant 5 cups) couscous (or raw cracked wheat)
2 Spanish onions, peeled and coarsely grated
olive oil
225g/½lb lamb, finely chopped
6 tablespoons tomato concentrate (purée)
salt and freshly ground black pepper
hot red pepper
100g/¼lb (½ cup) butter (or smen), melted

BOUILLON
1 Spanish onion, peeled and quartered
½ teaspoon powdered cumin
1 sprig thyme
100g/¼lb (½ cup) chick peas, soaked overnight and drained

1 To prepare *kefta* mix, sauté grated onions in 4 tablespoons olive oil until transparent, then add finely chopped lamb. Continue to cook, stirring constantly, until lamb has changed colour. Season with tomato concentrate (purée), and salt, freshly ground black pepper and hot red pepper to taste.

2 Bring 1.2 litres/2 pints (5 cups) water to the boil in the bottom of the *couscoussier*, and add the bouillon ingredients. Bring back to the boil.

3 Place muslin (cheesecloth)-lined top of *couscoussier* in place over the simmering bouillon, and add *couscous* (or cracked wheat). Cover and steam until *couscous* (or cracked wheat) and chick peas are tender, about 1 hour.

4 Transfer *couscous* (or cracked wheat) to a large, flat bowl, add melted butter (or *smen*), 2 tablespoons olive oil, and the cooked *kefta* mixture. Toss well with a fork, season with salt, freshly ground black pepper and hot red pepper to taste, then toss again. Serve immediately.

Serves 6

COUSCOUS K'DRA WITH CHICK PEAS AND RAISINS

700g/1½lb (scant 5 cups) couscous
1 roasting (broiler/fryer) chicken (or 1.4kg/3lb shoulder of lamb), cut into pieces about 100g/¼lb each
salt
100g/¼lb (½ cup) smen (or butter)

BOUILLON
100g/¼lb (½ cup) chick peas, soaked overnight and drained
4 tablespoons olive oil
4 Spanish onions, peeled and quartered
½ teaspoon each powdered saffron, cinnamon and sweet red pepper
¼ teaspoon hot red pepper
salt and freshly ground black pepper

VEGETABLES
8 carrots, scraped
8 turnips, scraped
8 courgettes (zucchini), scraped
16 strips grilled (broiled or barbecued) red pepper (or canned pimiento)

175g/6oz (1 cup) yellow raisins, washed and drained
175g/6oz (1 cup) black raisins, washed and drained
4 tablespoons chopped flat-leafed (Italian) parsley
4 tablespoons chopped fresh green coriander

1 Rub chicken pieces with salt, rinse well and pat dry. Place prepared chicken (or lamb) in the bottom of a *couscoussier* or steamer. Add all the bouillon ingredients, with salt and freshly ground black pepper to taste. Add 1.2L/ 2 pints (5 cups) water to cover, and bring to the boil.

2 Skim off any impurities, reduce heat to a simmer, then cover and simmer gently for 15 minutes.

3 Prepare the *couscous* as on page 184, and steam for 30 minutes (stages 1–4).

4 Remove *couscous* from steamer and rub with lightly salted water and *smen* (or butter) as on page 184 (stages 5 and 6).

5 Add carrots, turnips, courgettes (zucchini), pepper (or pimiento) strips and raisins to the bouillon. Stir in chopped parsley and coriander. Put *couscous* back in top of *couscoussier* (or steamer) and replace over the simmering bouillon. Continue to simmer for a further 20–30 minutes, or until chicken (or lamb) and vegetables are tender.

6 To serve *couscous*, heap steamed *couscous* in an even ring around the outside of a large heated serving platter. Arrange cooked chicken (or lamb) pieces and vegetables in the centre. Then spoon over chick peas and raisins and as much of the bouillon as you wish. Serve the remaining bouillon separately.

It is common practice in Morocco to flavour the extra bouillon as a sauce which guests use to give zest and flavour to the *couscous* as they eat. Add a teaspoon or two of *harissa* (see pages 65 and 66) to the bouillon; or add $\frac{1}{4}$ teaspoon each of sweet and hot red peppers, powdered cinnamon and ginger.

Serves 6–8

HADDA'S COUSCOUS WITH RABBIT

700g/1½lb (scant 5 cups) couscous
2 tender young rabbits (or 1 × 1.75kg/4lb rabbit), cut into serving pieces
salt and freshly ground black pepper
100g/¼lb (½ cup) smen (or butter)
1 medium-sized green pepper, seeded, cored and quartered
4 tablespoons chopped flat-leafed (Italian) parsley
4 tablespoons chopped fresh green coriander

BOUILLON
4 tablespoons olive oil
2 sprigs thyme
2 Spanish onions, peeled and quartered
4 cloves garlic, peeled
8 small turnips, scraped
8 small carrots, scraped
2 teaspoons sweet red pepper
1 teaspoon powdered cinnamon
½ teaspoon powdered saffron
¼ teaspoon hot red pepper
2 tablespoons tomato concentrate (purée)
100g/¼lb (½ cup) chick peas, soaked overnight and drained

SAUCE
¼ teaspoon each sweet and hot red peppers, powdered ginger and cinnamon
½ teaspoon tomato concentrate (purée)

COUSCOUS K'DRA WITH CHICK PEAS AND RAISINS *photographed in the Moroccan restaurant of the Palais Jamai, Fez.*

1 Season rabbit pieces generously with salt and freshly ground black pepper.

2 In the bottom section of a *couscoussier* or large steamer, combine rabbit pieces and all the bouillon ingredients. Pour over 1.2 litres/2 pints (5 cups) boiling water, and bring to the boil.

3 Skim off any impurities, then reduce heat. Cover and simmer for 15 minutes.

4 Prepare the *couscous* as on page 184, and steam for 30 minutes (stages 1–4).

5 Remove *couscous* from steamer and rub with lightly salted water and *smen* (or butter) as on page 184 (stages 5 and 6).

6 Add quartered green pepper and chopped parsley and coriander to the bouillon. Put *couscous* back in top of *couscoussier* (or steamer) and replace over the bouillon. Continue to simmer for a further 20–30 minutes, or until the rabbit pieces and vegetables are tender.

7 To make the sauce, strain off 300ml/$\frac{1}{2}$ pint (1$\frac{1}{4}$ cups) liquid from the stew. Pour into a small pan and flavour with the spices and tomato concentrate (purée). Taste and adjust the seasonings, adding a little more if necessary: the sauce should be quite strong in flavour. Reheat to boiling point.

8 To serve *couscous*, heap the grains around the sides of a large heated serving platter, smoothing it into an even ring. Arrange cooked rabbit pieces in the centre. Spoon over as much of the vegetables and juices as your platter will comfortably hold. Serve immediately, piping hot, handing hot sauce around separately so that guests may help themselves to a spoonful or two as they eat the *couscous*. Any remaining vegetables and juices can be kept hot, in reserve.

Serves 6–8

COUSCOUS AUX POISSONS

700g/1$\frac{1}{2}$lb (scant 5 cups) couscous
1.6kg/3$\frac{1}{2}$lb firm fleshed fish (pageot, daurade, merou, lotte (monkfish), etc.), cut into steaks or fillets
olive oil

BOUILLON
heads and bones of fish (if available)
2 Spanish onions, peeled and quartered
450g/1lb tomatoes, halved and seeded
$\frac{1}{4}$–$\frac{1}{2}$ teaspoon powdered saffron
1 sprig thyme
peel of $\frac{1}{2}$ fresh or preserved lemon (see page 64)
10–12 black peppercorns
4 tablespoons olive oil
4 sprigs each fresh green coriander and flat-leafed (Italian) parsley
4 cloves garlic, peeled
$\frac{1}{4}$ teaspoon hot red pepper
salt

SAUCE
125ml/4fl.oz ($\frac{1}{2}$ cup) olive oil
125ml/4fl.oz ($\frac{1}{2}$ cup) water
2–4 small garlic cloves, peeled and finely chopped
2 Spanish onions, peeled and coarsely grated
450g/1lb tomatoes, skinned, seeded and coarsely chopped (3 cups skinned, seeded and coarsely chopped tomatoes)
1 sprig thyme
$\frac{1}{2}$ teaspoon powdered cumin
$\frac{1}{4}$ teaspoon sweet red pepper
salt and freshly ground black pepper
harissa (optional)

1 In the bottom of the *couscoussier* or steamer, combine all the bouillon ingredients, adding salt to taste. Pour over 1.2L/2 pints (5 cups) water. Bring gently to the boil, and skim off any froth or impurities, then reduce heat. Cover and simmer for 15 minutes.

2 Prepare the *couscous* as on page 184, and steam for 30 minutes (stages 1–4).

3 In the meantime, prepare the sauce. In a medium-sized saucepan (or small casserole), combine all the ingredients, adding salt and freshly ground black pepper to taste. Bring to the boil, skim, lower heat and simmer for 20–30 minutes, adding a little more water if necessary. Reserve.

4 After the *couscous* has steamed for 30 minutes, remove from the steamer, and mix in a little olive oil. Rub the grains between the hands with a lightning movement to allow the air to get at it and to remove the lumps.

5 To complete the cooking, place fish steaks or fillets into the bouillon. Return *couscous* to muslin (cheesecloth)-lined strainer and steam above the simmering fish stew for 20–30 minutes more, fluffing the grains occasionally with a fork.

6 To serve, arrange the steamed *couscous* in a ring around the outside of a large heated serving platter. Pile fish in the centre and pour sauce over the fish, reserving a little to mix with some of the fish bouillon to moisten *couscous* before serving. A little *harissa* (see pages 65 and 66) may be added.

Serves 6–8

HOT SAUCE FOR COUSCOUS

Many Moroccans like to serve a *sauce piquante* (hot sauce) with *couscous*. It is usually served in a small bowl, and guests help themselves to a spoonful or two of the highly flavoured sauce, moistening the grains to add flavour.

1–2 teaspoons harissa (see pages 65 and 66)
1–2 tablespoons tomato concentrate (purée)
150ml/¼ pint (⅔ cup) broth from couscous

Mix the *harissa* with the tomato concentrate (purée) in a small bowl. Stir in the hot broth. Serve with *couscous*.

AZENBOU

This comforting highly flavoured cornmeal porridge, dressed with argan oil (or melted butter) and honey is a speciality of the south.

450g/1lb (generous 3 cups) cornmeal
salt
6–8 tablespoons argan (or olive oil)
¼ teaspoon each powdered cumin and sweet red pepper

GARNISH
argan oil and honey, or melted butter (or smen) and honey

1 In a large saucepan, bring 1.5 litres/2½ pints (6¼ cups) water to the boil. Dribble in cornmeal gradually, stirring constantly. When *azenbou* is cooked to the proper consistency (it should be almost thick enough to stand a spoon in it), remove saucepan from the heat and add salt to taste. A little argan or olive oil is stirred in with a hint of powdered cumin and sweet red pepper.

2 Just before serving, pour *azenbou* into a heated serving bowl and sprinkle with argan oil (or olive oil) and honey – or with melted butter (or *smen*) and honey.

Serves 6

17

THE WEDDING FEAST

Overwhelming evidence of the continuing richness and traditionalism of modern Moroccan life is the seven-day drama of the Moroccan wedding – a magic blend of Berber and Andalusian music, vivid costumes and swirling dances, set against the heady aromas of Moroccan cooking, spices and incense.

Marriages in Morocco are often arranged by the parents of the young couple who are to be married, especially in the country districts. But Azziz – in true western style – had fallen in love with the girl next door. The two young people had never dated, nor even spoken, but according to Azziz 'their eyes had said much'. Anyway, love it was, and the marriage was duly arranged. The fathers met; the bridal price was agreed; the date for the wedding set. It was to be a wedding in true Moroccan traditional style with the wedding preparations spread out over seven days of cooking for the great feast with literally hundreds of little cakes and honey-dipped sweets, great *b'stillas*, and *m'hannchas* prepared. In the kitchens, chickens by the score were to be simmered in countless *tagines* with preserved lemons and olives; forequarters of lamb were to be stuffed with mealy white *couscous*, raisins and nuts. And almonds were to be crushed by the hundredweight, and their milk cooled on ice to serve as drink. Rare spices were pounded in mortars; and sweet cakes of honey and nuts were twisted into fantastic shapes.

And most important of all, the ritual 'purification' of the bride: a series of ceremonies which – in seven days – was to take her from the unformed state of innocence to the fulfilled state of womanhood. Every night for seven nights she was led by her sisters and women friends to the *hammam* for a series of ritualistic baths. And each morning she returned home in a small procession accompanied by the excited beating of drums, singing and tambourines sounding through the streets to let her world know of her happiness. On the seventh day it was

ABOVE: *The richness and traditionalism of modern Moroccan life is brought magically to life in the seven-day drama of the Moroccan Wedding Feast – an exotic blend of music, costume, dances and the heady aromas of Moroccan cooking and burning incense.*

192

OPPOSITE: *From unformed state of innocence to fulfilled state of womanhood.*

time for the ritual of the sugar cones: a day when the hair-dresser, the make-up artist and the henna expert, specially engaged for the event, were to take over the entire house, with the womenfolk of the family and intimate friends to ready the bride-to-be for marriage.

First of all, the henna ceremony. The bride, dressed in traditional green and white, is seated in the room with the women. At her feet is a great brass tray containing the traditional bowls of henna, dried rosebuds, and cloves; sugar cones (symbol of purity); eggs (symbol of fecundity); and three small saucers each containing scented woods or spices to burn in a pungent incense designed to protect the bride from 'evil' spirits. While the *neqqacha* (the henna expert) works for hours covering her hands and feet with an intricate lace pattern of henna dye, the women sip tea, eat cakes, laugh, gossip and sing, chant and dance to the music of tambourines, tom-toms and the improvised metallic beat of a large pair of shears taken up by one of the guests to add to the joyous, almost pagan, festivities.

Then it is the turn of the hairdresser to wash her hair with henna, let it set in the sun like a great green mud pie before washing it out. Her hair is then scented with powdered dried rosebuds and cloves, and brushed with sprigs of wild marjoram dipped in rosewater before it is coiled and held in place with coloured combs and bright ribbons.

The make-up artist then begins to make-up the bride with creams and tinted pomades for her face and cheeks: applications of *kohl* to accent her eyes; red salves to redden her lips; and even tiny silver sequins and rhinestones applied in stylized geometric patterns on her cheeks. She is now totally transformed – half girl empress, half *geisha* – mysteriously glowing with Asiatic overtones; primaeval woman. Medea.

In the meantime, the sheep – a present of the bridegroom's family – is brought to sacrifice before the intimate members of the two families. The mother of the bride brings a brass tray holding dates and milk – symbols of hospitality – with a red and gold scarf over her shoulder. The scarf is placed over the sheep and the *Imam* expertly cuts its throat to the sound of drumbeats and tambourines, and the shrill ululations of the women expressing their excitement and happiness. As a final gesture, salt is sprinkled over the spot where the sacrifice took place to avoid the 'evil' eye.

During the whole day a fire has been tended so that the sheep – now skinned and dressed, anointed with oils and herbs and spices – may be spitted and slowly roasted over the embers to be ready in time for the wedding feast when family and guests will partake of a piece to bring the newlyweds happiness and good fortune.

It is late afternoon. Time for the groom to be taken to the

In the harem there is singing and dancing while the henna expert works for hours covering the bride's hands and feet with ritualistic, lace-like patterns of henna dye.

OPPOSITE (FROM TOP TO BOTTOM, LEFT TO RIGHT): *Hennaed hands and feet; one of seven changes of jewellery for the bride; metallic shears provide improvised music for the festivities; the bride's mother bearing traditional gifts for the sheep ceremony; the womenfolk, singing and chanting, go in search of the groom; the bridegroom returns from the Mosque.*

Little cakes and sweetmeats are served throughout the evening in traditional plaited straw baskets trimmed with red leather.

hammam by his brothers and his friends to prepare himself for the marriage night. The bride, her friends and the womenfolk of her family enjoy a last feast in her own home.

And now it is night. The groom, surrounded by the male members of his family and his friends, returns from the *mosque*. The women, with candles, lanterns and music, go to meet him in the crowded streets of the *medina*. The bride, now complete with henna-decorated hands and feet, carefully arranged and perfumed hair and exotically dressed in golden robes – her feet shod with tiny new slippers presented to her by the groom – is supported on each side by a *neggafate* (the wedding women hired to officiate as attendants to the bride) and gently led into the chamber where the festivities are to take place.

The groom, a hooded spectre from the Spanish Middle Ages in his white *burnous*, knocks at the studded door and begs admittance. He is met by the black *gnoua* orchestra who lead him triumphantly to his caparisoned bride where, before the guests, he kisses her for the first time, lightly on the forehead, and offers her a date and a sip of milk to drink. She repeats the gesture and they sit there happily as the musicians take over and the festivities begin. Steaming glasses of hot mint tea and little cakes – *ghoriba* of almonds and *smen*, honeyed *briouats* and *cornes de gazelle* – are passed around to the many guests who have been waiting for this moment. The music grows louder; one orchestra taking over from the other as the great dishes of sweetmeats are passed around and the guests begin to move, to sing, to dance and to gaze on the happy couple sitting on their throne in the centre of the feast.

Then the bride is taken away by her attendants to change her costume. There will be seven changes of costume in all, with subsequent changes of jewels and veils, during the night – each representing an area or province of Morocco. All the clothes, complete with jewels, scarfs and veils, are rented finery which come with the two *neggafates*.

At midnight, the feast is ready and the guests are summoned to various rooms around the central *riad*, to be seated on low divans placed around low octagonal tables, and the *b'stilla aux pigeons* is served, followed by forequarters of savoury lamb stuffed with *couscous*, raisins and almonds and chicken *m'hammar*, with a final taste of the sacrificial lamb, served in 'kneeling' position on a great brass tray. Dessert is a great sweet *m'hanncha* for each table, dusted with icing (confectioners') sugar and cinnamon, and accompanied by more sweetmeats.

It is now almost morning. The bride and groom – in one last burst of enthusiasm and energy – are swept up and carried at shoulder height among the guests with a fanfare of music, ululations and song, before disappearing finally to the privacy of the last few hours of the night.

18

CORNES DE GAZELLE AND OTHER MOROCCAN SWEETS

Moroccans, noted for their sweet tooth, are devoted to tissue-thin pastry wrapped around sweetmeat fillings of pounded almonds, dates or figs, flavoured with the distilled essences of orange blossoms or rose petals, and soaked in honey. Sweets such as *m'hanncha, kaab el ghzal, ghoriba* and *shebbakia* have brought a glimmer of delight to the eyes of jaded Moroccans ever since the times of the sultans and caliphs. Indeed, so expensive were sugar, nuts, rosewater and exotic spices in those far off days that only the sultans, caliphs and their favourites could afford them. And vast trays of sweetmeats and pastries were consumed, so legend has it, to the sound of music and poetry as fair-skinned maidens moved their well-rounded bodies to the sensuous sound of lutes and tambours.

Today, thanks to modern transportation and production methods, all that has changed and honey, sugar, almonds, walnuts, pistachio nuts and spices are within the reach of almost everyone. But it is interesting to note that the little cakes, pastries and rich sweets are not usually served at the end of a meal as they would be in Britain, but are reserved for special occasions and family celebrations when they appear in great abundance: weddings, births, name days and the many religious feast days scattered throughout the Moslem year.

Two of the most famous of these Moroccan sweets are *kaab el ghzal* (gazelle's horns), delicious crescent-shaped pastries stuffed with delicately flavoured almond paste and served either plain or dipped in orange-flower water and then coated with icing (confectioners') sugar; and *m'hanncha* (the coiled serpent cake),

ABOVE: *The sweets of the Arab world are famous. Pastry shops such as Benni's in Casablanca exhibit a variety of exquisite sweets and pastries.*

OPPOSITE: CORNES DE GAZELLE – *the crispy, almond-filled pastry crescents affectionately called 'gazelle's horns' – served with fresh dates.*

a flat round of baked almond-stuffed pastry, dusted with icing (confectioners') sugar and then decorated with a lattice of fine lines of powdered cinnamon. These two popular sweets, like the other little cakes, cookies and pastry-wrapped sweetmeats found in most Moroccan pastry shops, are usually served with steaming glasses of Moroccan mint tea at any time of the day when there are guests, or when the women of the house get together with neighbours for morning or afternoon tea.

Other sweet dishes in the Moroccan culinary repertoire are those sweets or puddings served just before the fresh fruits or fruit salads are presented at the end of a special feast. *Couscous sffa* (sweet dessert *couscous*) consists of a cone of steamed *couscous* grains garnished with trails of icing (confectioners') sugar and powdered cinnamon, often decorated with toasted almonds, raisins or fresh dates and served with warm or cold milk or buttermilk. *Keneffa* (sweet dessert *b'stilla*) is made of deep-fried layered leaves of *warkha* pastry, interspersed with a crunchy mix of ground almonds, icing (confectioners') sugar and powdered cinnamon, and served with almond milk, or more rarely, with an almond-flavoured custard; and *roz bil halib* (Moroccan rice pudding) is studded with sautéed pine kernels and/or raisins plumped up in orange-flower water.

Bennis, a famous pastry shop located in the Habbous section of Casablanca, just behind the Royal Palace, boasts the most mouth-watering selection of little Moroccan cakes and pastries I know. Here it is the custom to enter and choose three or four of each of the little cakes on view while a member of the Bennis family carefully sets them, like jewels, in cardboard boxes to take away. I often used to come here to choose delicious *ghoriba* (little lovers' cakes, not unlike our own macaroons in shape), available in several flavours; *cornes de gazelle*, both plain and sugared; stuffed dates; long, thin 'cigarettes' of *warkha* pastry wrapped around a filling of orange-flavoured almond pastry; tiny sesame cakes and *briouats*, triangular little pastries made by folding long strips of *warkha* pastry around almond paste (see page 204), or pounded dates or figs. Then, too, there are *shebbakia*, deep-fried pastry 'ribbons', which are soaked in bubbling hot honey before being sprinkled with toasted sesame seeds. *Shebbakia*, though a firm family favourite throughout the year in most Moroccan homes, is a 'must' as an accompaniment for the Ramadan 'break fast' soup, *harira*.

Spelling – a cause for confusion

It is in the realm of sweets, cakes and pastries especially that the phonetic French or English spelling of Moroccan dishes can become a problem: it is important to remember that Moroccan – in contrast to classic Arab – is a *spoken* language, and thus phonetic spellings can vary enormously. *B'stilla* – which is variously spelled *pasteeya, bisteeya, bstila, pastilla* or even *pastela* or *bastela* – is a case in point; as are *m'hanncha* (sometimes spelled *m'hancha*) and gazelle's horns (called *kab-aghzal, kab el ghzal* or even *kaab el ghazul*). The paper-thin leaves of home-made pastry are called *warkha* or *ouarka*; *sfenj* are often spelled *sfinges, sellou* is sometimes *slillou*; *shebbakia* are sometimes spelled *chebakia* or *chebbakiya*; *ghoriba* are also known as *ghoryba* or even *ghorayebah*; *briouats* are often seen as *braewats*; and the pastry envelopes called *rghaifs* as *rghayefs* or even *er ghaifs*.

Sounds confusing? It is. But relax: no matter how you spell the Arab names, you will find the results both delicious and different!

COUSCOUS SFFA
SWEET DESSERT COUSCOUS

700g/1½lb (scant 5 cups) raw couscous
2 tablespoons groundnut (peanut) oil
¼ teaspoon each salt and powdered cinnamon
175g/6oz (¾ cup) butter

GARNISH
powdered cinnamon
icing (confectioners') sugar
prunes, dates, raisins and/or sautéed almonds (optional)
milk

1 Place the raw *couscous* in a large bowl or tray, cover with cold water, then drain immediately. Stir with a fork, and let rest for 15 minutes.

2 Sprinkle the *couscous* with the oil mixed with 6 tablespoons water, and the salt and powdered cinnamon. Mix well with the palm of your hand until liquid is uniformly absorbed.

3 Put prepared *couscous* in the top part of a *couscoussier* and place over bubbling water. Steam for 30 minutes, then remove from the heat.

4 Return the *couscous* to the bowl or tray and mix in half the butter with your hands. The heat of the *couscous* melts butter as you rub it into the hot grains. Allow to cool and then sprinkle with 175ml/6fl.oz (¾ cup) water, mixing it well in with your hands. Leave *couscous* to absorb all the liquid, aerating it from time to time with your fingers.

5 Return the *couscous* to the top part of the *couscoussier* and cook over bubbling water for 15 minutes. Then transfer *couscous* to bowl or tray again. Add half remaining butter and mix again with hands. Return to top part of *couscoussier* and steam again for 30 minutes.

6 Return *couscous* to the bowl or tray for the fourth and last time; add remaining butter and mix in lightly with your hands.

7 Arrange hot *couscous* in a tall cone shape in a large warm serving dish, smoothing it evenly into shape with your hands. Decorate the cone with delicate trails of powdered cinnamon and icing (confectioners') sugar. Prunes, dates, raisins and sautéed almonds may also be used to decorate the *couscous*. Serve the *couscous* hot with additional icing (confectioners') sugar, powdered cinnamon and bowls of cool milk.

Serves 6–8

The legendary mound of crisp-fried warkha *pastry interleaved with pounded almonds, sugar and cinnamon called* KENEFFA — *as served at the Palais Jamai, Fez.*

KENEFFA
SWEET DESSERT B'STILLA

16 × 25cm/10 inch warkha pastry leaves (see page 85)

ALMOND GARNISH
salad oil, for frying
175g/6oz (1 cup) blanched almonds
2–4 tablespoons icing (confectioners') sugar
½–1 teaspoon powdered cinnamon

ALMOND CREAM
900ml/1½ pints (3¾ cups) milk
4 tablespoons ground almonds
3 tablespoons cornflour mixed with 6 tablespoons of the milk
6–8 tablespoons sugar
a pinch of salt
½ teaspoon vanilla essence (extract)
¼ teaspoon almond essence (extract)
2 tablespoons orange-flower water

1 Press two pastry leaves together carefully around edges to make eight circles.

2 To prepare almond garnish, place 4 tablespoons salad oil in a large, thick-bottomed frying pan (skillet). Add blanched almonds and fry, stirring constantly, until almonds are golden brown. Drain almonds (reserving oil for later use) and cool on kitchen paper (paper towels). When cold, chop coarsely and mix with icing (confectioners') sugar and cinnamon to taste.

3 To prepare almond cream, combine milk, ground almonds, cornflour (mixed with milk), sugar and salt in a saucepan and bring gently to the boil, stirring from time to time. Stir in vanilla and almond essences (extracts) and orange-flower water. Strain into a clean bowl and allow to cool.

4 About 1–2 hours before your guests arrive, add 4–6 tablespoons oil to the reserved oil in frying pan and heat. Fry *warkha* doubled circles until crisp and pale gold on both sides, adding more oil, as necessary. Do not let them brown. Drain on paper towels until ready to serve.

7 To assemble, place two crisp-fried *warkha* doubled circles in a large shallow serving bowl. Pour over a little thickened almond cream and sprinkle with 4–6 tablespoons of the almond garnish. Cover with two more doubled *warkha* circles, almond cream and almond garnish as above. Cover with another two *warkha* circles, almond cream and almond garnish as above. Repeat with last two *warkha* circles, some almond cream and remaining chopped almond garnish. Serve remaining almond cream separately.

Serves 4

GAZELLE'S HORNS
KAAB EL GHZAL

225g/½lb (1½ cups plus 2 tablespoons all-purpose) flour
2 tablespoons melted butter
1 tablespoon orange-flower water
1 egg yolk, beaten with a little water
200–300ml/7–10fl.oz (scant 1–1¼ cups) sifted flour

ALMOND PASTE FILLING
450g/1lb (2⅔ cups) blanched almonds
175g/6oz icing (1½ cups confectioners') sugar
3 tablespoons orange-flower water
1 egg, beaten
4 tablespoons melted butter
¼–½ teaspoon almond essence (extract)
½ teaspoon finely grated orange zest
¼–½ teaspoon powdered cinnamon

FOR SUGARED GAZELLE'S HORNS
orange-flower water
icing (confectioners') sugar

1 To make almond paste filling, combine almonds, icing (confectioners') sugar and orange-flower water in the bowl of an electric food processor, and process in short bursts until nuts are ground. Mix beaten egg with remaining ingredients, add to the almonds, and process again until well mixed.

2 Divide almond paste into 24–36 small balls then, with your fingers, roll each ball into a little sausage about 4cm/1½ inches long.

3 To make pastry, sieve flour into a large shallow bowl, and make a well in the centre. Add melted butter and orange-flower water. Mix dough, adding a little egg yolk and water until it is the consistency of bread dough.

4 Knead dough for 10–15 minutes, pulling it away from bowl, slapping it down and kneading it into bowl again with the heel of your hand, until dough is smooth and elastic.

5 Form dough into a loose ball and drop into a bowl of sifted flour; clean remains of sticky dough off your fingers on to ball of dough. Turn dough over in flour and leave until ready to roll out. Clean your hands, they'll be sticky.

6 To roll pastry, divide dough into two parts and cover one with a damp towel to keep it moist. Brush excess flour off the other and place on a floured work surface. Pat it loosely into a soft round. Brush off excess flour, turn dough over on floured working surface and, with a floured rolling pin, begin to roll dough out until it is a circle about 15cm/6 inches in diameter. Turn dough over, brush off excess flour and begin to roll out pastry from left to right of working surface, turning dough over from time to time and stretching it slightly as you roll, until pastry is very thin and about 60cm/2 feet long. With a pastry wheel cutter, cut pastry into an even sided strip 13cm/5 inches wide by 60cm/2 feet long. Repeat with remaining dough.

7 To assemble pastry 'horns', lay one pastry strip out on floured working surface, long sides facing you and space 12–18 little almond paste sausages out in the middle, along the length of the band, leaving 4cm/1½ inches between each sausage and at each end of the pastry band. Then using a rolling pin, roll out pastry on each side of sausages to the edges of pastry band, making pastry at edges as thin as you can.

8 Fold lower half of pastry over sausage shapes, bringing pastry edges together, and pressing them together gently with your fingers. Then, using pastry wheel cutter, make a cut in pastry half way between each sausage (as you would for ravioli); then cut a crescent shape around top of each sausage (2–3cm/¾–1¼ inches away from each sausage).

9 Preheat oven to moderate (350°F/180°C/Gas 4). Prick each pastry crescent with a needle (or a pin) to allow steam to escape while baking.

10 Place crescents (curved sides up) on a buttered pastry sheet and press rounded edges gently together. Brush pastry with egg yolk and water and bake in preheated oven for 15–20 minutes, or until pastry is crisp and light gold.

Makes 24–36 pastries

SUGARED GAZELLE'S HORNS
KAAB EL GHZAL MFENNED

This is perhaps my favourite version of this delicious little Arab pastry. In any case, it looks most attractive to serve both sorts on a tray.

To make them, just plunge newly baked pastry crescents one by one into orange-flower water and then roll them, while still wet, in a shallow bowl of icing (confectioners') sugar.

M'HANNCHA — *the 'serpent' cake – a slim coil of paper-thin pastry encasing a pounded almond filling, decorated with icing (confectioner's) sugar and trails of powdered cinnamon.*

M'HANNCHA
THE 'SERPENT' CAKE

6 × 25cm/10 inch warkha pastry leaves (see page 85)
softened butter
1 egg, beaten with 2 tablespoons water
icing (confectioners') sugar
powdered cinnamon

ALMOND PASTE FILLING
225g/½ lb (2 cups) ground almonds
100g/¼ lb icing (1 cup confectioners') sugar
1–2 tablespoons each water and orange-flower water
4–6 tablespoons melted butter, cooled
½ teaspoon each vanilla and almond essences (extracts)
finely grated zest of ½ orange (optional)

1 To make almond paste filling, combine ground almonds with sugar, water, orange-flower water and cooled melted butter. Add vanilla and almond essences (extracts) and, if desired, the finely grated zest of ½ orange. Mix well and knead until smooth. Chill.

2 Separate chilled almond paste into twelve even-sized segments. Roll each segment into a 'sausage' shape 1cm/½ inch thick. Preheat oven to 350°F/180°C/Gas 4.

3 Spread out two *warkha* pastry leaves, overlapping slightly. Place 4 almond paste 'sausages' in a row at the bottom of pastry leaves (about 5cm/2 inches from lower edge). Roll up the pastry tightly into a long sausage, tucking in ends after cutting away any excess pastry, to make a neat edge.

4 Brush a cake pan (or baking sheet) lightly with softened butter and arrange the *warkha*-covered 'sausages' in a tight coil starting at the centre of the cake pan (or baking sheet).

5 Repeat with remaining pastry leaves (two pastry leaves and four almond paste 'sausages' each time), continuing to form the coil (like a coiled snake) to the edges of the pan (see picture on the left).

6 Brush coil with beaten egg and water and bake in preheated oven until pastry is crisp and a pale gold in colour. Invert coil on the cake pan (or baking sheet) and bake for a further 10–15 minutes, or until pastry is crisp and golden.

7 To serve, invert pastry coil on to a large round serving dish and dust liberally with sifted icing (confectioners') sugar. Decorate with fine lines of powdered cinnamon in a lattice pattern over cake.

Serves 6–8

PÂTE DE DATTES

This date mixture and the almond one following, make delicious fillings for many Arab sweetmeats – and can be used as alternative fillings for *cornes de gazelle*, *m'hanncha* and *briouats* (see pages 102, 204 and 93).

Try this date mixture rolled into little balls, then rolled in icing (confectioners') sugar and powdered nuts as a sweet on its own.

450g/1lb dates, washed and stoned (2⅔ cups washed and pitted dates)
6–8 tablespoons groundnut (peanut) oil
6 tablespoons ground almonds
4 tablespoons ground peanuts
1–2 tablespoons orange-flower water
½ teaspoon powdered cinnamon
2 tablespoons honey

1 Bring water to the boil in the bottom of a *couscoussier* or steamer. Place dates in top section and steam for 15–20 minutes.

2 Transfer dates from steamer into a large mixing bowl. Add 2 tablespoons peanut oil to the hot dates and mash with a wooden fork or spoon.

3 Add ground almonds and peanuts with 4 more tablespoons peanut oil, and mash again until well mixed. Add orange-flower water, cinnamon and honey, and knead mixture with your fingers, moistening hands with water from time to time, until flavours are well distributed into mixture.

4 The date filling can be kept in a sterilized Kilner (Mason) jar for several days if protected from the atmosphere with a little oil.

PÂTE D'AMANDES

450g/1lb (2⅔ cups) shelled almonds
225g/½lb (generous 1 cup) sugar
2 tablespoons each water and orange-flower water
120ml/4fl.oz (½ cup) melted butter
1 teaspoon vanilla essence (extract)

1 To prepare almonds: bring a large saucepan of water to the boil, add almonds and leave for 2–3 minutes for skins to swell. Drain.

2 Remove skins from almonds by pinching each almond between your thumb and forefinger. Place peeled almonds in a large sieve and rinse with cold water. Drain.

3 Spread almonds out on a clean tea towel to dry overnight. (In Morocco they are allowed to dry in the sun for 2–3 days.) (They can be dried in a hot oven if necessary.) When almonds are completely dry, process them in a food processor.

4 To make syrup, combine sugar, water and orange-flower water in a medium sized saucepan. Cook over a low heat, stirring constantly, until sugar melts and bubbles begin to form.

5 Remove pan from heat, add melted butter and mix well. Gradually stir in ground almonds, then return to heat and work mixture to a smooth paste with a wooden spoon or spatula. Add vanilla essence (extract) and continue to stir until mixture begins to come away from bottom and sides of pan.

6 Remove from heat, pour into a large shallow gratin dish or baking pan, and leave mixture to cool. Cut into even-sized rectangles or diamonds.

Fatima preparing SHEBBAKIA *(honeyed pastry 'ribbons' sprinkled with toasted sesame seeds).* ABOVE, LEFT TO RIGHT: *Rolling out the pastry; trimming pastry with pastry cutter; cutting pastry into strips; deep-frying pastry 'ribbons'.*

OPPOSITE: *Moroccan cuisine is rich in honey-dipped sweets and pastries.* TOP ROW: SHEBBAKIA *and* RGHAIF, CENTRE: *'cigars' of* warkha *pastry filled with* pâte de dattes; BOTTOM: BRIOUATS.

HONEYED PASTRY 'RIBBONS'
SHEBBAKIA

1 tablespoon dried (active dry) yeast
½–1 teaspoon salt
1 tablespoon sugar
4 tablespoons warm water
5 tablespoons melted butter
5 tablespoons olive oil
2 eggs
8 tablespoons orange-flower water
4 tablespoons vinegar
900g/2lb plain (scant 6½ cups all-purpose) flour
1 pinch powdered saffron, dissolved in 150ml/¼ pint (⅔ cup) warm water
oil, for deep-frying
900ml/1½ pints (2½ cups) clear honey
8 tablespoons sesame seeds, lightly toasted

1 In a medium-sized bowl, mix yeast with salt and sugar, and sprinkle in the warm water. Stir until well mixed, then set aside in a warm place for 15 minutes.

2 Mix melted butter with olive oil in a small bowl.

3 In a mixing bowl, beat eggs with orange-flower water, then add vinegar and butter and oil mixture. Beat again until well mixed.

4 Sift flour into a *gsaa* or large shallow bowl (I use a wide wooden salad bowl), and make a well in the centre with your hand. Slowly pour the flavoured egg and fat mixture into the flour, stirring constantly with your hand until mixture is well amalgamated. Then add the yeast mixture and beat with your hand until it is a fairly stiff sticky dough, adding only as much saffron water as necessary.

5 Knead the dough well, by pushing down and forward with the heel of your hand – it will be very sticky – folding the dough over on to itself each time. Knead in this way until dough is smooth and elastic.

6 Divide the dough into six equal pieces, and clean your hands. Take one piece of dough, dust it lightly with flour, and pat it gently into a ball. Using a floured rolling pin, roll dough out on floured working surface (1) and (2) or pastry board, turning dough over occasionally to keep it from sticking, into a rectangle about 20 × 25cm/8 × 10 inches. Then, with a pastry wheel, trim edges of rectangle evenly. (3) Quarter rectangle into four rectangles of 10 × 12.5cm/4 × 5 inches. Then cut each into five or six 'ribbons' leaving 6mm/¼ inch of pastry uncut on top and bottom edges of each pastry (dough) rectangle (4).

7 Heat oil in deep fryer. Heat honey in a saucepan deep enough to protect you if honey boils up when cooking.

8 Pick up every other strip of one rectangle at the top with your fingers, and join top ends of 'ribbons' loosely together. When you pull pastry (dough) away from the working surface, the 'ribbons' will elongate slightly.

9 To fry, gather every other strip in your fingers (as above) and then bring the lower opposite corners together to form a sort of loose 'rosette' shape. Fry 2 or 3 'ribbon' parcels at a time in the hot oil until just gold, not too brown or they will get tough.

10 Drain them then drop them into the hot honey. As soon as the honey boils up again, remove cakes to a cake rack to drain. Sprinkle immediately with lightly toasted sesame seeds. Proceed as above with remaining pastry.

Another version – also called *shebbakia* – is made by pressing the batter through a pastry tube (round nozzle) or even through the hole in the bottom of an earthenware flower pot, to make a series of 'flower' shapes in the hot oil. These, too, are dipped into boiling honey and sprinkled with sesame seeds as above.

Makes 24

SELLOU

This is a traditional sweet – much loved by Moroccans – served at Ramadan, at baptisms, and at special parties. It is a very rich, sugary-brown powder of pounded almonds, baked flour and sugar, flavoured with sesame and anise seeds and cinnamon. Guests help themselves to a spoonful or two when eating other sweets.

450g/1lb flour (3 cups plus 2 tablespoons all-purpose) flour, sifted
225g/½lb (1 cup) butter
100g/¼lb (scant 1 cup) sesame seeds
100g/¼lb (⅔ cup) almonds, chopped
2 tablespoons groundnut (peanut) oil
1–2 tablespoons anise seeds
100g/¼lb (generous ½ cup) sugar
½–1 teaspoon powdered cinnamon

GARNISH
icing (confectioners') sugar
whole almonds, or sugared or slivered almonds

1 Place sifted flour in a large thick-bottomed frying pan (skillet) and cook over a medium heat, stirring constantly, until flour has turned golden brown. Remove from heat. (Or bake in the oven at 350°F/180°C/Gas 4.)

2 Melt butter in a medium-sized saucepan, add browned flour, and cook over a medium heat, stirring constantly, until sauce is thick and caramel coloured. Do not let it burn. Remove from heat.

3 Grill (broil) sesame seeds in a pan without fat until golden. Sauté chopped almonds in oil until golden. Combine sesame seeds, chopped almonds and anise seeds, and process in a food processor until smooth.

4 In a bowl combine the flour and butter mixture and the processed seed mixture. Add sugar and cinnamon and mix well. Allow mixture to cool for at least 2 hours.

5 When ready to serve, arrange this powdery mixture in a pile on a serving dish and decorate with trails of icing (confectioners') sugar and whole, sugared, or slivered almonds.

ALMOND MACAROONS

225g/½lb (2 cups) ground almonds
225g/½lb icing (2 cups confectioners') sugar
finely grated zest of 1 lemon
4 egg whites

GARNISH
blanched almonds

1 In a small saucepan combine ground almonds with icing (confectioners') sugar. Stir in finely grated lemon zest and cook over a very low heat, stirring constantly, for 10–15 minutes. Remove from heat and leave to cool.

2 Beat egg whites until stiff and add gradually to almond and sugar mixture. Place in a piping bag.

3 To bake macaroons, place a piece of waxed paper on a baking tray and pipe small macaroons on paper 5cm/2 inches apart. Place a blanched almond on top of each macaroon. Bake in preheated oven (350°F/180°C/Gas 4) for 20 minutes, or until macaroons are cooked through but have not taken on colour.

ROZ BIL HALIB
MOROCCAN RICE PUDDING

1.2 litres/2 pints (5 cups) milk
50–75g/2–3oz (about ⅓ cup) rice
2 tablespoons ground rice
175g/6oz (scant 1 cup) sugar
100g/¼lb (1 cup) ground almonds
¼ teaspoon almond essence (extract)
½ teaspoon vanilla essence (extract)
2 tablespoons orange-flower water

GARNISH
powdered cinnamon
pine kernels, sautéed in butter until golden, or raisins, soaked in orange-flower water

1 In a saucepan, bring 900ml/1½ pints (3¾ cups) of the milk gently to the boil. Add rice, lower heat and cook until rice is tender, adding a little water, if necessary.

2 In a small bowl, combine ground rice and enough cold water to mix to a smooth paste. Pour remaining milk into it and stir well.

3 Pour ground rice mixture into saucepan with rice and cook, stirring constantly, until the mixture comes to the boil again. Then add sugar and ground almonds and simmer over a low heat, stirring constantly, until the mixture thickens.

4 Remove saucepan from the heat, and stir in essences (extracts) and orange-flower water. Leave to cool for a few minutes. Pour into a shallow serving dish and chill in the refrigerator for several hours.

5 Just before serving, remove serving dish from the refrigerator, sprinkle with powdered cinnamon and decorate with sautéed pine kernels or soaked drained raisins.

Serves 4–6

GHORIBA 1
FLOUR AND BUTTER BASED MACAROONS

225g/½lb (1 cup) butter
1 teaspoon vanilla essence (extract) (or orange-flower water)
100g/¼lb icing (1 cup confectioners') sugar, sifted
225g/½lb (1½ cups plus 2 tablespoons all-purpose) flour, sifted

GARNISH
icing (confectioners') sugar
blanched, halved almonds

1 In a small saucepan, melt the butter over a low heat. Skim off any froth and pour the melted butter into a large mixing bowl, leaving residue in the bottom of the pan. Place mixing bowl in the refrigerator until butter solidifies.

2 Remove mixing bowl from the refrigerator and beat butter with a whisk or wooden spoon until it is creamy and pale coloured. Add vanilla essence (extract) (or orange-flower water) and beat in icing (confectioners') sugar, a little at a time.

3 Beat in sifted flour, a little at a time, until mixture is stiff.

4 Knead dough in bowl until it becomes pliable. Cover bowl with a tea towel and leave to mature in the bowl for 15 minutes.

5 Remove dough from the bowl and roll out on a lightly floured surface to a long thin sausage about 4cm/1½ inches thick. Cut into 20–24 segments and then roll each segment into a ball.

6 Lightly oil the palms of your hands and flatten each ball, passing mixture from hand to hand, into a round 2.5–4cm/1–1½ inches in diameter.

7 Place biscuits (cookies) on a buttered baking sheet, far enough apart so they can spread while baking. Place a blanched almond in centre of each, and sprinkle with icing (confectioners') sugar. Bake for 15–20 minutes in preheated oven (350°F/180°C/Gas 4) or until golden. Remove and set aside to cool. They can be stored in an airtight tin when cold.

Makes 20–24

GHORIBA 2
ALMOND AND SUGAR BASED MACAROONS

150g/5oz icing (1¼ cups confectioners') sugar
1 small egg, beaten
225g/½lb (2 cups) ground almonds
finely grated zest of 1 lemon
1 teaspoon vanilla essence (extract)
¼ teaspoon powdered cinnamon

GARNISH
icing (confectioners') sugar

1 In a large mixing bowl, combine icing (confectioners') sugar and beaten egg, and beat until mixture is white.

2 In a medium-sized bowl, combine ground almonds and remaining ingredients, and gradually mix into beaten sugar and egg mixture.

3 Knead dough in bowl until it becomes pliable. Cover bowl with a tea towel and leave to mature in the bowl for 15 minutes.

4 Remove dough from the bowl and roll out on a lightly floured surface to a long thin sausage about 4cm/1½ inches thick. Cut into 20–24 segments and then roll each segment into a ball.

5 Lightly oil the palms of your hands and flatten each ball, passing mixture from hand to hand, into rounds 2.5–4cm/½ inches in diameter.

6 Place biscuits (cookies) on a buttered baking sheet, far enough apart so they can spread while baking, and sprinkle with icing (confectioners') sugar. Bake for 15–20 minutes in preheated oven (350°F/180°C/Gas 4) or until golden. Remove and set aside to cool. They can be stored in an airtight tin when cold.

Makes 20–24

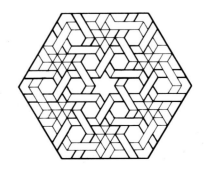

Summer fruit platters

Great platters of fruits are a joy during the summer months in Morocco. Melons are particularly delicious whether striped watermelon, or canteloupe or honeydew. Cut into individual pyramids and served with quarters of lemon, they are delicious chilled (served alone or with other fruits), liberally decked with cubes of ice.

In the summer there are ripe green and purple figs in all the markets and on sale along the roads, artfully arranged pyramids of brightly coloured fruits in spanking new, straw baskets. Yellow and red plums abound at this time of year, as do luscious peaches and purple and green grapes. And, for a brief period, tiny orange-red pears appear in the markets with great fat bananas and Barbary figs (prickly pears, the fruit of a cactus) for a few pence a pound. My own courtyard boasts great hands of home-grown bananas and a lime-scented thorn lemon to add a spicy lemon flavour to fruit salads and drinks. And on the other side of the garden is my lone fig tree: not a profound producer, but the fruits are the more treasured for that. Later in the year, we have mandarins, tangerines, lemons and oranges.

Peaches are served on their own, peeled and dusted with crushed sugar and ground cinnamon. Bananas are cut into thick slices, covered with chilled *crème fraîche* and dusted with crushed sugar and ground cinnamon; or tossed in a fragrant bath of orange and lemon juice and orange-flower water, and dusted with icing (confectioners') sugar. Figs are cut into quarters, doused with honey and garnished with chopped toasted almonds, with perhaps a hint of rosewater added, to lend a touch of Eastern enchantment. Oranges are peeled, cut into elegant cartwheels and bathed in lemon juice, orange juice and orange-flower water. Just before serving they are garnished with a scattering of chopped fresh dates and slivered green almonds. A recipe from the south dresses them with almond-blossom honey and garnishes the dish in spring with individual orange blossoms and green almonds.

Pomegranates are often served, as are loquats and Barbary figs to add a touch of glamour to the fruit dessert tray. Dark red, almost brown strawberries are sold in the markets; they have a full rich flavour. And fresh dates from the south seem to be almost always available.

A platter of freshly picked oranges from the riad.

MOROCCAN ORANGE SALAD

6 ripe oranges
12 dates, stoned and chopped
12 blanched almonds, slivered
orange-flower water (or lemon juice and icing (confectioners') sugar)
powdered cinnamon

1 Peel oranges, removing all pith, and slice crossways. Place in a salad bowl and garnish with chopped dates and slivered almonds. Flavour to taste with orange-flower water (or lemon juice and icing (confectioners') sugar).

2 Chill, then just before serving, sprinkle lightly with powdered cinnamon.

Serves 6

MOROCCAN PEACH DESSERT

The peach – first cultivated in China, arrived in Morocco via ancient Persia – as did melons and pomegranates. This dessert is delicious served with cream or ice cream.

4 large ripe peaches
4 tablespoons sugar
2–4 teaspoons rosewater

GARNISH
powdered cinnamon
fresh mint leaves
whipped cream or ice cream

1 Peel peaches and slice into a large shallow mixing bowl. Sprinkle with sugar and rosewater and mix well.

2 Place bowl in refrigerator for at least 2 hours.

3 Just before serving, sprinkle with ground cinnamon and leaves of fresh mint. Serve with whipped cream or ice cream.

Serves 4

ABDESLAM'S FRESH FRUIT SALAD – *a refreshing mixture of strawberries, diced apple, pear and banana, garnished with fresh mint leaves and flavoured with orange and lemon juice and orange-flower water.*

ABDESLAM'S FRESH FRUIT SALAD

2 ripe dessert apples
2 ripe dessert pears
juice of 2 oranges
juice of 1 lemon
2 bananas
2 tablespoons orange-flower water
icing (confectioners') sugar
16–20 strawberries, hulled and halved
24–36 mint leaves

1 Peel and core apples and pears. Cut them into eighths and then into thin slices.

2 Combine sliced apples and pears in a fruit bowl and add orange and lemon juice to prevent fruit from discolouring.

3 Peel bananas and slice thinly. Add to fruit in bowl and toss gently. Add the orange-flower water, and icing (confectioners') sugar to taste.

4 Add the strawberry halves to fruit salad. Garnish with fresh mint leaves and chill until ready to serve.

Serves 6

Moroccan drinks

Moroccan wines are a legacy of the French rule in Morocco. And although Moslems do not drink wines or alcohol in any form – it is strictly forbidden by the Koran – they have no aversion to producing them. You will find many agreeable reds, whites and rosés in all the major Moroccan cities, which are excellent accompaniments to the rich Moroccan cuisine. My own favourites are Gris de Boulaouane, a dry, light and fruity rosé; Valpierre (*blanc de blancs*), a dry white from the region of Zaërs near Rabat; Guerrouane, a rich, fruity red wine from Ait-Yazem near Meknes; and Toulal, both red and white, from the plains near Guerrouane. The Moroccans themselves drink excellent cooling waters instead – Sidi Harazam (still) and Oulmes (sparkling) – as well as the national drink, *nâa-naa* (*thé à la menthe*), freshly brewed mint tea made with Chinese green (gunpowder) tea, sprigs of fresh mint and cane sugar.

Non-alcoholic drinks made with milk or buttermilk and the juices of fresh fruits and almonds are also firm favourites: milk flavoured with orange-flower water or rosewater, or the milk of pounded almonds; water flavoured with orange or lemon juice, pounded sugar and orange-flower water; the juice of pomegranates, watermelon, grapes or strawberries flavoured with orange-flower water or rosewater.

One of my favourite fresh-tasting drinks is made from white grapes passed through a fine sieve and lightly flavoured with powdered cinnamon and orange-flower water. Another is bruised mint leaves and sugar plus a hint of rosewater with chopped ice and equal quantities of milk and Oulmes.

An even more exotic drink from the Middle Ages, is made by burning a little gum arabic in the ashes of a charcoal brazier and placing an upturned earthenware jug over it to allow the smoke captured by the upturned jug to impregnate the jug with its magical flavour. Then chilled water, lightly flavoured with orange-flower water, is added. The drink is left in a cool place (covered) to infuse before drinking.

Two new freshly-made drinks to be found in the *cafés* or milk bars which abound in every city are combinations of milk and diced bananas or apples, or a whirl of avocado and milk. Add to these a plethora of bottled fizzy orange and lemon drinks and the ubiquitous Coca-Cola and you have a fair idea of the drinks available.

Fresh-tasting chilled fruit juices and fruit-flavoured milk drinks are popular in Morocco.

213

19

A LAST TASTE

A bowl of chilled fresh fruits – a salad of Moroccan strawberries – photographed in front of a Moroccan mural.

Khadija, Azziz' beautiful new wife, is the latest addition to the household. She is young, virtually untrained, knows little about cooking. She has yet barely learned the rudiments of washing and ironing, her daily task. Azziz has to help her with the cleaning of the house but she is always smiling, and I am happy for her. And happy, too, that she is untrained and I can teach her Moroccan cooking. She will be a willing pupil. I can see she is already interested. As is Azziz. They will cook together in harmony. All the recipes in this book. Neither can read, of course, neither French nor English. (I'm not even sure they can read Arabic.) But they will learn as I teach them – and show them – and correct their tastes. This is after all what I do best.

Already – in the few weeks since their wedding – I have taught them the basic precepts of salad making: the correct dosages for a perfect salad dressing in the Moroccan manner (with olive oil, vinegar, finely chopped fresh garlic, fresh green coriander and flat-leafed or Italian parsley), and just how much freshly ground black pepper, hot red pepper, sweet red pepper and salt to use; how to slice the sweet red onions and fiery green peppers thinly; how to slice the fat, richly flavoured tomatoes and the apple-flavoured cucumbers a little more thickly; and how to garnish the salad with diced anchovies and plump black olives. Making salad is an art.

Then come the *chermoula* dressings for fish, for chicken, for brochettes of lamb; how to stuff green peppers, tomatoes, aubergines (eggplant) and onions with *kefta* and rice; how to make a purée of potatoes in the French way using *crème fraîche* (available in the market in the Gueliz), mixed with water for lightness; and how to cook perfect *pommes frites*, as well as a country-style lamb *tagine* (a Moroccan version of Irish stew but with carrots, turnips and potatoes as well as skinned, seeded and diced tomatoes, onion and finely chopped garlic and fresh green coriander). All this they have now learned.

Yesterday, I taught them one of my favourite dishes – *tagine du pauvre*, lentils simmered in olive oil and a light stock with leftover lamb bones and chopped onions, carrots, tomatoes, and garlic to add substance and flavour. Here the seasoning is all: the right combination of hot red pepper, sweet red pepper, black pepper, salt and cinnamon. Delicious. I like to eat it as a main course when I am alone, or as an appetizer salad with wedges of ripe tomato and black olives and a spicy, herb-flavoured vinaigrette dressing for a company meal the next day. And I am alone tonight. Dinner is at the low table in the *riad*. Azziz sprinkles rose petals and tiny geranium flowers on the table. Stubby little candles set in tin lanterns from the local *souk* are the only light. Other lanterns glimmer softly in the trees.

Dinner is two eggs poached in a hot cheesy cream with a sprinkling of cumin and hot red pepper, followed by the lentil *tagine*. I smile with pleasure to see how well it has turned out. Azziz smiles, too. He is proud. A second helping (*noblesse oblige*), and then the cooling refreshment of chilled fresh fruits. This is followed by a glass of fragrant mint tea with a touch of *verveine* in it and absinthe (for happiness and, I suspect, for health).

I am content as I make my way up to the moonlit terrace to study the stars, secure in the knowledge that another sweet, pricklingly pungent glass of tea will follow me. And then to bed – for tomorrow it is an early start for Casablanca – and then a plane to London to deliver this book – *Taste of Morocco* – for publication.

Marrakech, January 1987

A second helping: noblesse oblige.

INDEX

Page numbers in *italic* refer to the illustrations and captions

PHOTOGRAPH ACKNOWLEDGEMENTS

All photographs are by Michelle Garrett with the exception of those listed below, which are by John Stewart:
pages 1, 2, 14/15, 19, 22, 34, 35, 37–41, 44, 49, 50, 52, 62, 65, 67–72, 78, 84–6, 91, 93, 96–9, 104, 112, 117, 128, 134, 135, 137, 139, 146–8, 164, 165, 167, 169, 171, 186, 192, 198, 204, 206, 207.